M&A Disputes

M&A Disputes

How They Happen, How to Resolve Them, How to Avoid Them

Heiko Daniel Ziehms

Wolters Kluwer

Published by:
Kluwer Law International B.V.
PO Box 316
2400 AH Alphen aan den Rijn
The Netherlands
E-mail: lrs-sales@wolterskluwer.com
Website: www.wolterskluwer.com/en/solutions/kluwerlawinternational

Sold and distributed by:
Wolters Kluwer Legal & Regulatory U.S.
920 Links Avenue
Landisville, PA 17538
United States of America
E-mail: customer.service@wolterskluwer.com

ISBN 978-94-035-4446-5

e-Book: ISBN 978-94-035-4496-0
web-PDF: ISBN 978-94-035-4506-6

For Alba Lucia, Laura and Sara

About the Author

Heiko Daniel Ziehms is a Partner and Senior Managing Director of FTI Consulting in London. He focuses on the quantification of damages and forensic accounting analyses in M&A, joint venture and other commercial disputes and provides transaction advisory services.

Mr Ziehms was appointed as a financial and accounting expert in a large number of disputes. He has worked on matters in DIS, HKIAC, ICC, ICSID, LCIA, SIAC, Swiss Rules and VIAC arbitration forums, ad hoc arbitrations and the courts, including some of the most complex corporate disputes in Europe valued up to several billion euros. He is experienced in giving oral expert testimony. He has advised on several hundred transactions, including 'landmark' deals.

He was listed among the world's foremost expert witnesses in the tenth edition of *Global Arbitration Review's GAR 100*. He has also been recognised by Who's Who Legal for several years among the leading expert witnesses for arbitration worldwide, where he is ranked as a 'Thought Leader', and among the leading consulting experts for damages and forensic accounting.

Mr Ziehms holds an MBA from the Haas School of Business at the University of California at Berkeley and a graduate degree in Business from the University of Bamberg, Germany. He is a Certified Fraud Examiner and qualified and previously worked as a Certified Public Accountant (CPA)

Table of Contents

List of Abbreviations

ASC	Accounting Standards Codification (as issued by FASB)
ASU	Accounting Standards Update (as issued by FASB)
CAPM	Capital Asset Pricing Model
DCF	Discounted Cash Flow
EBIT	Earnings Before Interest and Taxes
EBITDA	Earnings Before Interest, Taxes, Depreciation and Amortisation
FASB	Financial Accounting Standards Board
IAS	International Accounting Standard
IASB	International Accounting Standards Board
ICC	International Chamber of Commerce
IFRS	International Financial Reporting Standards
M&A	Mergers and Acquisitions
MAC	Material Adverse Change
PE	Private Equity
POC	Percentage of Completion
PPA	Purchase Price Adjustment
RIM	Residual Income Model
SPA	Sale and Purchase Agreement
US GAAP	US Generally Accepted Accounting Principles
WACC	Weighted Average Cost of Capital
WIP	Work in Progress

List of Figures

List of Figures

List of Tables

Foreword

M&A transactions play a significant role in both domestic and cross-border economic activity. Much has therefore been written on the subject. Similarly, a body of research examines the success of completed transactions, focusing on operational implementation and the achievement of anticipated benefits from the integration of two businesses. In contrast, there is surprisingly little structured examination of M&A-related disputes. Such disputes can, at worst, frustrate a deal entirely or, in instances less extreme but still important, adversely affect the post-transaction environment and hence the prospects of a successful acquisition.

The first edition of M&A Disputes and Completion Mechanisms in 2019 filled the gap in the literature on M&A disputes to great effect. Since the date of the first edition, the complexity of transactions has continued to rise to encompass increasingly extensive datasets as the digitalisation of businesses and business models broadens, regulatory reach grows (much of it new and evolving, to cover wide-ranging issues under the ESG umbrella as well as emerging considerations around data and privacy), and enterprises report a sense of accelerating business cycles and increased unpredictability. All of this has occurred against the backdrop of the COVID-19 pandemic, the end of a low-interest rate environment and the aggressive return of inflation, the energy crisis, and rising geopolitical uncertainty. The burden of dealing with these developments in an acquisition has, however, continued to fall on the financial information and related reporting on which transactions are founded, the assessment of the deal price, and the terms of the Sale and Purchase Agreement (SPA) that govern the transaction and the rights and obligations of the parties.

This second edition of Heiko's book is, therefore, both timely and welcome, given it can draw on a new set of experiences and observations taken from a period where the scope for M&A disputes has intensified.

This edition follows the same format as its predecessor in addressing two central themes: the 'mechanics' of a transaction, namely the processes by which completion is intended to occur and the component financial elements of the processes; and the valuation of transactions, including the related assessment of damages.

An analysis of overall deal mechanics helps explain how M&A disputes can arise, often at the intersection of accounting information and decisions and the associated valuation of specific assets and liabilities or the overall business. Chapters 3 to 10 step through the issues and cover completion processes, and individual considerations affecting balance sheet items such as net debt and working capital, earn-out mechanisms, revenue recognition, and fraud.

Having identified where and how M&A disputes can arise, it is necessary to consider how to resolve them. This brings into focus dispute resolution processes such as arbitration, litigation, and expert determination (typically of specific technical points, such as in the last case, adjustments to the purchase price). Often, resolution of M&A disputes involves an award of damages. Chapter 11 orients the reader by addressing valuation principles, standards of value, and valuation methods – all of which need to be understood when assessing value and frameworks for calculating loss. The chapter helpfully explains the role of accounting information in presenting the underlying economic activity of a business and in informing a valuation. Chapter 12 engages with damages analysis specific to M&A disputes and addresses the legal principles governing the compensatory framework, questions of value versus price, and the specific interactions of these two measures in different contexts such as warranty claims, misrepresentation actions, and the quantification of indemnities.

It is vital to understand how to avoid or minimise the potential for M&A disputes, which can often be achieved through small and simple measures. Chapter 14 distils these 'lessons learned' into a short, practical commentary drawing on the author's extensive experience in M&A and related disputes.

For those of us involved in transactions, valuation, or dispute resolution – whether as principal, adviser, independent expert, or resolver of M&A disputes – Heiko's book is an authoritative guide to the issues. As a technical treatise on a comprehensive range of accounting, corporate finance, and legal topics and sub-topics germane to M&A disputes, the book addresses theory and practice with admirable depth and balance.

Mark Bezant, June 2023

Preface

The idea for this book goes back almost fifteen years. It originated from a series of presentations and workshops to law firms, investment banks, private equity firms, and corporate M&A departments. The contents expanded considerably over time, shaped by the collective experience of my colleagues and me in M&A-related disputes, transaction advisory services engagements, and countless hours of discussions with a broad group of professionals and academics. I began writing almost ten years ago, and the precursor to this book, *M&A Disputes and Completion Mechanisms*, was published in 2019. On account of the many new developments in M&A disputes, even in the space of a few years since that first publication, what was originally intended as a second edition has turned into a new book.

This book, like its predecessor, starts from a set of ideas in corporate finance that underpin the structure of deals, their valuation, and the measurement of damages. They include the role of capital structure;[1] the relationship between risk and return;[2] the no-arbitrage principle;[3] the relationship between accounting figures and 'value';[4] and insights from behavioural finance.[5] Whether explicit or implicit, the analysis rests on these propositions.

The data that are available suggest that causes of M&A disputes – including breaches of contractual obligations and fraud – are far more prevalent than many participants in M&A transactions may expect.[6] A high 'base rate' for potential disputes meets with a rapidly changing M&A landscape. To put the pace of change into context, consider recent developments and their implications for M&A disputes. Here are six.

1. For example, §2.01 [A], §7.05 [B] [3], §11.04 [B] [2] [b].
2. §4.04 [B] [4] [b], §7.05 [B], §11.04 [B] [1].
3. §4.04 [B] [4] [b]; §4.04 [E], §11.04 [B] [2].
4. §11.01.
5. While I do not claim expertise in this area, the analysis acknowledges the importance of behavioural biases for many M&A disputes, *see, e.g.*, §11.05 [A] and Chapter 14.
6. *See* §14.02 for references.

1. A Record-Breaking M&A Market Followed by a Wave of M&A-Related Disputes

An unprecedented wave of M&A activity peaked in 2021: total global deal value amounted to USD 5.9 trillion, an increase of 64% compared to 2020[7] and the highest ever recorded, driven by exceptionally high valuations and fuelled by access to cheap financing.[8] More recently, M&A activity has slowed significantly,[9] and markets have experienced significant volatility in energy prices in 2022 and a series of shocks to the banking system in 2023.

A period of exceptionally high valuations does not mean that markets, or individual acquisition targets, are overvalued. However, high-value deals and the steep decline that followed mean an increased scope for disappointment for the parties. Buyers can be disappointed when it becomes clear that an acquisition target will fall short of the expected returns that had been 'priced into' the bid. Sellers can be disappointed in some cases when a significant shortfall against expectations means lower-than-expected earn-out payments. Disappointment breeds disputes.

2. The Resurgence of Inflation and Rising Yields

The resurgence of inflation and the end of 'secular stagnation' have changed important aspects of M&A deals and related assessments of damages. After almost half a century of decreasing bond yields, the trend reversed between the second half of 2019 and mid-2021 for government bonds (depending on geography) when yields started to rise. Government bond yields are often an important building block in the cost of capital assumption used by experts. Valuations in Europe with valuation dates between 2019 and the end of 2022 often had to deal with negative government bond yields. A year later, they are at 300 basis points or higher. In disputes, this not only means higher cost of capital but can also make the choice of valuation date far more significant. If that choice is between the locked box date, signing and closing, then longer closing periods can make this effect even more pronounced.

3. An Increase in Fraud Cases

Allegations of fraud have always been an important aspect of M&A disputes. The authors of a recent study estimate that 10% of large publicly traded firms are committing securities fraud every year in normal times,[10] and that, on average only approximately one-third of corporate frauds are detected.[11] These figures relate to

7. Refinitiv Perspectives, Dealmakers ring out 2021 as the year of M&A, available at https://www.refinitiv.com/perspectives/market-insights/dealmakers-ring-out-2021-as-the-year-of-ma.
8. Reuters, Global M&A volumes hit record high in 2021, breach USD 5 trillion for the first time, 31 December 2021. https://www.reuters.com/markets/us/global-ma-volumes-hit-record-high-2021-breach-5-trillion-first-time-2021-12-31/.
9. *See Sharp fall in global dealmaking brings pandemic-era frenzy to a halt*, Financial Times, 29 December 2022, available at https://www.ft.com/content/fe4f0017-8e41-44ae-85db-55b09157b379.
10. With a 95% confidence interval of 7% to 14%.
11. Dyck, A., Morse, A. and Zingales, L. *How Pervasive Is Corporate Fraud?* Review of Accounting Studies, 2023. A result from the same study is that accounting violations, less severe than alleged securities fraud, are even more prevalent, with an average annual pervasiveness of 41% (although not all are necessarily severe misrepresentations).

corporates generally, many (presumably) without M&A activity in any given year – and hence without the pressure, opportunity and rationalisation associated with M&A that one might expect to increase the risk of fraud meaningfully. In addition, the data analysed in the study goes back decades, whereas more recent periods with exceptionally low borrowing costs, trillions worth of pandemic stimulus money (often with very limited oversight), and abundant liquidity on corporate balance sheets have created an environment where fraud may well be more prevalent than these figures suggest. Fraud can be cyclical, bred in times of ample liquidity and more likely to be uncovered when that liquidity dries up. The section on fraud covers recent examples.

4. The Rise of Warranty & Indemnity Insurance

Warranty & Indemnity (W&I) insurance aims to protect the parties in a transaction against loss resulting from breaches of representations and warranties. The insured party is compensated for covered claims by an insurer. Traditional policies cover warranties included in the Sale and Purchase Agreement (SPA) whereas newer forms of W&I insurance extend the coverage to 'synthetic warranties', whereby a buyer can obtain protection for matters that a seller will not (or cannot) warrant in the SPA.

W&I insurance is a significant innovation that has experienced rapid growth in recent years and is now a feature of many M&A transactions.[12] This has introduced new complexities in many M&A disputes. For example, differences between damages clauses in the SPA and the insurance contract can require different approaches to the valuation of damages, even where both relate to the same (alleged) breach.

5. Increasing Third-Party Funding

Third-party funding is the financing of litigation or arbitration by an otherwise unrelated institution, often a specialised funder. The funder usually receives a share of any payout (funding arrangements can otherwise be flexible). Third-party funding has existed for decades, but it has become more important in recent years, and analysts expect significant further growth: according to one estimate, the global market was worth USD 11.5 billion in 2019 and is expected to grow to USD 24.1 billion by 2028.[13] While historically common in investment arbitration or class actions, third-party funding is also used to fund M&A-related disputes. The approaches funders take to financing decisions can affect M&A disputes in different ways: funders are highly selective as to the disputes they fund and may be more likely to involve specialised experts. Further, the arbitration process can be more tightly structured than those without third-party funding.

12. American Bar Association, *Private Target Mergers and Acquisitions Deal Point Studies* (2017, 2019, and 2021). For private M&A activity within the United States, the percentage of deals that mentioned representation and warranty insurance (RWI, the U.S. term for this type of insurance), increased from 29% in 2017 to 52% in 2019 to 65% in 2021. Similarly, 2021 saw an increase in insured transactions in European markets, especially for higher-value deals in the UK (*see* CMS European M&A Study 2022, 55 and 56).
13. https://www.researchnester.com/reports/litigation-funding-investment-market/2800.

6. A Long-Term Trend Towards Arbitrating Disputes

Most of the private M&A disputes emerging from the recent record market are being resolved through arbitration. By one recent estimate, more than 75% of SPAs have arbitration clauses.[14] Statistics published by arbitration institutions show that shareholder, share purchase or joint venture agreements represent a significant fraction of their overall caseload. For example, these types of agreements represented 14% of the cases administered by the LCIA in 2021.[15]

Arbitration more generally has experienced steady, long-term growth over the past decade. By one estimate, international arbitration filings worldwide grew steadily at more than 3% a year from 2010 to 2019 and increased by 9.9% in 2020.[16] A record period for M&A, already driving related disputes, has met with an acceleration in the rise in the popularity of arbitration, placing M&A disputes among the most relevant triggers of arbitrations.

Beyond these, new themes that can be expected to play a role in M&A disputes in years to come include data privacy and cybersecurity as well as environmental litigation.

The book develops some of these recent trends in greater depth. For example, recent valuations have brought into sharper focus the issue of value versus price, discussed in §11.05 [A]. This could be among the more important issues facing courts and tribunals as they decide the next generation of M&A disputes. Other material that discusses recent developments includes supplier finance (now a feature of many disputes, *see* reverse factoring (*see* [§4.04 [A] [5]]), material adverse change clauses [§1.05 [B]]), and many other aspects of damages valuation.

The focus of the book is technical, with an emphasis on financial and accounting aspects of M&A disputes. Much of the analysis deals with how disputes arise and how they can be resolved, whether in expert determination, arbitration or litigation, and the measure of damages to be used in this context. A number of chapters also offer lessons as to how disputes might be avoided. These are captured in a set of recommendations in the last Chapter, 14, which is also the least technical chapter in the book. If you find the topics of interest but do not have the time to read the entire book then consider reading only this chapter.

14. Elsing/Pickrahn/Pörnbacher/Wagner, *M&A-Streitigkeiten vor DIS-Schiedsgerichten*, V (C.H. Beck, 2022).
15. LCIA 2021 Annual Casework Report, available at https://www.lcia.org/LCIA/reports.aspx.
16. International Arbitration after the Pandemic, An FTI Consulting Report – published in March 2022, p. 3.

‘Apparently there is nothing that cannot happen.’ – Mark Twain

Acknowledgements

My gratitude begins with two former colleagues who edited the book. I was extremely fortunate to have them. John Winepress, a former KPMG Transaction Services Partner, went through an early draft of the manuscript of *M&A Disputes and Completion Mechanisms* word by word and made many helpful suggestions. I am grateful for the generosity with which he gave his time and inspired by the breadth and depth of his knowledge.

Anna Baird (of Baird Forensic) is a former colleague at FTI and Berkeley Research Group who edited the new material since the publication of *M&A Disputes and Completion Mechanisms* in 2019. Anna is a forensic accounting and valuation expert in her own right. Her superb technical knowledge and sense of what works in writing were invaluable (any mistakes that remain are entirely mine).

I am very grateful to Mark Bezant for the kind and generous Foreword.

M&A disputes often play out at the intersection of different professional and academic disciplines, including corporate finance, law, forensic accounting and behavioural economics. The text has benefitted from many colleagues, clients and friends from across these disciplines who found time in their busy schedules for helpful and clarifying discussions that developed my own thinking. I am grateful to Silke Burzle-Brayley (FTI Consulting) who provided valuable comments on legal aspects of damages, Dr Markus Altenkirch (Baker McKenzie), Dr Oliver Beige, Jonathan Berger (FTI Consulting), Professor Stephen Penman (Columbia University), Mike Pilgrem (FTI Consulting), Professor Gerhard H. Wächter (Wächter Law) and Tim Warren (FTI Consulting) who all commented on various aspects of the damages or fraud sections, or pointed me to relevant literature. I am very grateful for their contributions. My gratitude also goes to many other colleagues at FTI Consulting, including Kami Zargar for input on the completion accounts process and expert determination, Dr Meloria Meschi and Bruno Campana for comments on the section on event studies and Marion Duffy for comments on the sections on pensions and leasing. Again, all mistakes that remain are mine alone.

I am also grateful to James Lumley for editing some of the less technical sections, to Danish Ishtiaq who improved the graphs in the book, and to Finn Pfeifer for excellent proofreading.

Thank you also to many other FTI Consulting colleagues for support or discussions on topics in the book: Mark Bezant, Veronica Böhmer, Nick Childs, Alexander Davie, David Eastwood, Timothy Gardiner, Jane Harley, Steve Harris, Patrick Hébréard, John Hudson, Basil Imburgia, Nikki Gordon Jones, Dr Ekaterina Lohwasser, Noel Matthews, Natasha O'Kane, Henry Pannell, Tracey Stretton, and Sherrill Taggart.

I am indebted to my co-authors of past publications: Maren Burtoft, Matthias Breimhorst, Erik van Duijvenvoorde, Sean Fishlock, Thomas Goslich, Roman Gültlinger, Phil Hersey, Abigail Harris, Anna Hartley, Thomas Kunder, Dr Ekaterina Lohwasser, Fabian Peters, Thomas Pfeiffer, Dr Shireen Meer, Wilhelm Mickerts, Julia Noyer, Edmond Richards, and Eduard Saura. The book draws on our joint publications, at times significantly.

I would also like to acknowledge the many former colleagues and clients and academics who contributed to the book *M&A Disputes and Completion Mechanisms*. They include Professor David Teece and Danny Ryan of Berkeley Research Group and the late David Saunders. In addition: Chaitanya Arora, Christian Axmann, Vipul Barbhaya, Stefan Bödeker, Thomas Brown, Alexandros Christou, Nataliya Das, Piers de Wilde, Ron Evans, Giovanni Foti, Daniel Galante, Abigail Gammie, Adam Garside, Sarah Glover, Mustafa Hadi, John House, Julius Huckabee, Susanna Ingalls, Mark James, Ben Johnson, Amy Kingdon, Leontine Koens-Betz, Alexander Leslie, Amy McLaughlin, Matthew McSheaffrey, Matthias Odrobina, James Rusden, Christophe Schmit, Ayumi Ukita-Schneider, Rebecca Stadward, and Sally Wilks. Thank you in particular to the experts who shared their experience from M&A disputes in private arbitrations that would not have been accessible otherwise. I have ensured that any details remain confidential.

Others who contributed to the first edition and to whom I am grateful include: Dr Peter Grindley (Berkeley Research Group) for comments on economic aspects of transactions, Rolf Brien (MITCAP Partners) for sharing insights into bidding processes, Roula Harfouche (HKA) and Adam Kramer (3 Verulam Buildings) for comments on the sections on damages valuation and breaches of warranties, Professor Siegfried H. Elsing (Orrick) for pointing me to relevant literature on damages, Olaf W. John (Mercer) for comments on the discussion of pensions, Professor Jennifer Chatman (the Haas School of Business at UC Berkeley) for pointing me to behavioural research into decision-making, Sarah Keeling (StoneTurn) for comments on risks in emerging market transactions, as well as Michael Betten, Lou Tricarico (Macquarie), Markus Schneider (Grant Thornton), Gregor Klenk (Goodwin Procter), Dr Dirk Oberbracht (Gibson Dunn), and Noah Ojetola for providing valuable input. Thank you also to Professor Stephen Penman of Columbia Business School (Columbia University) for comments on damages valuation and for writing *Financial Statement Analysis and Security Valuation*.

I have co-presented many of the topics in this book in numerous seminars and workshops to law firms, investment banks, private equity firms, and corporate M&A

departments. I have enjoyed these presentations tremendously and benefited from the experience of my co-presenters and the participants. The most frequent co-presenters were Gregor Klenk of Goodwin Procter, Dr Martin Neuhaus and Dr Harald Selzner of Noerr, and Dr Dirk Oberbracht of Gibson Dunn.

Experiencing the generosity with which all these busy professionals and academics shared their time and knowledge was among the most rewarding aspects of writing this book.

I would also like to thank the team at Wolters Kluwer for their guidance and encouragement, including Eleanor Taylor, Kiran Nasir Gore and Claire Chouzenoux, and the team at Newgen, including Gayathri Ravi, R. Srinivasan, Shamli Chapalge, E. Dhanalakshmi and Farzana.

Most of all, I am grateful to my wife Alba Lucia for her love, support and encouragement. This book is dedicated to her and our daughters Laura and Sara.

Heiko Ziehms, London, September 2023

CHAPTER 1

Introduction

§1.01 BACKGROUND AND PURPOSE OF THIS PUBLICATION

In the course of an M&A transaction, the key protagonists, be they the principals or their advisers, deal with a myriad of complex matters. They often have to make decisions against the backdrop of an unrealistic deadline, imperfect (despite, often voluminous) information, and a shrewd other side. In making these decisions, they deal with complex technical issues spanning a variety of specialist fields of knowledge, such as: corporate finance, accounting, law, taxation, banking, operations, environmental, and strategy. This can make decision-making tricky, and it is easy in these circumstances to create outcomes that are open to disagreement and that end up in legal disputes. These outcomes – to the extent they relate to financial and accounting matters – are the principal focus of this book.

Research by economists and practitioners working in the field of mergers and acquisitions (M&A) shows that a high number of deals fail.[17] The causes cited for such failure are varied: a lack of strategic fit, poorly executed integration, clash of cultures, and insufficient understanding of the target company's market, to name a few. A post-M&A dispute is another factor often associated with a failed transaction: at best, it can take the gloss off a deal. At worst, it can threaten the viability of both the acquirer's own business as well as that of the acquired company.

It is difficult to think of another corporate activity that wastes as much management time and costs as much money, without furthering – indeed, often hindering – the operating activities of the business as a post-deal dispute. Disputes can take years to resolve and cost many millions of pounds, euros, or dollars. In short, they should be avoided.

17. For an overview, *see* Ioannis C. Thanos and Vassilis M. Papadakis, *Unbundling Acquisition Performance*, in David Faulkner, Satu Teerikangas, Richard J. Joseph (eds) *The Handbook of Mergers & Acquisition*, 121 (Oxford University Press 2014).

It is not always possible in the highly charged circumstances of a deal to find the time to contemplate, much less debate, issues from a theoretical point of view, to think through a problem conceptually, and to go back to basics. This publication tries to link practical matters back to corporate finance theory and accounting conventions and thus provide a grounding in these disciplines that underlie most transactions and their completion mechanics.

Understanding why disputes happen starts with the conceptual framework of the 'deal mechanics' – a term used here to embrace the completion mechanism (*see* §1.03 below) – and their interface with the valuation of the target company, the acquisition structure, and the sale and purchase agreement (SPA). Beyond this conceptual framework, the book draws on a large number of actual cases of post-M&A disputes to identify precisely where things go wrong. Lessons learned from past disputes can help identify situations which might otherwise lead to them being repeated; they can also be instructive, where a dispute has already arisen, in forming a view as to how to resolve it.

The principal focus of this publication is on financial and accounting matters in the context of M&A disputes. It should be emphasised that it is not the intention to prompt a discussion of accounting issues outside this context; these are covered exhaustively elsewhere. Further, this is not a legal textbook. When legal questions are discussed, it is only to provide context and explain relevant financial or accounting aspects of completion mechanisms and their related disputes.

The book is aimed at M&A practitioners, be they corporate M&A departments, PE, sovereign wealth funds or other investors, as well as investment bankers, lawyers, accountants, and other professionals who advise them. It is also intended for those who deal with post-M&A disputes: judges, arbitrators, litigators, Warranty and Indemnity (W&I) insurers, and third-party funders. Whether they possess extensive or relatively little experience in the field, these busy people would find the discussion here of benefit to them.

§1.02 WHAT GOES WRONG?

Disputes often arise at the intersection of different professional disciplines. Take accounting. Much in accounting relies on professional judgment, both of the accountant and others. For example, accounting for a long-term construction project may require estimates by engineers as to the degree of completion. These estimates can affect reported earnings and working capital. Reported earnings, in turn, can be the basis of a buyer's valuation. If a buyer uses a market approach and an earnings multiple of, say, ten, then a dollar increase in those earnings (if considered recurring and cash-relevant) can increase the valuation of the enterprise by an amount that reflects a similar multiple (all else being equal). The very same estimate may affect the working capital figure at closing and lead to a dollar-for-dollar purchase price adjustment. Much can go wrong here: estimates of the degree of completion can be overly aggressive, earnings inflated, or working capital overstated. The buyer overpays, possibly even more than once: the effect of the same (overstated) degree of completion may be included in both earnings and working capital at closing (*see* §9.03 [B]). The professionals involved in reviewing the technical estimates would have been different from those analysing the accounting, and again from those valuing the target or drafting the SPA. The exchange of information across disciplines is not always straightforward.

The occurrence of an unexpected event around closing is another important factor in many M&A-related disputes. This could be the disruption to a customer relationship, unexpected volatility in supplier or financial markets, or sudden changes in regulations. Examples include recent shocks to energy markets, disruption to credit markets during the financial crisis of 2007 to 2009 (§4.04 [C]), rapidly falling prices in the markets for ships (§3.04 [A]), a cyberattack (§1.05 [B]), the discovery of fraud (§10.01), or unforeseen regulatory decisions (§8.03 [A] [2]).

The effect of disruption can be exacerbated when it meets with vague measurement concepts or ambiguous wording in the SPA (§12.04 [D]). The combination provides a fertile feeding ground for those seeking to disagree over the determination of a purchase price adjustment (§4.04 [C] [5]), the basis of an earn-out (§8.03 [A] [1]), the counterparty of an exclusivity agreement (§1.05 [A]), an alleged material adverse change (MAC) (§1.05 [B]), or the value of shares of subsequent steps in an acquisition which the buyer has an option to acquire.[18] There is often a trade-off between getting a deal done while accepting some ambiguity – which can be constructive in a negotiation (*see* §14.02 [A]) – and resolving difficult technical matters satisfactorily by investing enough time to ensure that concepts and the wording in contracts are as clear as possible.

A response sometimes heard when particularly complex topics arise in the course of a transaction is the claim that such issues do not really matter in the context of the deal. Comments such as 'at the end of the day, there is only one purchase price and it doesn't matter how you get there', or an almost exclusive focus on 'the big picture', are not uncommon. Those who raise legitimate concerns are sometimes branded 'deal killers'. While the big picture is clearly important, many disputes arise not necessarily out of 'big picture' problems, but because the parties got the technical minutiae wrong. A successful transaction can be forgiving. However, when things start going wrong, and one party starts looking – usually with more time and better access to information than was available when the deal was negotiated – technical oversights and errors very often come to light. Marry in haste, litigate at leisure, to paraphrase.

A benefit of the recent growth of W&I Insurance is that insurers publish data on the frequency of claims. While limited to insured transactions, the statistics are informative. One recent survey suggests that the average reported claim frequency per policy exceeded 20% for all deal sizes except the smallest category of deals worth less than USD 100 million (17%).[19] Other surveys report somewhat lower figures.[20]

18. *Cavendish Square Holdings BV v. Makdessi* [2015] UKSC 67.
19. M&A: Elevated claim levels put focus on due diligence, AIG Claims Intelligence Services, 2021. The survey suggests that claims of financial statements warranties are the most common type of contractual breach, followed by tax and compliance with laws. It covered the period to the end of 2019, i.e., before the COVID-19 pandemic.

Nonetheless, a dispute is not a remote possibility but a real risk, and reducing it is a good investment.

Having said that, however perfect the deal mechanics, some transactions cannot be saved. Factors such as the unequal balance of power between buyer and seller, information asymmetries, behavioural biases, or a cultural mismatch can play a significant role in the lead-up to disputes. Even deals acclaimed as a marriage made in heaven end, sadly, in tears and, sometimes, divorce. Those are for others – perhaps behavioural economists – to analyse.

§1.03 DEFINITIONS AND COMMONLY USED TERMS

Throughout this publication, the term 'deal mechanics' is used to refer to a range of completion mechanisms, completion accounts, purchase price adjustments, and locked box arrangements. For the sake of clarity, these terms are defined below:

- Completion mechanism: a transaction procedure involving completion accounts and purchase price adjustments or, alternatively, a locked box.
- Completion accounts (or 'closing date accounts'): the accounts drawn up as on the completion date, by either purchaser or seller, in accordance with the provisions of the SPA, in order to establish, under the terms of the SPA, the purchase price adjustments to be made to the preliminary (or provisional) purchase price agreed by the parties.
- Purchase price adjustments: the adjustments to the preliminary purchase price to reflect the actual values in respect of, most commonly, net debt and working capital and, in some transactions, certain other defined items which are added to or deducted from the preliminary purchase price, to calculate the final purchase price from which equity value is derived.
- Locked box: the arrangement whereby the parties to a transaction agree on a fixed price with no subsequent adjustments, based on a balance sheet date before signing. The date is often that of the last audited financial statements. This avoids the necessity to prepare completion accounts. The purchase price is fixed based on that historical balance sheet date and reflects, *inter alia*, the levels of cash, debt, and working capital at that date. Locked box transactions are economically, though not legally, backdated transactions.

§1.04 CASES

The cases referred to in this book have two sources:

(1) A proprietary data set of over sixty cases with well over 1,000 individual claims. These are primarily international arbitration cases which the author

20. Insights into W&I Insurance Claims in Asia, What half a decade of data tells us, Marsh Insights, April 2020. This survey reports that the average rate of notification of all policies in the last five years in Asia was approximately 15%.

and his colleagues have worked on over the last twenty years. Given the confidentiality of these cases, they have not provided any specific information on any actual case. In all instances, names and details have been changed in order to maintain confidentiality.

(2) Cases in the public domain which the author references as appropriate.

It should also be pointed out that the discussion of the cases in this book, which come from a variety of different legal jurisdictions, relate to financial and accounting questions, not points of law.

§1.05 TYPES OF M&A DISPUTES

An M&A-related dispute is defined here as any dispute, whether litigated, arbitrated, mediated, or prosecuted, arising from the sale of one business, or part of one business, to another, or a merger of two businesses.

Most M&A-related disputes occur after closing. However, disputes can arise during all stages of a deal as shown below in Figure 1.1.

Figure 1.1 Transaction Timeline

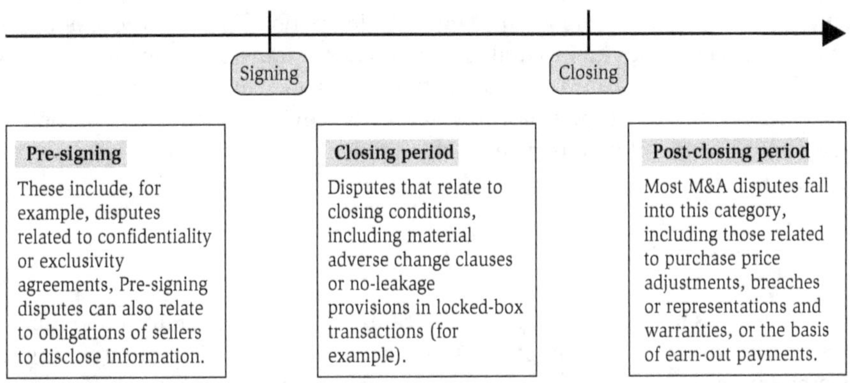

[A] Pre-signing

Typical disputes that arise in the period before signing relate to binding parts of (otherwise often non-binding) documents, such as letters of intent, non-disclosure agreements, break-up fees, or exclusivity agreements. They can also arise over sellers' disclosure obligations.

An example of a pre-signing dispute is *Gemini v. AmeriPark*, which related to an exclusivity agreement that was part of an (otherwise non-binding) indicative offer.[21] The case is discussed in §13.04.

[B] Closing Period

The purpose of closing conditions is to ensure that legal and other requirements have been satisfied and that, when control is transferred to the buyer, the business is the one that the buyer contracted to buy. Closing conditions often include regulatory approval, financing, 'bring-down' of representations and warranties, or the non-occurrence of a MAC (to name only a few). Closing conditions vary significantly by transaction. There are also geographical differences, reflecting differences in the typical allocation of risk between the parties in different parts of the world. As it takes time to meet the closing conditions, signing and closing usually do not occur on the same day, at least for complex transactions.

One type of dispute that arises during this period relates to MAC clauses. These clauses aim to protect the buyer by providing a mechanism to terminate a transaction before closing in the event of a MAC. MAC clauses are usually either closing conditions or sellers' representations (or sometimes both).

SPAs also often include covenants that require the target company to conduct its business in the ordinary course during the closing period. Their purpose is to protect the buyer from surprises in the conduct of the seller or target management, and thus to ensure it receives the business in substantially the same condition as it was when the parties signed the SPA. In the past few years, the covid pandemic has brought MAC clauses and conduct of business covenants into sharper focus. They are discussed in Chapter 13.

[C] Post-closing

Most of the cases in this book fall into this category. Post-closing disputes (other than those related to earn-outs (Chapter 8)) are usually initiated soon after closing, often triggered by unexpected liquidity needs of the target business which in turn leads to a forensic review.

It is fair to say that, in the absence of unexpected liquidity needs or other triggering events (such as a whistle-blower coming forward), many potential causes of post-M&A disputes go unnoticed.[22]

21. An exclusivity agreement is an agreement that the buyer and seller in an M&A transaction only deal with each other to the exclusion of other parties for a certain period of time while they negotiate a deal.
22. This observation is also consistent with recent research findings. *See* the discussion of detection likelihood in Dyck, A., Morse, A. and Zingales, L. *How Pervasive Is Corporate Fraud?* Review of Accounting Studies, 2023, 6.

CHAPTER 2

The Value of the Firm, Capital Structure, and the Completion Mechanism

§2.01 OVERVIEW

[A] The Value of the Firm and Capital Structure

A firm engages in operating, investing, and financing activities. It does so with the intention of generating value and providing a return to investors who have acquired claims on the firm for the distribution of future surpluses. The two principal types of investors are the shareholders and the debtholders, their claims being on the firm's equity and debt, respectively.[23] These claims may be tradeable in the capital markets (such as shares on a stock exchange) or not tradeable (such as many partnership interests).

In a perfect market and in the absence of taxes, the value of the firm is independent of how the claims on it are divided among the different investors.[24] The capital structure itself is irrelevant: the present value of two potentially uncertain income streams equals the sum of their separate present values.[25] However it is

23. There are other claims, but these two are sufficient for the purpose of this analysis. The separation of firm financing and production decisions goes back to the Fisher Separation Theorem. *See* Rubinstein, *A History of the Theory of Investments*, 55 (Wiley 2006).
24. Franco Modigliani and Merton Miller (Modigliani-Miller's Proposition I), *The Cost of Capital, Corporation Finance and the Theory of Investment*, American Economic Review June 1958, Vol. 48, No. 3, 261–297.
25. This is called the 'Law of the Conservation of Investment Value' by John Burr Williams, *Theory of Investment Value*, North-Holland Pub. Co., 1956. John Burr Williams preceded Modigliani-Miller. *See* Rubinstein, *A History of the Theory of Investments*, 128 (Wiley 2006).

apportioned between the respective claimants (the shareholders and debtholders), the value of the firm does not change.[26]

The relationship between firm value and the value of the claims on the firm can be stated as follows:

(1) Value of the firm = Value of debt + Value of equity

In a transaction, the value of the firm is commonly referred to as 'enterprise value', but also as the 'headline price' (often in the letter of intent issued at the early stage of a deal), the 'value of the operations', or the 'cash and debt free' value. These terms refer to the operating assets and liabilities, excluding financing items, such as surplus cash and financial debt.[27]

The relationship between the value of the firm and the claims on it is also expressed in the principal accounting (or balance sheet) equation:[28]

(2) Net Operating Assets = Equity + Net Debt.

While the balance sheet equation uses accounting (or book) values, it is of the same form as equation (1). It links accounting, a man-made construct, to the theory of corporate finance. The difference is only in the way assets, liabilities and equity are measured.[29] The book will return to this difference in the discussion of damages in Chapter 11.

[B] The Equity Value Bridge

In a share deal, the buyer and seller ultimately have to agree on the price for the equity. While a number of valuation approaches are available, the starting point for valuation in most (though not all) transactions is enterprise value, to which adjustments are made for debt and debt-like items and for cash and cash equivalents in order to arrive at a value for the equity. In practice, cash and debt-like items are usually combined under one heading, 'net debt'.

This is depicted in Figure 2.1 in a simple version of what is known as the equity value bridge.

26. With taxes and the risk of bankruptcy, capital structure decisions are not irrelevant.
27. In the analysis of operating and financing activities, investing cash flows are considered to be operating cash flows, and the two combined form free cash flow, the cash returns of the operations. Investing in operating assets is an operating activity.
28. Assuming 'clean-surplus' accounting. *See* Stephen H. Penman, *Financial Statement Analysis and Security Valuation*, 42 (4th ed., McGraw-Hill Education 2009).
29. *See* Stephen H. Penman, *Financial Statement Analysis and Security Valuation*, 42 (4th ed., McGraw-Hill Education 2009). From this equation it is easy to derive the 'clean surplus' for equity book value as the change in book value of equity equals earnings minus dividends. This property is in accordance with Modigliani Miller.

Figure 2.1 Equity Value Bridge

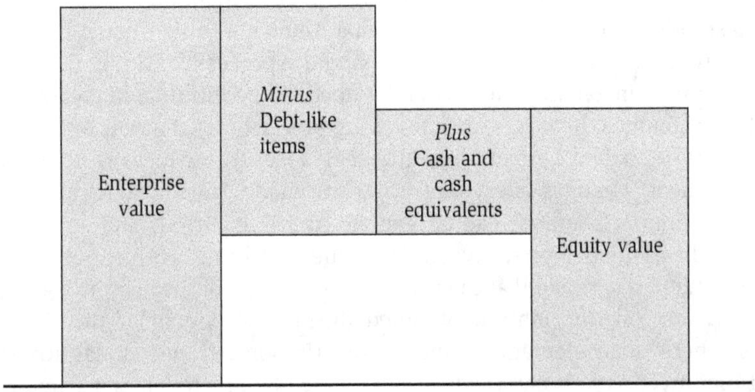

Enterprise value is typically measured by discounting free cash flows or using a multiple-based method, such as a multiple of Earnings before Interest and Taxes (EBIT) or Earnings before Interest, Taxes, Depreciation and Amortisation (EBITDA).[30]

Enterprise value encompasses all the operating assets and liabilities necessary to carry on the business. It assumes, critically for transactions, an appropriate, or normal, level of working capital at the date on which closing takes place (or other relevant date). The level has to be agreed between the parties. The normal level of working capital that the parties agree upon is commonly referred to as the 'reference value' or 'target value', with any variances from this being reflected in an adjustment.

Enterprise value also assumes that capital and revenue expenditure, both operating items, have been maintained at appropriate levels and that the business is not 'underinvested'. What level of investment is considered 'appropriate' is a matter for negotiation between the parties.

Hence, as well as an adjustment in respect of net debt, the final purchase price in a transaction will typically also incorporate adjustments in respect of working capital and, less frequently, capital and revenue expenditure. These are collectively referred to as purchase price adjustments. They are discussed in outline later in this section and in depth in Chapters 4, 5 and 6.

To the layman, purchase price adjustments may seem quite straightforward. However, even in a relatively uncomplicated transaction, an inordinate amount of time and effort can be expended, particularly by the accountants and lawyers acting for each side, in rehearsing the various arguments as to whether an item should or should not be treated as an adjustment and how it should be measured.

30. Some valuation approaches value the equity, e.g., the dividend discount model and the discounted net abnormal earnings models. However, these are less commonly used in practice.

[C] The Uncertainty Inherent in a Transaction

Ultimately, the buyer and seller have to reach an agreement on the items to be treated as purchase price adjustments, namely: what items are to be treated as adjustments, how they are to be defined and measured, and the process for doing this. All this – or at least a detailed mechanism to this end – needs to be formulated clearly in the SPA. One of the difficulties, however, is in knowing precisely what assets and liabilities will be on (or off) the balance sheet when the deal closes. A business is not static; it (and its balance sheet) changes every day: sales are made, inventory levels rise and fall, creditor accounts are settled, capital expenditure is incurred, and so on. The latest independently verified figures available to the purchaser are probably the audited financial statements prepared at the previous year end. For more up-to-date figures, he or she will rely on information obtained during the course of the due diligence. Inevitably there is an element of uncertainty (in some transactions, anxiety) in the mind of the buyer as to what assets and liabilities he or she will get when ownership transfers. This concern may become heightened once the SPA is signed: there is generally no going back.

[D] The Transaction Timeline

The timeline of a transaction where signing and closing occur on different dates is shown in Figure 2.2.

Figure 2.2 Transaction Timeline

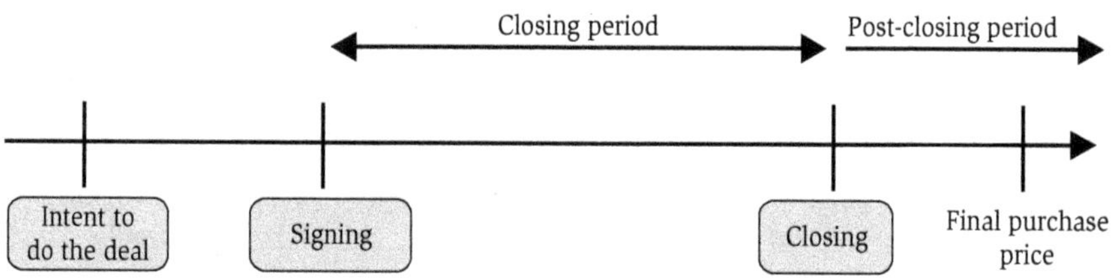

Examples of closing conditions include governmental or regulatory approvals, transaction financing, third-party and shareholder consent, bring down of representations and warranties, the retention of key employees, and the non-occurrence of MACs (to name only a few). Closing periods can range from a few weeks to several months, and in some cases can even be significantly longer, for example in regulated industries or where significant antitrust reviews are involved.[31]

The existence of this interval between signing and closing, whose length can be difficult to predict accurately, gives rise to further uncertainty as to the precise assets

31. For example, the acquisition of Alstom's power and grid businesses by GE required regulatory approval in over twenty countries and regions, taking approximately eighteen months from the announcement in April 2014 to closing in November 2015.

and liabilities to be transferred at closing. The longer the closing period, the greater the uncertainty. However, significant changes can occur even in short closing periods.

[E] The Purpose of the Completion Mechanism

The purpose of a completion mechanism is to set out a clear and unambiguous process which will ensure that the parties to the SPA obtain what they bargained for. Ironically, many post-M&A disputes originate from disagreements over the very mechanisms that were put in place precisely for this purpose. A sound completion mechanism should ensure that both buyer and seller get what they understood they negotiated, resulting in a 'clean' transaction.

More often than not, the main concern (at least up to completion) is on the part of the buyer. The buyer will seek to incorporate into the SPA measures to safeguard his or her interests, including for the period from signing to completion, during which the target business remains under the stewardship of the seller. This is not limited to financial and accounting matters; the buyer will usually be protected by covenants concerning the operation of the business during the closing period.

One of the buyer's principal worries here is that the seller could 'extract value', or that value could 'leak', between signing and closing, and that this is not reflected in the final purchase price, resulting in the buyer taking over a business worth less than what they believed they were getting.

If the SPA does not contain a completion mechanism that adjusts the purchase price or prevents value leakage, then there are a number of ways in which a seller could potentially extract value. These include:

- Dividend payments.
- Adjusting transfer prices used in transactions between related parties.
- Intercompany charges.
- Management compensation.
- Advisory fees.
- Waiving liabilities.

Value leakage is discussed further in §7.03.

Leaving aside the possibility of a seller's less than honourable intentions, it is sensible for both parties to protect themselves from being disadvantaged as a result of movements in the balance sheet in the period leading up to closing. While the buyer's concerns probably outweigh those of the seller during that time, the boot is rather more on the other foot when it comes to the preparation of completion accounts, as shall be seen later.

Traditionally, the solution to the problems outlined above has been to prepare a set of completion accounts. These incorporate the various purchase price adjustments, computed on the basis agreed by the parties and documented in the SPA, and result in the establishment of the final purchase price.

However, an alternative approach emerged in the early 2000s, namely the 'locked box'. In this scenario, the parties agree on a fixed price in the SPA with no subsequent purchase price adjustments.

Figures 2.3 to 2.5 show the two principal completion mechanisms that are available in a private M&A transaction, the purchase price adjustment and the locked box, as well as a combination of the two, a hybrid completion mechanism. Each option is discussed further below.

Figure 2.3 Purchase Price Adjustments

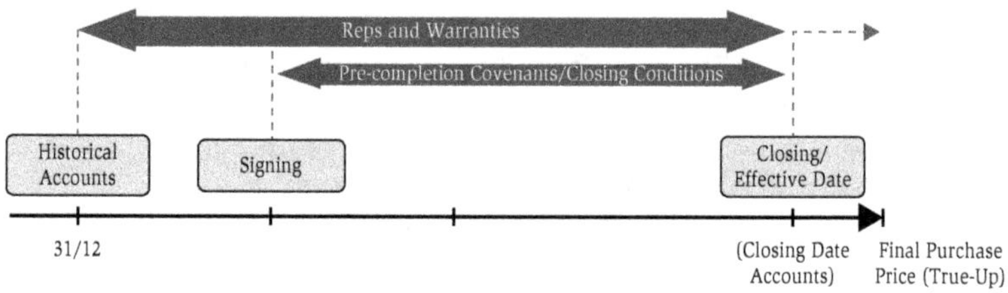

Figure 2.4 The Locked Box

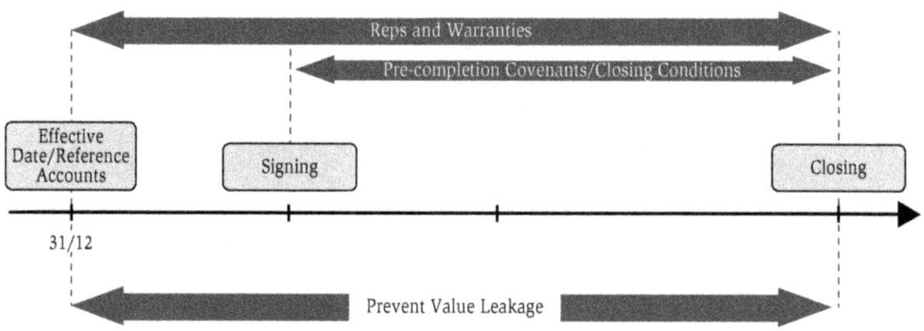

Figure 2.5 Hybrid Completion Mechanism

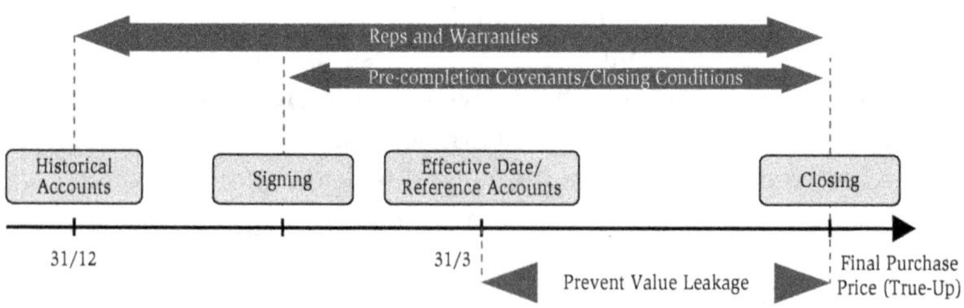

[F] Relevance of Items Leading to Purchase Price Adjustments in a Locked Box Transaction

The purpose of a locked box mechanism is to eliminate adjustments to the purchase price subsequent to closing by computing an equity value based on a historical balance sheet, i.e., prior to the closing date. The agreed equity value is a fixed purchase price that is not subject to any post-closing adjustments. It is a final price.

The term 'purchase price adjustments' typically refers to adjustments made to the preliminary purchase price following the completion accounts process. It should be noted that similar adjustments are made or should be made, when agreeing the fixed purchase price in locked box transactions, only that they are incorporated into the fixed purchase price.

The use of the term 'purchase price adjustments' here is, therefore, generic: it refers to transactions involving completion accounts as well as to those made in agreeing the fixed purchase price with a locked box mechanism.

Example: Enterprise Value, Equity Value, and Double Counting[32]

The case shows how the interaction between the individual elements of the equity bridge in Figure 2.1 above can lead to confusion and double or triple counting. This is a divorce case. The aspects of interest here concern the valuation of the husband's business, a machinery and equipment maker. His former wife was entitled to one-half. The dispute was over the valuation of the shares.

The aggregate balance sheet of the husband's company is shown in Table 2.1.

Table 2.1 Balance Sheet as at 31 December 1995

	EUR Thousand
Manufacturing facility (building)	132
Other assets	54
Total liabilities	–492
Net assets	–306

At 31 December 1995, the company reported negative net assets of EUR 306,000. According to a property expert, the fair value of the manufacturing facility (with a book value of EUR 132,000) amounted to EUR 319,000.

An expert valued the business at EUR 260,000 (enterprise value). The expert then deducted the negative net assets, arguing that a buyer of the business would be willing to pay a positive amount only if the net asset value was not negative. Accordingly, the equity value amounted to – EUR 46,000 (=260,000–306,000). Note that this figure counted the facility twice, once in enterprise value and again in the deduction of the

32. BGH, 8 September 2004 – XII ZR 194/01, NJW-RR 2005, 153, OLG Koblenz, 13 July 2001 – UF 248/00, OLGR Koblenz 2002, 152, (simplified here). *See also* the discussion in: Wächter, *M&A Litigation*, 3rd ed. 2017, RWS Verlag Kommunikationsforum GmbH, p. 665.

book value of net assets.[33] Nevertheless, possibly because the resulting equity value was a negative number, the judge at first instance decided to add to the equity value the fair value of the manufacturing facility of EUR 319,000. The value of the shares was thus determined as - EUR 46,000 + EUR 319,000 = EUR 273,000. By adding the fair value of the facility, the resulting value now included the manufacturing facility three times, with three different amounts:

- the book value of EUR 132,000;
- the value included in the enterprise value of EUR 260,000; and
- the fair value of EUR 319,000.

The first Court of Appeal[34] decided to eliminate the book value of the facility from the negative net assets which is calculated as - EUR 306,000 - EUR 132,000 = - EUR 438,000. It determined that the equity value amounted to EUR 260,000 (EV) - EUR 438,000 = - EUR 178,000. The court then added to this subtotal the fair value of the manufacturing facility of EUR 319,000 to obtain EUR 141,000. As the book value of the facility had been removed, this valuation of EUR 141,000 counted the facility twice.

The German Federal Court of Justice (BGH) sent the case back to the lower court instructing the court to review whether the manufacturing facility was a necessary part of the operations. This suggests that the value of the facility could only be added if it was determined that it was not part of normal operations. (It is not clear how the lower court ruled.)[35]

§2.02 PURCHASE PRICE ADJUSTMENTS: OVERVIEW

[A] Introduction

As discussed above, purchase price adjustments represent adjustments between enterprise value (a debt and cash-free basis with a normal level of working capital and investments in fixed assets) and equity value (after the deduction of net debt at closing).

In a 'traditional' transaction involving a completion accounts process, purchase price adjustments are made to a preliminary purchase price by measuring (subsequent to completion) the relevant balance sheet items at the closing date. In a locked box transaction, such adjustments are made based on a historical balance sheet, i.e., at a date prior to closing. Purchase price adjustments are summarised in Table 2.2.

33. The book value of net assets is a negative figure, it includes the positive book value of the facility (EUR 132,000).
34. OLG Koblenz 2002, 152 - FamRZ 2002, 1190.
35. BGH 8 September 2004 - XII ZR 194/01, NJW-RR 2005, p. 155.

Table 2.2 Purchase Price Adjustments

Adjustment	*Purpose*
Net debt	To arrive at a debt-free, cash-free valuation
Working capital*	Primarily protects buyer against a seller reducing working capital to decrease net debt
Capital expenditure*	Protects buyer against a seller slowing down capital expenditure to decrease net debt
Revenue expenditure*	Used, notably, in businesses where certain revenue expenditure, e.g., marketing, research and development, are key metrics. Protects buyer against a seller cutting expenditure to reduce net debt
Net assets/equity	Typically used instead of – sometimes as a 'floor' in addition to – a net debt adjustment. Far less prevalent in recent years
Enterprise value	Used in relatively rare cases where there is unusual uncertainty over enterprise value

*Used in combination with net debt adjustment.

Each of these adjustments is discussed briefly below. More detailed analysis, together with examples of disputes arising from these adjustments, is included in later chapters.

Earn-outs should not be confused with purchase price adjustments which have a different purpose from addressing changes in the closing period. Earn-outs are deferred compensation, whereas purchase price adjustments are not, only they are calculated at closing. Earn-outs are discussed in Chapter 8.

[B] Net Debt Adjustment

The net debt adjustment results in a valuation on a 'cash-free, debt-free' basis. Thus, the buyer is compensated for the level of debt taken over at closing; similarly, the seller is compensated for any surplus cash (free cash) in the business at closing.

[C] Working Capital Adjustment

Since variations in cash and debt are, in part, directly attributable to changes in the level of working capital, a net debt adjustment typically requires a corresponding adjustment in respect of (net) working capital. Net working capital and net debt represent the most common combination of purchase price adjustments.

The basic purpose here is to protect the buyer from actions by the seller that maximise the cash – or minimise the net debt – position of the target business at closing by reducing net working capital. This is achieved as the buyer pays – on a dollar-for-dollar basis – for working capital in excess of a level that is agreed by both parties to be 'normal' (commonly referred to as the working capital 'reference value' or working capital 'target'). Correspondingly, the buyer receives a purchase price reduction for any shortfall against the reference value. If the completion mechanics work properly, every movement in net debt that relates to working capital is offset by the working capital adjustment, so that the net purchase price is unaffected.

[D] Capital Expenditure Adjustment

A seller may be motivated to slow down capital expenditure in order to maximise the cash position of the target business at closing. As a consequence, the buyer would obtain an 'underinvested' business with an artificially high cash position (which it would pay for as part of the net debt adjustment).

The rationale behind a capital expenditure adjustment is that it offsets this higher cash position by correcting for any shortfall in expenditure in the closing period compared with an agreed amount of aggregate capital expenditure (or reference level). The adjustment may be limited to a decrease in the purchase price, or go both ways and also increase the purchase price if capital expenditure is higher than the reference level. Adjustments in respect of expenditure incurred in excess of the agreed reference value are often subject to a ceiling in order to protect the buyer from expenditure it considers excessive. A capital expenditure adjustment is also used in some cases to give buyers some influence over long-term investment decisions even before closing (if specific expenditures are identified in the SPA), although this can run into issues of 'gun jumping' (*see* below §6.01).

[E] Revenue Expenditure Adjustment

Purchase price adjustments in connection with revenue expenditure feature relatively rarely in transactions. Similar to the working capital and capital expenditure adjustments, the rationale is to protect a buyer against a seller attempting to improve the target entity's net debt position. The difference is that revenue expenditure adjustments protect against other ways the net debt position could be influenced that are not already captured by either of those other adjustments. More common examples relate to marketing or research and development expenditure (against reference values) which is discretionary or can be delayed.

[F] Net Asset Adjustment

The net asset or equity adjustment (both terms are used interchangeably in this publication in the context of purchase price adjustments) calls for a price adjustment in respect of the difference between net assets and an agreed reference value at closing. A surplus over the reference value increases the purchase price; a deficit reduces it. The idea is to capture the net effect of changes between signing and closing in the book value of equity. This equates the change in the commercial value of the equity, the owners' residual claim against the assets, with the change in book value.

Net asset adjustments used to be fairly widespread but have become rare in recent years.[36] This probably has to do with an increasingly sophisticated market that has exposed the problems associated with these adjustments.

One such problem is that many changes in the book values of assets have nothing to do with 'value' as understood in the context of a transaction and, consequently, should not lead to a purchase price adjustment. The book value of net assets is not the same as value transferred on closing. Consider a non-cash one-off write-down of goodwill or a change in accounting policies to capitalise internal costs (such as development expenditure). Both result in a change in net assets. Should a buyer, however, pay more (or less) because of these and other items that may have nothing to do with value?[37]

A practical problem has to do with the fact that, since equity represents total assets less total liabilities, it is impacted not only by how each balance sheet item is accounted for but also by accounting choices concerning the income statement. The SPA, therefore, must specify accounting rules not only for a limited number of net debt and working capital items but for all balance sheet and income statement items. The SPA has, *inter alia*, to limit arbitrary accounting choices that underlie the determination of book values at closing; a simple reference to consistency or GAAP invariably does not suffice. Further, the SPA has also to include a definition of normalised earnings in a manner that ensures that only components to which the parties agree should result in an adjustment to the price. In theory, this means the parties must be in a position to anticipate any and all items that could affect net income, so as to ensure they do not result in an adjustment; in a sense, they have to 'normalise' the net income of the closing period. In the author's experience, normalising unknown income - and expenditure - of a future period, is difficult, to say the least.

In practice, the more thoroughly the parties define balance sheet items in the SPA to ensure that a net asset adjustment captures only those items that are relevant to value, the more closely those remaining will resemble net debt and working capital items. The result should, theoretically at least, be very similar: a mechanism that captures only items for which it is appropriate to have a dollar-for-dollar adjustment. The difference, however, is that the starting point for a net asset adjustment is all balance sheet captions, from which those not relevant to value have to be excluded, a process more complex (if done properly) than simply specifying a smaller population of items relevant for adjustment.

36. An exception are transactions involving financial institutions, for which debt and net assets have a different significance from other firms. For these, net asset adjustments are common.
37. One might argue that an impairment write-down of goodwill reflects a change in expectations of the financial performance of an acquired business, and that this change can be of relevance to value. However, it is far from clear that this should lead to a dollar-for-dollar purchase price adjustment.

Due to these problems, net asset adjustments increase the scope for potential disagreements between the parties considerably.[38] Similar problems arise with warranties of net assets or minimum equity. Since net asset adjustments are rarely used today, they are considered here only in the context of specific disputes.

[G] Adjustments to Enterprise Value

The purpose of the purchase price adjustments outlined so far is either to derive an equity value from enterprise value or to take account of, say, a level of working capital at closing that does not correspond to underlying enterprise value assumptions. Occasionally a party to a transaction (usually the buyer) sees the need for a purchase price adjustment that changes what might be described as the 'intrinsic' enterprise value. It is rare for this kind of adjustment to be agreed to and almost never a good idea.

An enterprise value adjustment may be mooted when a valuation is based on the results of a period for which figures are considered critical to the valuation but are not yet available, for example, when a financial year ends during the closing period (and is not, therefore, available at signing).

The problem with an adjustment to enterprise value is that it can make the final purchase price difficult to predict, and easy to disagree on since minor changes to, say, EBITDA can translate into major changes to price (through the multiple). In one instance of this nature, the purchase price was subject to adjustment depending on the recalculation of the gross margins of certain contracts entered into by the target business prior to closing and its income for a defined period.[39]

If a party is unable to come to a conclusion about the value of the business at the time the deal is signed, then the information it is waiting for arguably weighs too heavily in the valuation; as such, any adjustment overstates the importance of the information, which usually relates to a comparatively short period (relative to the many years of a going concern's future trading). Additional, apparently critical, information is still required to value the business. Conceivably, in these cases, signing is simply taking place too early.

[H] Acquisitions Carried Out in Steps

Some acquisitions are performed in steps whereby the buyer initially acquires less than 100% of the share capital (although often a majority interest) with an option to buy the balance of the shares in a subsequent step or series of steps.

In these cases, the purchase price adjustment should correspond to the percentage of the shares acquired in each step. It is usually necessary first to determine 100% of the purchase price adjustment and then to reduce it by the fraction not acquired. This generally applies to all types of purchase price adjustments. For example, if the

38. For an example of an equity adjustment in a post-M&A dispute *see* ICC Case 11587 in the following section.
39. ICC Case 11587, discussed in the following section.

initial acquisition is a 70% interest in the target entity, and a net working capital adjustment on a 100% basis is USD 10 million, then the purchase price adjustment at the time of the initial acquisition step is USD 7 million.

If the parties instead adjusted for 100% in a 70% acquisition, then the buyer would pay for the entire working capital surplus (in the example above) but would not be entitled to 100% of any future distributions from this excess working capital.

For subsequent steps in the acquisition process, the parties should, theoretically, re-measure both the reference value and the working capital at the relevant date of these steps.

In practice, it may be unrealistic to renegotiate the working capital reference value or re-measure the working capital position in subsequent acquisition steps, especially with multiple steps involving only minor amounts. The parties may therefore agree on fixed adjustments for all acquisition steps at the outset. In such cases, sellers may need to consider protecting themselves from changes the buyer may effect to working capital after gaining control.

§2.03 THE LOCKED BOX: THE PRINCIPAL IDEA

The concept of the locked box first appeared in PE auctions in Europe in the early 2000s and has since come to be adopted in a wide range of transactions. It is a popular completion mechanism in Europe and the norm for many PE transactions. It continues to be less common in the US and Asian Pacific markets.[40] This has led to situations in the past in which US buyers who participated in an auction process in Europe were asked to bid on a locked box basis with which they were unfamiliar. However, the use of the locked box is increasing in the US and Asia Pacific.[41]

The locked box is an alternative way of dealing with the uncertainties of the balance sheet at closing. The parties agree on a fixed price in the SPA with, usually, no subsequent adjustments. The fixed price is an equity price, calculated based on the balance sheet at a date before signing, frequently that of the last audited financial statements. This date is referred to as the 'effective date' or the 'locked box date'. The balance sheet at this date is the 'effective date balance sheet' or 'locked box balance sheet', and the period between the effective date and closing is the 'locked box period'. The purchase price is fixed on the basis of the effective date balance sheet and reflects the levels of cash, debt, and working capital at that date, after which the (acquisition target) 'box' is 'locked', so that no value may 'leak', other than in relation to matters specified in the SPA. There is no true-up at closing. The SPA has leakage protections.

The locked box has the following principal advantages:

- It is easier for a seller to assess bids in an auction process.

40. A smarter way to get deals done, *International Survey: Identifying International Market Practice for Equity Value Adjustments and Sale and Purchase Agreements*, Grant Thornton, November 2017, p. 5.
41. *Ibid.*

- It avoids the, often time-consuming, negotiations over defining in the SPA the bases of accounting to be applied to the completion accounts;
- It avoids the preparation and review of the closing date accounts and subsequent discussions, which result in (frequently downward) adjustments to the purchase price.

However, there are also potential downsides to a locked box approach. As the final purchase price is fixed and there is no true-up at closing, the due diligence on the reference date accounts is usually more important than in completion accounts processes, where the buyer also gets to review financial information as at closing. At the same time, strong sellers and competitive bidding processes – which make a locked box transaction more likely – tend to mean more restricted access to information during the due diligence phase.

Another disadvantage of locked boxes can be that the SPA naturally does not contain a collaborative resolution process similar to the completion accounts process for a purchase price adjustment (*see* Chapter 3). A collaborative resolution process provides the parties an opportunity to agree on a compromise before needing to involve an independent expert to make a determination. Locked box SPA disputes, while less likely to occur overall, are therefore more likely to head straight into litigation or arbitration.

Locked box agreements are economically, but not legally, backdated transactions. A way to view the retroactive transfer of economic interest is that the seller effectively manages the target company for the benefit of the buyer and that profits generated by the target business between the effective date and closing accrue to the purchaser. To compensate for this, the SPA usually specifies an interest rate (sometimes called a daily profit charge) to be applied to the fixed purchase price. The locked box interest charge is discussed in more detail in §7.05.

The locked box is often considered to be seller-friendly (even though there are circumstances in which it can be buyer-friendly).[42] This links its popularity to the relative strengths and weaknesses of sellers and buyers during the M&A cycle: during cyclical peaks, in a seller's market, the locked box tends to be more popular than during downturns, when buyers are in stronger positions.

§2.04 HYBRID COMPLETION MECHANISMS

Some completion mechanisms incorporate aspects of both purchase price adjustments and the locked box. For example, this is the case when a fixed purchase price is agreed, but there is nevertheless a reason or need to adjust for an item at closing (e.g., an intercompany balance), or, alternatively, when a purchase price adjustment is linked to a date when annual financial statements are prepared, but closing takes place a few days later. This latter case might occur when, for example, closing is proposed in early

42. For example, in the rare case that the buyer knows the target management well, and loyalties have already shifted.

January for a target business with a year end on 31 December, and the parties wish to use the year-end accounts as the basis for closing; this requires locked box type 'value leakage' protections for the period between 31 December and the closing date.[43]

43. Sellers should consider in this case whether closing could occur before 31 December in which case it is the seller, not the buyer, who may require protection against leakage.

CHAPTER 3

The Completion Accounts Process and Expert Determination

§3.01 INTRODUCTION

While the transaction negotiations are in train, the subsequent preparation of completion accounts (alternatively called 'closing date accounts') can tend to be relegated to little more than a process not unlike the annual preparation of accounts for audit – a necessary but routine, indeed tedious formality, to be undertaken at a later date. The completion accounts process, up to final agreement between the parties, can be time-consuming, especially when it requires time to settle disagreements during which there continues to be uncertainty over the final purchase price. This is among the reasons for the growing use of the locked box transaction.

As the completion accounts are the basis of the purchase price adjustment and the calculation of the final purchase price, they have a central role in any transaction with a purchase price adjustment. This chapter covers the key aspects to consider in mitigating problems arising from completion accounts.

§3.02 OVERVIEW OF COMPLETION ACCOUNTS PROCESS

The arrangements for the preparation and finalisation of completion accounts are set out in the SPA and typically follow the process shown in Figure 3.1.

Figure 3.1 Completion Accounts Process Overview

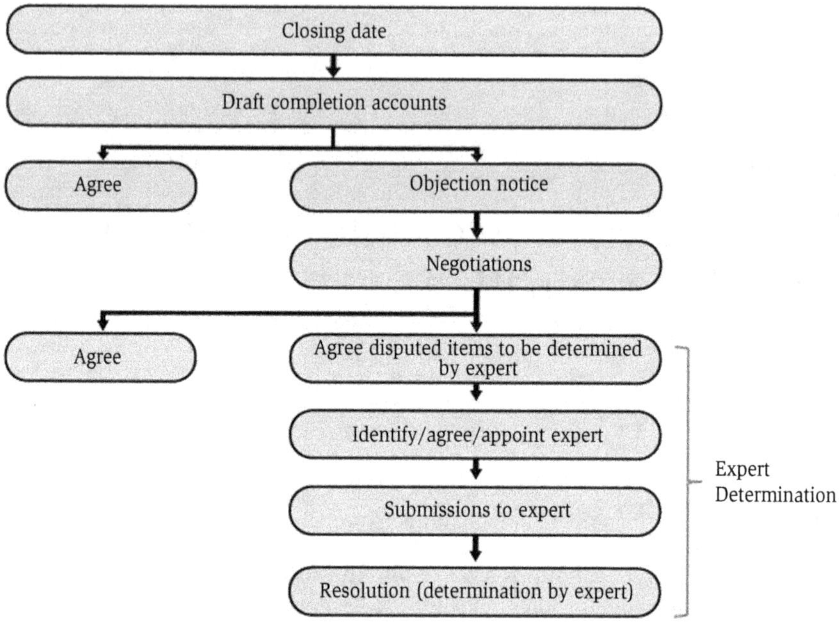

The completion accounts process starts when after closing, one party (more often the buyer) prepares draft completion accounts and the resulting calculation of the purchase price. The SPA usually sets out a defined period during which the draft completion accounts must be delivered to the other party.[44] This period typically ranges somewhere between twenty business days from closing for a straightforward transaction to ninety days or more (often less in the minority of deals in which the seller prepares) for a complex transaction in which the preparation of the completion accounts requires the consolidation of single-entity accounts of (multiple, international) subsidiaries. An example of wording that may be used in SPAs is as follows:

> As soon as practicable, and in any event, no later than thirty Business Days after the [Closing Date], the [Purchaser] shall procure that the Company prepares and delivers to the Seller, for its review, drafts of the Closing Accounts and the Final Purchase Price Statement drawn up in accordance with paragraph [].

Once the draft completion accounts and purchase price calculation have been delivered, the receiving party has the opportunity to review these. The review period is contractually predetermined and is usually shorter than the period for preparation of the completion accounts. If the reviewing party agrees with the draft accounts, then the final purchase price is determined on this basis, and the process is complete. If the

44. The SPA may specify interest for the period until the actual delivery or finalisation, which can be relevant in case the draft completion accounts are not delivered when required.

receiving party does not agree with all or part of the completion accounts, then the next step in the process is for the receiving party to prepare an objection notice (also called dispute notice or notice of disagreement) in which it details the areas of disagreement. Objection notices are written statements that can run into hundreds of pages when there are many areas of disagreement and many individual legal entity accounts on which the consolidated completion accounts are based.

The objection notice is followed by a period of negotiations – the resolution period – during which the parties attempt to reconcile their differences on the contentious items. The resolution period can be around fifteen business days for a straightforward completion process or significantly longer if more complex. The idea is that the parties negotiate in good faith to eliminate or narrow areas in dispute. If the parties reach agreement on all contentious points at the end of this period, then the final purchase price is determined, and the process ends. If, on the other hand, they do not resolve all differences, then the disputed items are referred to an expert for determination of the final completion accounts and purchase price. The expert may be predetermined in the SPA, or the parties may agree in the SPA only the process by which the expert will be determined. If the parties agree to name a single expert in the SPA (a firm or an individual), they should ensure that the expert is not conflicted, and further consider that this can make the expert determination more expensive later on in the event it is required.

The SPA should set out clearly and comprehensively the mechanics for each step, including:

- Who prepares the accounts and in what time frame?
- The time available to the recipient for review and for arranging access to people involved in the preparation of documents.
- The process for agreeing or not agreeing the accounts, including how objections are to be notified to the other side and the requisite time frame.
- The process for resolving disputes (again, with time frame).
- In the event of the parties failing to reach an agreement, the provisions for resolving any dispute(s) through the engagement of an independent third party, including how such a third party is to be selected, the nature of the role they are to play, and the extent of their involvement. This third-party process is often referred to as an 'expert determination'.[45]
- How the respective parties' costs are to be borne, including those of the independent experts.
- The cut-off date until which new information can be considered in the completion accounts.

45. An expert determination is also sometimes referred to as 'arbitration'. However, in this book the term 'arbitration' is used to mean a form of dispute resolution after any expert determination.

An example of wording in the SPA for the review and objection process is as follows:

> No later than the last day of the Review Period, the Seller shall serve a written notice on the Purchaser stating whether or not it agrees with the Draft Documents. In the case of any disagreement, the notice (the 'Objection Notice') shall specify in reasonable detail each matter or item in dispute and, to the extent practicable, any adjustments which the Seller considers should be made to the Draft Documents.
>
> During the Review Period, the Purchaser shall, upon reasonable notice and during normal business hours, allow the Seller (and its agents or advisers) to access and review the Company's working papers relating to the preparation of the Draft Documents and such books and records of the Company as the Seller (or its agents or advisers) may reasonably require for the purpose of reviewing the Draft Documents.
>
> If, during the Review Period, the Seller:
>
> (1) serves a written notice to the Purchaser confirming its agreement with the Draft Documents, they shall, with effect from the date of service of such notice, constitute the Closing Accounts and the Final Purchase Price Statement and shall be final and binding on the Parties; or
>
> (2) fails to serve an Objection Notice, the Draft Documents shall, with effect from the expiry of the Review Period, constitute the Closing Accounts and the Final Purchase Price Statement and shall be final and binding on the Parties.
>
> If the Seller serves an Objection Notice in accordance with paragraph [] of this Schedule, the Parties shall, during the period of fifteen Business Days commencing on the date of service of the Objection Notice (the 'Resolution Period'), seek in good faith to reach agreement on the disputed matters. If, before the Resolution Period expires, the disputed matters are:
>
> (1) resolved by the Parties in writing, the Draft Documents (revised as necessary to reflect the Parties' agreement) shall constitute the Closing Accounts and the Final Purchase Price Statement, and shall be final and binding on the Parties with effect from the date of their agreement; or
>
> (2) not resolved by the Parties in writing before the expiry of the Resolution Period, then the Parties shall require the disputed matters to be referred to the Expert for determination in accordance with paragraph [] of this Schedule.

§3.03 WHO PREPARES?

The issue of who prepares the completion accounts is not necessarily a given. In a majority of cases, the buyer is the natural choice as the buyer is in control of the business (including the accounting function) after closing. However, there can be a certain logic, usually put forward by the vendor, for their side preparing the accounts, on the grounds that their staff (at least up to completion) are familiar with the accounting policies and practices applied in the past. This logic may apply in particular to carve-out transactions where, prior to the transaction, accounting information was prepared by corporate headquarters. While the exception, in these situations there can be a reason for the vendor to prepare the completion accounts. In other situations, as the buyer will be unfamiliar with the target's accounting processes, it may be hesitant to enter into a potentially contentious process, under time pressure. In complex transactions, PE buyers may feel that they do not have the time or resources immediately after closing to prepare the completion accounts. However, these cases are exceptions, and it is more often the buyer who prepares.

In the course of most transactions, staff will transfer from the ultimate employ of the seller to the buyer. Consequently, staff who in the past have prepared accounts for one party will be asked to do so for the other. Senior management should be aware of the concomitant sensitivities involved and should expect a shift in loyalty on the part of those individuals. The question of who prepares may, therefore, also involve a consideration of the timing at which loyalties shift from seller to buyer.

There is a distinct 'first-mover' advantage to the preparer of the completion accounts. The party who prepares gets to bring its own evaluation of judgmental areas (e.g., allowances for doubtful debts or inventory) to the first draft of the accounts, and it is for the non-preparer to object (with an explanation of the basis for the objections). Similar to negotiations, the first explicit mention of a figure often serves as an 'anchor' in the rest of the process, from which the other side needs to move away. In addition, the preparer is usually afforded more time to prepare the accounts than the non-preparer has to object. However, more time may mean more effort and cost involved in preparing which can be a disadvantage.

Another advantage to a buyer who prepares is that it helps ensure that the seller is kept out of business after closing to a greater extent than if the seller prepares.

The right to prepare can therefore be an important tactical advantage, and the question of who prepares can be a negotiating point when the SPA is drafted.

A disadvantage of preparing the completion accounts may be the difficulty of knowing or anticipating what approach the other side will adopt during the completion accounts process. For example, a preparer who takes a 'middle-of-the-road' approach may be confronted with an overly aggressive stance taken by the other side unexpectedly (*see* below §3.08 [E]), and there is a risk that the outcome is different from one where both parties would have adopted either middle-of-the-road or extreme positions.

Whichever side cedes, the preparation of the accounts should safeguard its interests by, as a minimum, ensuring that it and its advisers will have sufficient time to review the accounts, as well as satisfactory access to people and documents. Securing access rights requires specific wording in the SPA, such as whom the party may speak to (including the target's advisers), what records it has access to, and even whether it has the right to make photocopies, etc.

§3.04 BASIS OF PREPARATION OF THE COMPLETION ACCOUNTS

[A] The Accounting Hierarchy

It is sometimes proposed to simply use generally accepted accounting principles (International Financial Reporting Standards (IFRS), US Generally Accepted Accounting Principles (US GAAP), or local accounting rules) as the basis for the completion accounts. It may come as a surprise to non-accountants that two accountants given the task of preparing a set of accounts in accordance with 'generally accepted accounting principles' could come up with two entirely different results. Yet, as known from numerous high-profile corporate debacles, within the framework of accounting principles the preparer of accounts is afforded considerable scope for manoeuvre: generating accounting outcomes is not like solving a math equation. Consequently, the basis on which completion accounts are to be prepared has to be laid down in (for some, excruciating) detail in the SPA.

The basis of preparation usually follows a hierarchy of accounting rules to be applied to the completion accounts, as displayed in Figure 3.2. The usual order, as shown here, is that specific rules prevail over past practice and past practice over generally accepted accounting principles. However, sometimes the order of past practice and GAAP is reversed (*see* section [B] below).

Figure 3.2 The Completion Accounts Hierarchy

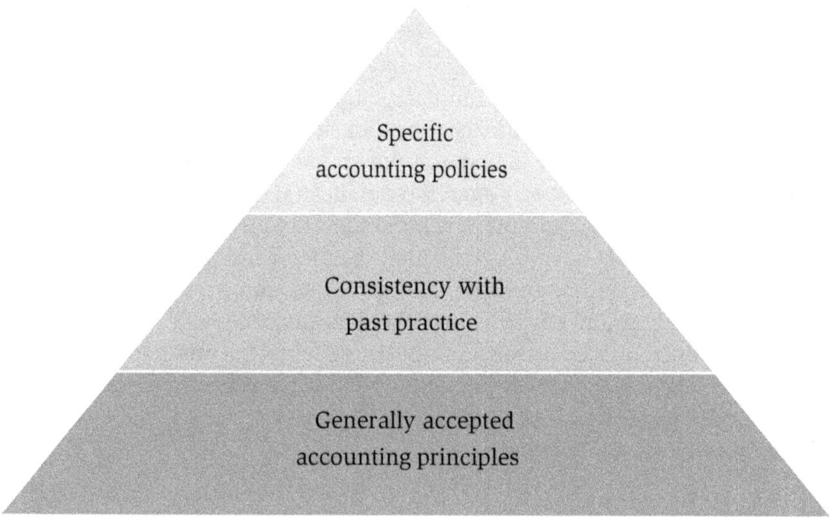

Specific accounting policies and measurement rules. These may have no regard for the way the target entity's accounts have been prepared in the past (usually the last sets of audited financial statements). For example, the rule for creating an allowance against doubtful debts may be that there will be an allowance against any account receivable which is unpaid within the period of credit granted, or where cash has not been received by a specified date after completion. This is regardless of how the target entity has hitherto computed the allowance. Another example of a specific measurement is the dollar amount deduction for a defined benefit pension deficit (*see* below §4.04 [C]). Such rules aim to provide no room for judgment. Specific accounting policies also typically specify cut-off dates for the consideration of post-balance sheet events.

Consistency with past practice of the target entity or vendor group. Where no specific rule of measurement is laid down, then the respective accounts caption will be determined on a consistent basis as it has been in the past (usually audited financial statements). The preparer of the completion accounts may not use a new set of accounting practices, measures or categorisations different from those applied in the past (on which the target entity was valued), including the exercise of discretion. This is to protect against unexpected changes that would favour one party.

In accordance with *generally accepted accounting principles* (e.g., IFRS, US GAAP, or local GAAP). This usually refers to the GAAP relevant to the target entity before the transaction which is also frequently the basis on which the buyer analysed and valued the target business.

As can be seen, the further down the hierarchy, the more scope the preparer generally has to apply their judgment. The application of the above hierarchy can be illustrated by a simple example using inventory allowances as displayed in Table 3.1.

Table 3.1 Basis of Preparation: Hierarchy of Measurement – Inventory Allowances

Basis of Measurement	*Application*
Specific measurement rules	Allowance is made in full (against the gross amount) for items where the quantity on hand exceeds total Movements [a defined term] in the last six months before the date of the completion accounts
Past practice	Past practice was that allowance was made in full for items where the quantity on hand exceeds total Movements in the last twenty-four months
Generally accepted accounting principles	Inventory is stated at the lower of cost and net realisable value

In considering the appropriateness of past practice and stated accounting policies, it is advisable, where the target entity has been issued with an accounting manual (e.g., if it is part of a group of companies preparing accounts on a uniform basis), to ascertain whether the rules set out in the manual form an acceptable basis for the completion accounts and whether the target entity does indeed follow those rules. The accounting hierarchy can also reference the written accounting guidance of the target group.

In addition to limiting the scope for judgment (and therefore dispute), the use of specific measurement rules can be helpful when staff are transferring from one owner to another and are being asked to adopt a different approach to preparing the completion accounts.

Furthermore, while in the example above it is referred under 'past practice' to allowances being computed in a mechanistic way, it is common for them to be determined based on management's judgment. While a seller will quite reasonably defend the preparation of completion accounts prepared on a similar basis as in the past, an aggressive buyer can, equally reasonably, be expected to seek adjustments which have a dollar-for-dollar impact on the final purchase price. The term 'consistency' therefore needs to be carefully defined.

Lastly, it is often appropriate to specify that the accounting rules in force at the time of signing are relevant to the preparation of the completion accounts in order to avoid disagreement in the case of changes in GAAP.

Example Completion Accounts Dispute (High Court of England and Wales)

The case of *Mihail Tartsinis v. Navona Management Company*[46] (English Commercial Court) is a curious case which provides some lessons on how *not* to go about preparing completion accounts.

Briefly, the plaintiff and a fellow businessman sold to Navona shares in a company that owned a fleet of ships. The key issue in the transaction was the fleet and to what extent a decrease in its underlying value should lead to a purchase price adjustment. While the fleet was reported in the accounts of the target company at net book value, the parties apparently did not dispute, during the course of their negotiations, that this was considerably higher than the underlying market value (which had recently fallen). What amounted to completion accounts were issued by Navona showing (incorrectly, as it should have been written down) the fleet at an unadjusted net book value rather than the lower market value. As a consequence, the seller claimed a price adjustment to reflect the higher net book value, which the buyer refused to accept, asserting that the value of the vessels relevant to the determination of the purchase price was the lower value that had been used to calculate the provisional purchase price under the SPA and which represented an assessment made by the parties of the vessels' market value. Legal proceedings ensued.

In the event, the court 'rectified' the contract. After considering the evidence, it concluded that there was pre-contractual agreement over the (lower) value of the fleet and substantially dismissed the plaintiff's claim. This dispute will be discussed further in §11.03 where standards of value are discussed.

While the case contains some interesting legal issues, from the narrow point of view of completion accounts and related matters, lessons include that it is important to reach an agreement between the parties about the basis on which the completion accounts are prepared, including the relationship between accounting numbers and the commercial value transferred. This is an important theme in many post-M&A disputes,

46. *Mihail Tartsinis v. Navona Management Company* [2015] EWHC 57 (Comm).

and the discussion will return to the distinction between the accounting value of an asset or liability and its commercial value several times: in the context of accounting choices and commercial value (§4.02 [C]), damages valuation (§11.01), and breaches of accounting warranties §12.01 [A].

Another important lesson is the broader point that those involved in a transaction should act in a 'joined up' manner so that there is clarity among the entire deal team, which in this context extends to whoever ultimately prepares the completion accounts on the matters involved, including:

- Clarity as to the basis on which the target entity's accounts have been drawn up in the past, any shortcomings, and the consequences for how the completion accounts are to be drawn up.
- Ensuring that the SPA (and more specifically, the purchase price adjustment mechanism) is drafted properly to reflect what is intended by the parties.
- Procedures to ensure that the completion accounts are reviewed before release.

[B] GAAP Override

A further important issue that can arise is how to deal with items that are consistent with past practice yet are non-GAAP compliant. A target entity that draws up its accounts in accordance with local GAAP may not convert these to make them comply with say, IFRS, on the grounds of materiality. It may also be the case that the target has made an accounting error in the historical accounts that may or may not be corrected in the completion accounts.

The issue then relates to the order of items (2) and (3) in the hierarchy above. The hierarchy can be reversed, meaning the parties agree that generally accepted accounting policies prevail over consistency. This is called a 'GAAP override'. Whether or not to agree to a GAAP override can be a significant decision in a transaction, as it determines, for example, whether an accounting error in the accounts prior to closing must be corrected in the completion accounts if it is discovered during the preparation or review of the completion accounts.

The reason one party (usually the buyer) may prefer a GAAP override is that it provides protection against unknown errors in the target's accounts, especially in situations where due diligence access was very limited or where there is already a suspicion on the part of the buyer that the seller's historical accounts may be incorrect, but the buyer cannot determine this conclusively during the due diligence.

The disadvantage of a GAAP override is that the correction leads to a one-off effect that is (usually) unexpected and may result in a decrease or increase to the purchase price that has nothing to do with 'value'. This can lead to economically unjustified changes to the final purchase price.

A GAAP override is generally an exception, and the parties more often agree to the hierarchy as it is shown above (i.e., consistency prevails over GAAP). This means that accounting errors in the historical accounts (usually the last audited financial statements prior to closing) will be carried forward in the completion accounts.

Standard SPAs usually include some version of the accounting hierarchy. However, if a clear hierarchy is missing, then a dispute is more likely. These disputes continue to occur.

A hierarchy should be clear and unambiguous, as *Shafi v. Rutherford*, the case discussed below, demonstrates.

Example of an Error Correction in the Completion Accounts (High Court of England and Wales): *Shafi v. Rutherford*[47]

Shafi v. Rutherford is generally considered an important decision for those who perform expert determination. Ms Sofia Shafi and Dr Alexandra Rutherford formed a company in 2007 to start a joint dental practice, each party initially holding 50% of the shares. The new company leased equipment. In 2009, the parties decided to part company, and Ms Shafi agreed to sell her 50% interest to Ms Rutherford. The SPA included a purchase price adjustment with the following provision:

> In the calculation of the Completion Liabilities, liabilities shall include any and all sums paid at or payable by reference to the period up to and including the Completion Date including but not limited to [certain specific matters].[48]

Operating leases were not included in Completion Liabilities under this definition, whereas finance lease liabilities were included to the extent they were payable as specified in the provision.

The SPA further contained the following hierarchy:

> 1.2 The draft completion accounts shall;
> 1.3 be prepared in accordance with the specific accounting policies and principles set out in Part III of this schedule so that, in the case of any conflict, such policies and principles shall override the provisions of paragraphs 1.4 and 1.5;
> 1.4 subject to paragraph 1.3, be prepared in accordance with the accounting policies, principles, practices and procedures adopted by the Company in the preparation of the Accounts, which include the policies set out in paragraphs 1, 2, 3 and 5 of Part III of Schedule 4, so that, in the case of any conflict, such policies, principles, practices and procedures shall override the provisions of paragraph 1.5;
> 1.5 where none of the accounting policies, principles, practices or procedures referred to in paragraphs 1.3 and 1.4 deal with the matter, be prepared in accordance with generally accepted accounting principles in the UK as applicable to small companies as at the Completion Date.[49]

In the company's 2008 annual accounts, the equipment leases had been (incorrectly) accounted for as operating leases. The leases were also treated as operating leases in the draft completion accounts.

47. *Ms Sofia Shafi v. Dr Alexandra Rutherford* [2014] EWCA Civ 1186.
48. *Ibid.*, para. 13.
49. *Ibid.*, para. 11.

The parties could not agree on the completion accounts, and the matter was referred to expert determination. The expert determined that the relevant leases should have been treated as finance leases all along and that, therefore, the 2008 accounts had not been prepared in accordance with relevant UK GAAP. However, the expert considered that there was no mechanism under the agreement for him to amend the 2008 accounts and decided that he could not take into account in the purchase price adjustment a finance lease liability which resulted from correcting the lease accounting.[50]

Legal proceedings ensued. The main issue concerned the proper construction of paragraph 1.4 of the SPA, specifically whether the incorrect lease accounting treatment had to be carried over into the completion accounts. This is a question of hierarchy. The judge concluded that the completion accounts should have reflected the corrected accounting treatment of the leases:

> given that they were to be prepared in accordance with the accounting policies, principles, practices and procedures adopted in the preparation of the accounts, such accounts having been expressly stated to have been prepared on the basis of [relevant GAAP].

And further:

> when clause 1.4 referred to 'the accounting policies, principles, practices and procedures adopted in the preparation of the Accounts', it was referring to the policies et cetera used by the profession generally on which those accounts are stated to be drawn up, not to the way in which the company has actually applied those policies.[51]

At issue was therefore whether the hierarchy in paragraph 1.4 meant that the liabilities of the company should be computed by reference to correct accounting policies, supplemented if necessary by reference to practices adopted, or alternatively according to such policies except where contradicted by the actual treatment of those liabilities in the 2008 accounts where that treatment was incorrect. The Court of Appeal found that the judge had correctly accepted the first of these alternatives. The completion accounts were to provide the final adjustment between the parties of the consideration for the sale of the shares. The court saw no reason why in those circumstances, the parties would have wished to carry forward erroneous accounting treatment of liabilities.[52] The error correction prevailed, a 'GAAP override'.

§3.05 SUBSEQUENT EVENTS AND LIMITATIONS OF THE USE OF NEW INFORMATION

The cut-off date until which new information can be considered in the completion accounts can be an area of dispute if it is not specified in the SPA. The longer the

50. *Ibid.*, para. 22.
51. *Ibid.*, para. 27.
52. *Ibid.*, para. 40.

completion accounts process, the more opportunity there is for new information to surface. Where the SPA is silent on the cut-off date, the question of what information can be taken into account can then become a key area of completion accounts disputes.

On the one hand, it can be argued that, in arriving at commercially relevant values, any additional information that becomes available over the completion accounts process resolves uncertainty and therefore results in a more reliable set of accounts.[53] An argument consistent with this view is that changes to the completion accounts as new information becomes available do not necessarily mean that earlier drafts of the accounts were incorrect, only that better information has since become available. Hindsight can be useful, despite 'competing with the much more sought after and potentially lucrative ability to accurately forecast the future'.[54]

On the other hand, accounting estimates are usually based on the limited information available at the time. Without a clear cut-off date, the parties risk a cycle of updating the completion accounts leading to continuous changes of the purchase price adjustment, in extreme cases until the last moment when the dispute is resolved, the last syllable of recorded time.[55] In this cycle of updating, information asymmetry often favours one party, usually the buyer, who has better access to information. While buyers will argue that it is only fair to be able to use all information that becomes available and reflect it in the final purchase price, sellers may be concerned that the buyer can use information selectively and that only bad news comes to light. This is why sellers may feel they need protection from an expert determination 'by ambush', with information surfacing late in the process.[56]

One situation that leads to this kind of dispute is if the parties agree to extend the original period to prepare the completion accounts but do not address the cut-off date. Buyers may then consider information that surfaces during the extension period, whereas sellers argue that such information should not be considered.

Accounting standards contain guidance on events after the reporting period. This can be of relevance when the accounting hierarchy makes reference to GAAP (*see* above §3.04 [A]). For example, International Accounting Standard (IAS) 10.3 distinguishes between adjusting and non-adjusting events:[57]

- An adjusting event is an event after the reporting period that provides evidence of conditions that existed at the end of the reporting period.
- A non-adjusting event is an event after the reporting period that is indicative of conditions that arose after the end of the reporting period.

---

53. For example, information about the collectability of receivables that only comes to light after the relevant balance sheet date.
54. Kroll, *Wearing Blinders to Avoid the Use of Hindsight Post-Closing*, 21 June 2019, available at https://www.kroll.com/en/insights/publications/expert-services/wearing-blinders-to-avoid-use-of-hindsight-post-closing.
55. William Shakespeare, Macbeth, Act 5 Scene 5.
56. *See* A. Vincent Biemans and Gerald M. Hansen, *M&A Disputes*, John Wiley & Sons, 2017, 124.
57. US GAAP distinguishes between Type 1 'recognised subsequent events' and Type 2 'nonrecognised subsequent events', broadly comparable with IAS 10[92]s adjusting and non-adjusting events. *See* Mergers & Acquisitions Disputes, AICPA Forensic and Valuation Services Section Practice Aid, 2012, American Institute of Certified Public Accountants, NY, 33.

IAS 10.8 requires an entity to make an adjustment in its financial statements for an adjusting event, whereas, according to IAS 10.10, no adjustment is made for a non-adjusting event (even though a disclosure may be required (IAS 10.21)).

In summary, it is usually appropriate to include a clause in the SPA which limits the period in which events can be considered in the completion accounts (and to ensure that this cut-off provision takes precedence over GAAP). A common date used is the delivery of the first draft of the completion accounts by the buyer or seller.

Example of a Dispute over Information that Became Known after Closing (International Arbitration)

The target company reported a trade receivable related to a long-term construction contract for an infrastructure project in Eastern Europe. The receivable was part of working capital at closing. The seller had not recorded an allowance against the receivable in the last set of accounts before the sale and stated that it had expected the customer to pay in full. During the completion accounts process, the parties at first continued to consider the receivable to be fully recoverable.

Approximately two months after closing, the relationship between the target management and the customer deteriorated. The customer claimed that there had not been sufficient progress on the project. Target company management accepted that the project was behind plan and agreed to discount the invoice – which was still unpaid – by 50%. It wrote down the receivable accordingly.

A dispute had developed for other reasons, and in this context the buyer revisited the accounting treatment of the receivable in the completion accounts and argued that the problems had already existed at closing, but that the seller had withheld relevant information. In the buyer's view, the carrying value of the receivable should have been reduced by 50% at the time of closing.

The seller argued that the project had not been behind plan at closing and that the partial write-down was, in essence, the result of the buyer's own poor project management. In the seller's view, the receivable was fully recoverable at closing. The SPA did not include provisions relating to the cut-off date for the completion accounts. (The dispute settled.)

§3.06 TO AUDIT OR NOT TO AUDIT?

There is no requirement for completion accounts to be audited. However, it is sometimes proposed that – instead of agreeing in the SPA the process set out above in §3.02 – the completion accounts should simply be audited by a third party. The idea is that an independent external auditor will use an objective and fair approach to determine the purchase price adjustment, removing conflict and that an audit might also provide a degree of comfort. Another idea sometimes advanced is that at the end of the completion accounts process described in §3.02, the final completion accounts should be audited.

While it is true that an audit might provide a degree of comfort, notably to the party who has not prepared the accounts, it is usually not the appropriate mechanism to resolve the completion accounts process. As the audit procedures must be separate from the preparation of the accounts, and the auditor must be different from the person who prepares the accounts, an audit still leaves open the question of which party prepares. Moreover, it is far from clear what criteria an independent auditor should apply to achieve a fair outcome. For example, if the party that prepares exercises all individual areas of judgment at the extreme end of a permissible range (under the accounting rules specified in the SPA) in order to maximise or minimise the purchase price adjustment, should the external auditor accept all such accounting choices? Alternatively, on what basis should the auditor reject them? An audit also raises practical questions: who does the independent auditor talk to when auditing the accounts, and where are these individuals' loyalties placed?

An auditor will also work to a certain materiality level. This may make it difficult for the accounts to be contested and for dollar-for-dollar adjustments to be won.

Provided the basis of preparation has been satisfactorily nailed down and the non-preparer and their advisers have sufficient time and access to people and documents, then this should suffice.

§3.07 DISPUTE RESOLUTION

Disagreements over completion accounts can occasionally lead to high-profile, high-value disputes, as in *Chicago Bridge & Iron Co. v. Westinghouse Electric Co. LLC*, and unusual transaction in which the buyer, Westinghouse, presented a net working capital calculation that amounted to over USD 2 billion less than the estimated pre-closing net working capital amount.[58] How these disputes are to be resolved is an area in which the lawyers advising on a transaction will typically lead. Here are some of the principal areas to consider:

- Expert determination versus arbitration. As a general rule, a process involving an expert is less time-consuming than arbitration and, hence, less costly. In cases involving completion accounts, because there is perhaps one or at least a limited number of specific issues to be resolved and this falls readily within the capacity of the expert (usually a member of the relevant professional body), it is often appropriate to appoint an expert. Typically, submissions are made to the expert by either side over the course of the process, ordinarily with a right of reply, and a decision follows within a relatively short space of time.
- The SPA should specify that only the issue or issues being contested are to be considered (not, for example, the full completion accounts, which could potentially open up other issues not contested by the parties). The authority of the expert determiner should be limited. This was a lesson of *Chicago Bridge & Iron Co. v. Westinghouse Electric Co. LLC*.[59]

58. Chicago *Bridge & Iron Co. v. Westinghouse Electric Co. LLC*, 2017 WL 2774563 (Del. 28 June 2017).
59. *Ibid.*

- The SPA should also specify that the expert determination cannot go beyond the positions of either party. That is, if one party claims that an item leads to an adjustment of USD 70 million, and the other party claims that it is only USD 40 million, then the expert determination should generally not fall outside of this range.

An in-depth discussion of the advantages and disadvantages of appointing an expert or commence arbitration and their respective roles is beyond the scope of this publication.[60] There are usually also differences in the law of the country by which any agreement is to be governed and disputes dealt with.

§3.08 OTHER ASPECTS

[A] Accounting Input into SPA Draft

Those tasked with financial due diligence for the buyer should provide input into the basis of the completion accounts including the accounting definitions in the SPA. They should be instructed to analyse, during the due diligence phase, the basis on which the target company's historical accounts have been prepared, the basis on which they should have been prepared, and the basis on which the completion accounts should be prepared, as well as highlight any key discrepancies to the deal team. Otherwise, there is a risk that like will not be compared with like. Care should be taken when agreeing the terms of any purchase price adjustment mechanism to ensure that any input from the financial due diligence team is duly accounted for in the drafting of the SPA and the completion accounts mechanism. In particular, if any specific item is to be treated differently from the rest, this must be clearly stated.

[B] Preparation of a Full Balance Sheet

The completion accounts are schedules with cash, debt, working capital, capital expenditure and other items. They may be limited to the items that are part of the purchase price adjustments as defined in the SPA, or alternatively represent a full balance sheet, including balance sheet items that do not lead to an adjustment. From the perspective of the recipient of the draft accounts it is generally preferable that the schedules amount to a complete balance sheet and not be limited to the items that lead to an adjustment. This serves primarily as protection for the party that does not prepare or has less access to information, as it is easier to identify items that should have been included in an adjustment but were omitted. For example, items may have been moved outside of the adjustments, and a full balance sheet with some detail will enable the other party to identify such items and reconcile individual items into the trial balance.

---

60. *see* John Hudson, Kami Zargar and Heiko Ziehms, Post-completion M&A disputes: two paths to resolution, in GAR European Arbitration review 2023 (forthcoming) for further reading.

[C] Materiality

A further factor to consider is materiality. Other than where specific measurement rules are applied that result in a definitive value being reached, the broader basis of measurement would typically involve consideration of materiality. An example would be where a target entity is a division of a group and the divisional accounts are drawn up to a higher level of materiality than those of an individual company (whose accounts are subject to an individual audit opinion).

A dollar-for-dollar purchase price adjustment may be appropriate even if it would not be material in the context of the group's or even the target's individual financial statements. Materiality thresholds can be agreed in the SPA. It is necessary to distinguish these from a collar amount around an adjustment (*see* §5.05).

[D] The Preliminary Purchase Price

Another aspect of the completion accounts relates to the preliminary purchase price (or estimated purchase price), the amount usually paid at closing. When the final purchase price is determined, only the difference to the preliminary price is paid (by whichever side owes it).

One consideration in setting the preliminary purchase price is that in the event it is determined by the seller's (good faith) estimate, the buyer may need to ensure that the estimate is within a pre-agreed range and does not exceed the available equity and debt financing. It is generally preferable to owe a final payment rather than to be a creditor. A buyer will usually attempt to agree a preliminary purchase price that is lower than the expected final price. This can be particularly important if the other party is a special-purpose vehicle or based abroad.

[E] Approaches to the Completion Accounts Process

Most strategic investors and PE sponsors do not take an overly aggressive approach during the completion accounts process as there are usually reputations and continuing relationships to consider. However, there is a small minority of investors who can be very aggressive in their attempt to maximise or minimise the final 'cash event' in the acquisition process.

If a party asks its internal deal team or external advisers to look for ways to maximise or minimise a purchase price adjustment, it is fair to assume that it will find something. The other side should then prepare for the next steps in the completion accounts process.

CHAPTER 4
Net Debt

§4.01 OVERVIEW

Net debt is deducted from (and, if applicable, net cash added to) enterprise value to arrive at equity value. There is no definition of net debt laid down in law or accounting standards; identifying what is, and is not, to be included in net debt in a transaction is a matter for the parties to negotiate and document in the SPA.

In practice, many items may be considered to have the characteristics of debt, although the case for some is more clear-cut than for others.

To provide a flavour of what we are concerned with, items listed below have been treated as net debt. They are ranked starting with what might be considered to be 'harder' (relatively uncontentious) items usually included in any definition of net debt, progressing to 'softer' items (those less commonly treated as such):

- Bank and other (explicitly) interest-bearing debt.
- Debt factoring and similar financing.
- Finance leases.
- Accrued interest.
- Derivative securities.
- Pension obligations; Supplier finance.
- Non-controlling (minority) interest.
- Employee loans.
- Intercompany balances.
- Break costs (e.g., of leases) and early debt repayment penalties.
- Cash that is working capital in nature, e.g., cash in tills (which would not form part of 'cash' within net debt) or cash that cannot be taken out of the business, i.e., trapped cash.
- Deferred revenue/prepaid amounts.
- Capital expenditure creditors.
- Restructuring costs.

- Effects of converting foreign currency debt at the spot rate.
- Dilapidation provisions.
- Accrued bonuses.
- Warranty provisions.
- Other customer-related claims, including unusual or excessive credit notes and unidentified receipts which may have to be repaid.
- Other contingent liabilities (to the extent not covered through indemnities).
- Current tax assets and liabilities.
- Operating leases (if flipping from operating to finance benefits one side).
- Early retirement provisions.
- Unrealised foreign exchange losses.
- Deferred tax assets and liabilities.

The merits or otherwise of these items can be debated (and frequently are), particularly those closer to the foot of the list. Whether they are ultimately included in net debt usually comes down to the respective negotiating positions of buyer and seller.

Before discussing individual adjustments at greater length, including those that commonly feature in legal disputes, it may first be helpful to consider some conceptual matters.

§4.02 CONCEPTUAL MATTERS

[A] Interest-Bearing Debt

It is sometimes suggested that a starting point for classifying items as net debt in a transaction is whether they are interest-bearing, and this definition of net debt is sometimes agreed in letters of intent. However, although explicitly interest-bearing debt (such as bank debt) is invariably treated as net debt, the use of the term 'interest-bearing' is not without problems. For example, is debt-factoring interest-bearing (there is a financing cost associated with factoring, but it is not necessarily reported in financial statements as interest)? On the other hand, a defined benefit pension obligation (commonly treated as debt) is not, strictly, interest-bearing (companies report an interest cost in their financial statements, but no cash interest is paid). Should it be considered 'interest-bearing'?

The term 'interest-bearing' is, therefore, not necessarily instructive in itself.

[B] Financing Versus Operating Items

Where there is usually consensus is that items relating to financing activities should be treated as net debt. It is, therefore, no surprise that they are among the 'hardest' items in the list in §4.01 above. However, net debt often also includes liabilities of an operating nature.

One might ask why, if items relate to operations, they should be deducted in the equity value bridge: are they not already reflected in enterprise value, the present value of net operating cash flows? The answer is: if the valuation model reflects these in enterprise value, then there are, indeed, no grounds on which to deduct them as net debt. In practice, however, that is often not the case as valuation models do not unfailingly capture the cash effects of operating items. For example, a net debt adjustment for a pension liability effectively introduces an element of accrual accounting for an operating item into a discounted cash flow (DCF) valuation.[61] More generally, long-term obligations extending many years into the future exceed the forecast horizon of DCF models that usually extend out perhaps five or seven years and then assume a terminal value.

In the case of pension obligations, a net debt deduction transfers the economic burden of past commitments that have not, as of the transaction date, become 'cash-relevant', from the buyer to the seller (who incurred the cost, and the liability, but not the cash outflow). Incurring the non-cash cost generated benefits for the seller. Continuing with the example of unfunded defined benefit pension obligations, these represent pension promises to employees (instead of cash payments) in return for services they provided to, and which benefited, the seller. The work performed by and compensation to the employees are part of the operating activities of a business. The associated liability (the future payment of compensation for past service) is an operating liability. It is similar in nature to a liability for unpaid salaries or wages except that any cash-out may occur many years hence.

If the business is sold at the time the pension promise becomes 'cash-relevant' (albeit potentially many years after closing), the buyer will ultimately bear the economic burden of employees' work which benefited the seller. Unless the obligations have been funded involving assets that are not required in the normal course of business, the buyer will service them with cash that would otherwise be available for distribution to the shareholder (i.e., the buyer) or other uses. A net debt deduction moves the present value of the future economic cash burden from buyer to seller.

Other examples of potential net debt items that arise from operating activities are discussed later in this chapter. While there are different accounting rules and valuation issues for each, the underlying rationale – moving the economic burden from buyer to seller by deducting the value from the purchase price – is the same.

[C] Accounting Choices and Value

Accounting is by fiat, that is to say, accounting rules are created by standard setters or lawmakers. Accounting rules specify how assets and liabilities should be valued in the accounts. The resulting accounting, or book values, are not necessarily the same as economic value. The relationship between accounting, or book values, and economic value is discussed below in §11.01.

Returning to the equity value bridge, in concept, all its components, including net debt, should be measured at fair value, even if they are derived from accounting figures. How these components are accounted for should theoretically not be relevant

61. The point will be revisited below at §11.04 [B] [2] [c].

to the net purchase price adjustment and the final purchase price. Their carrying values in the balance sheet are only the starting point for the measurements at which they adjust the purchase price (albeit a convenient starting point because accounting figures are readily available).

Secondary effects of accounting choices can, however, have direct relevance to value and need to be considered separately, again at fair value. For example, tax payments are made on the basis of taxable income according to tax accounting rules. The financial accounts may be the basis for debt covenants. Such secondary effects should therefore enter into the enterprise valuation or the purchase price adjustment so that they are reflected in the equity value. The discussion of deferred taxes in §4.04 [I] is an example.

It is worth considering how the carrying values of items in a balance sheet compare to their fair values:

- *Items whose book value typically equates to fair value at the reporting date.* These include cash and cash equivalents, short-term investments and marketable securities, trade creditors, and financial borrowings (though interest rates may fluctuate and, with them, the value of the liabilities); they are short-term and forever revolving.
- *Items whose book value does not equate to, but approximates fair value.* These include receivables (subject to estimates for unrecoverable amounts), inventory (at the lower of cost and market), investments recorded under equity accounting, accruals, and provisions (which are subject to specific accounting rules, for example, pension obligations, and management estimates).
- *Items whose book value often differs substantially from fair value.* These include long-term debt securities (investments held to maturity that are reported at historical cost) and some provisions. Other examples, albeit with less relevance for completion mechanisms, include tangible and intangible assets other than goodwill (recorded at historical acquisition cost less depreciation or amortisation, subject to impairment reviews), and goodwill (recorded at historical cost, subject to impairment reviews).
- *Items not recorded in the balance sheet at all.* Items with possible relevance for completion mechanisms include many types of off-balance sheet liabilities such as leases (if classified as operating), factoring (if the receivables are 'derecognised'), and commitments and contingent liabilities (e.g., if probability thresholds are not met or a loss cannot be reasonably estimated).

§4.03 INTERACTION WITH WORKING CAPITAL

For a purchase price adjustment mechanism to work properly, a seamless interaction between the individual adjustments is necessary. A basic interaction between the net debt adjustment and working capital is between cash and individual components of working capital. Most day-to-day transactions of a business affect both. For example, a consequence of the receipt of funds from customers is that cash increases (net debt decreases) and trade receivables decrease (working capital decreases). The effects offset each other. Cash payments to suppliers and trade payables interact similarly.

To the extent that a change in cash stems from a change in working capital, a properly functioning completion mechanism means that the working capital adjustment neutralises the change in cash (net debt) exactly so that there is no impact on the net purchase price. At closing, it does not matter whether a particular receivable has already been converted into cash, or if a particular trade payable has already been paid. Consequently, accelerating collections from customers, deferring settlement of trade payables, or liquidating inventories will not affect the net purchase price if the working capital and net debt adjustments interact properly (assuming, of course, that the working capital reference value is set at an appropriate level – more on this in Chapter 5).

When things go wrong in completion mechanisms, it is often here. A typical problem is that an item is captured twice, both as working capital and as net debt (e.g., a capital expenditure creditor). Alternatively, an item may not be captured at all (e.g., an accrual for outstanding supplier invoices), giving the seller an opportunity to manipulate the cash or the working capital position prior to closing – as a consequence of which the buyer overpays. A seamless interaction reduces the risk of a post-deal dispute.

Many items can be treated as alternatively net debt or working capital. However, the economic outcome is often not the same. For example, if deferred revenue is included in the definition of working capital, then only amounts above those included in the reference working capital lead to a reduction of net working capital at closing (and to the purchase price). This is a different outcome from a dollar-for-dollar net debt deduction (as long as any amount of deferred revenue is included in the reference value). If the parties agree to treat an item as working capital in the completion accounts but it is not included in the reference value (e.g., because it has never been reported in the past), then in theory this would achieve the same economic result as a net debt deduction. However, in practice, it may still not lead to the same outcome. A significant working capital adjustment resulting from such an item may cause the other party to look for offsetting items elsewhere in working capital during the completion accounts process – an option that is not readily available for a net debt deduction. From the perspective of a buyer, it is therefore generally preferable to include an item in the definition of net debt rather than working capital.

§4.04 INDIVIDUAL NET DEBT ADJUSTMENTS

[A] Factoring

[1] Introduction

Debt factoring is among the more complex issues encountered in completion mechanisms and one that can be difficult to think through conceptually. This is primarily because treating factoring appropriately (as debt) also has implications for the treatment of working capital.

Factoring is, in essence, the sale of receivables by a business to a third party (a factor) at a discount. The benefit to the business is that it converts its receivables into cash immediately. Factoring not only generates cash but also gives companies the ability to manage the balance sheet and cash flow at a specific reporting date or during a reporting period.

There are different types of factoring arrangements, and these need to be considered in determining the appropriate accounting treatment. The relevant accounting standards are:

- IFRS: IAS 39 and IFRS 9 (although these make no specific reference to factoring).
- US GAAP: FASB ASC 860-10.

The key issue is whether the factoring arrangement is recourse or non-recourse:

- Non-recourse: the factor bears the risk of uncollected invoices. In general, this is accounted for as a sale of the receivables, which are 'derecognised' (i.e., to say, removed from the balance sheet, as if the customer had paid). This is a common type of off-balance sheet financing.
- Recourse: the factor does not take the risk of uncollected invoices. Depending on the terms, the accounting treatment may be on- or off-balance sheet. Under IFRS, receivables are generally 'derecognised', meaning they are no longer recorded on the balance sheet if substantially all of the risks and rewards of ownership have been transferred, with control as a secondary test.[62] Factoring with recourse will more often fail the risks and rewards test than non-recourse factoring and is more often accounted for as a loan (i.e., on-balance sheet). Under US GAAP, the accounting treatment is determined by FASB Accounting Standards Codification (ASC) section 860-10-40.

[2] Factoring in the Context of the Transaction

If the company in receipt of the finance retains the receivables on its balance sheet and records a liability, the treatment in a transaction is usually uncontroversial: the liability, readily visible in the balance sheet, is treated as net debt. There is no impact on working capital since the factored receivables have not been derecognised.

Disagreements over the treatment of factoring in a transaction tend to arise when factored receivables are off-balance sheet – that is to say when they are derecognised. The cause of such disagreements is sometimes that the respective parties (and their

62. James M. Wahlen, Jefferson P. Jones and Donald Pagach, *Intermediate Accounting: Reporting and Analysis*, Cengage Learning 2016, 6.31.

advisers) find it difficult to consider such amounts as debt because they are not (by definition) visible in the balance sheet.

When a seller argues against a net debt deduction, they often raise the following objections:

- The company has always factored and can continue to factor after closing if the buyer wishes to; factoring is 'part of the business'. However, the fallacy is easy to expose. The fact that a specific type of financing has been in place before closing and may continue to be in place is not relevant to whether it is considered as debt. A company may have had bank debt for many years which may remain in place after closing. Such borrowings are not somehow less 'debt-like' simply because they have been there for a long time or will continue to be there.
- Considering balance sheet effects, factoring gives the same result as customers paying (albeit early, and ignoring any discount and other charges). It looks like an operating, not a financing transaction, a seller would argue. If that is the case, why treat it as debt? However, such an impression is given only by how the factoring is accounted for – and the accounting should not matter. It may look as if the customer has paid early, but they have not. Rather, the factoring arrangement has generated liquidity to make it look as if that were the case. The liquidity comes not from the customer, but from the factor (with an inherent financing cost), similar to a loan or other asset-backed financing; it just does not look that way in the balance sheet after the payment is made.

[3] Factoring and the Completion Mechanism

Factoring, then, is a financing transaction and the associated liability should be included in net debt. This offsets the increase in the cash position resulting from the factoring arrangement which the buyer pays for, dollar-for-dollar (since it reduces net debt).

However, the mechanics do not end there. A factoring arrangement under which the receivables have been derecognised results in lower working capital (all else being equal). If the target business has factored in the past, its historical working capital, as reported, will have been artificially low and will, as a consequence, understate its true working capital needs. To correct this, that is to reflect in the reference value the true working capital needs of the business, the factored receivables have to be added back to reported working capital on a pro-forma basis in order to establish accurate working capital levels (including averages) as well as reference working capital.

It is sometimes argued that it is not necessary to add back factored receivables as described above, or to include factoring liabilities in net debt; and that allowing variations in factored receivables to resolve themselves through the working capital adjustment, without an adjustment to net debt, achieves the same economic outcome. That is not the case. This can be demonstrated by means of a simple example.

[4] Factoring: Example

The example considers the impact on the net debt and working capital adjustments of the following possible combinations:

- A working capital adjustment where factored receivables are added back (option 1) or not added back (option 2), both to the reference value and closing working capital.
- A net debt adjustment which includes factored receivables at closing (option 3) or excludes them (option 4).

Table 4.1 sets out the development of working capital of a target company. It is assumed that:

- the company factors 90% of its receivables at any time;
- these receivables are derecognised upon being factored;
- working capital consists only of trade receivables;
- there is no debt other than in relation to factoring;
- the average working capital is also the agreed reference working capital (i.e., the reference value).

Table 4.1 Factoring Example Monthly Development

	January	*February*	*March*	*April*	*Average (Mean)*	*Amount at Closing*
Gross trade receivables	100	90	80	70	85	100
Less: factored receivables	(90)	(81)	(72)	(63)	(76.5)	(90)
Net reported trade receivables	10	9	8	7	8.5	10
Cash in target company due to factoring	90	81	72	63	n/a	90

Table 4.2 displays the results of each of the four permutations set out above together with the consequences for the final purchase price.

Table 4.2 Factoring Example: Results

	Permutation	*Working Capital Adjustment*	*Factoring Debt*	*Cash Balance from Factoring*	*Net Impact on Purchase Price*
1.	Factored receivables included in working capital; factoring liability included in net debt	15.0	(90.0)	90.0	15.0
2.	Factored receivables NOT included in working capital; factoring liability included in net debt	1.5	(90.0)	90.0	1.5
3.	Factored receivables included in working capital; factoring liability NOT included in net debt	15.0	0	90.0	105.0
4.	Factored receivables NOT included in working capital; factoring liability NOT included in net debt	1.5	0	90.0	91.5

Each permutation results in a different net purchase price for each combination of adjustments. This shows that the deduction cannot be resolved through the working capital adjustment alone. The only 'clean' solution is option 1 above, where an adjustment is made against a working capital reference value to which factored receivables are added back and which includes the amounts factored in factoring debt. It is the same outcome as if no factoring were in place. This result is consistent with the purpose of a purchase price adjustment, which is to neutralise the effect of changes to the price from financing transactions before closing. It is, therefore, the only outcome that ensures that the seller transfers the value the buyer pays for. It can be surprising that factoring does not 'resolve itself' in the working capital adjustment, neither in the simplified example above nor, usually, in real life.

This treatment sometimes runs into the following objection: the buyer is being asked to pay for 15.0 of surplus working capital (against a reference value of 85.0 if factored receivables are added back) but receives only 1.5. The balance of 13.5 has already been sold (by way of factoring), and the buyer will not collect the 13.5 after closing, even though they paid for it. The adjustment of 15.0, however, seems to suggest that the buyer should expect to receive 15.0, not 1.5. Is the buyer, therefore, overpaying by 13.5?

The answer is no. It is true that the buyer obtains only 1.5 in working capital, despite paying for a working capital adjustment of 15.0. However, the buyer also obtains a higher cash balance at closing than without factoring. It is higher by exactly 13.5 (the difference between factored receivables at closing and the reference amount, or 90% of 100 less 90% of 85.0), that is, the buyer pays 15.0 for working capital even though it only obtains a surplus of 1.5 against the reference value, however, it also obtains 13.5 more in cash than without factoring. The buyer does not pay for this extra cash because of the net debt deduction. It pays 15.0 as part of the working capital adjustment and obtains 15.0 in value.

Many times in transactions factoring is not dealt with appropriately, and in each case this means that someone overpays. It is safe to assume that this will often go unnoticed.

Example of a Dispute involving Factoring and Reverse Factoring (International Arbitration)

The example relates to a major fraud case. The target group routinely used a local subsidiary to record sales of goods to a business partner and supplier in a neighbouring country before each month-end, only to re-purchase the goods from the partner immediately at the beginning of the following month (the goods were never actually shipped).

The sale-and-repurchase transactions occurred routinely just before each month-end; the amounts involved depended on the liquidity needs of the subsidiary at any given month-end. The trade receivables that the subsidiary recorded upon the sale were immediately factored.

Upon repurchasing the goods a few days later, the subsidiary received (electronic) invoices from the partner and recorded trade payables. It transferred the invoices to a financial institution as part of a reverse factoring transaction (see next section). This transfer occurred within a few days of receiving the invoices, and, once transferred, the subsidiary reclassified the related payables from 'trade' to 'other'. The financial institution settled the business partner's invoices without delay, while granting the subsidiary an extension in payment days – what had been average payable days of approximately thirty turned into over ninety.

The reverse factoring arrangement generated liquidity both for the subsidiary (by effectively extending payable days by over 60) and for the business partner that recorded the sale-and-repurchase transaction on top of its normal supplier relationship and was paid immediately by the financial institution. The business partner, who was also a supplier, granted the subsidiary additional discounts – part of the cost of the financing transaction.

The arrangement was, in substance, an asset-based lending transactions. The subsidiary effectively borrowed against inventory. Once the inventory had been derecognised (it was never physically moved as part of these transactions), it sold the receivables to a financial institution, a factor.

The financial institutions involved in the factoring and reverse factoring transactions were unaware of the scheme. The target group had been sold as a healthy, profitable business, when in reality it was on the verge of collapse, using the sale-and-repurchase transactions to stay afloat.

[5] Reverse Factoring

Reverse factoring is a type of financing arrangement in which a third-party financing company (a factor) settles a supplier's invoices in the first instance, instead of the debtor, often a large corporate. There can be different ways to structure this financing transaction. A typical one involves the accelerated payment of the supplier, net of fees. The buyer (the debtor) subsequently pays the original amount to the financial institution, usually again with extended terms. From the supplier's perspective, the arrangement accelerates the collection of receivables. It can also generate liquidity for the debtor due to the extension of payment terms. The cost of the arrangement is at least partially borne by the supplier, either through a fee to the factor or by receiving less from the factor than it was due from the debtor (a discount).

Reverse factoring is depicted in Figure 4.1.

Figure 4.1 Reverse Factoring

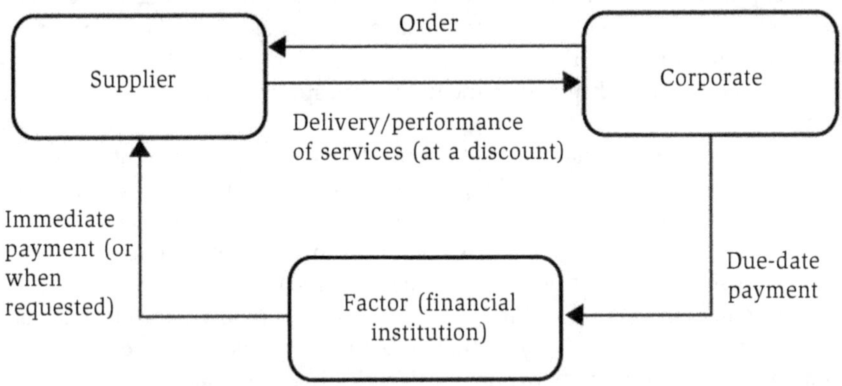

Reverse factoring is also known as 'supplier finance', 'structured payable arrangement' or 'vendor payable programme'. One of its purposes is can be to allow a smaller supplier (or group of smaller suppliers) to benefit from the better credit rating of a larger corporate customer.

Reverse factoring has seen rapid and aggressive growth over the last decade. A way to illustrate this is the relative number of mentions of the term in publications, which is shown in Figure 4.2 below.

Figure 4.2 Mentions of the term 'Reverse Factoring'

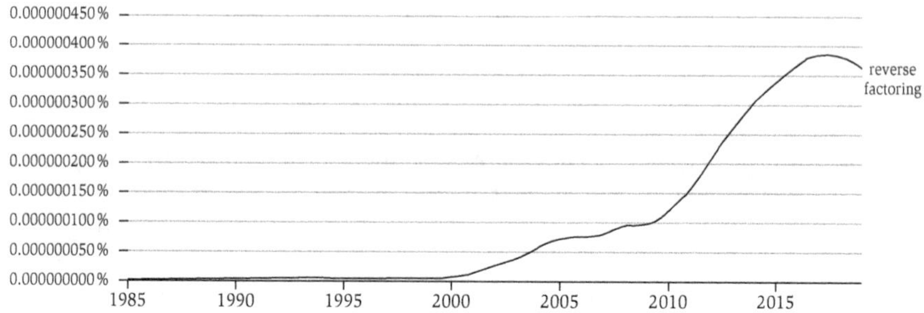

Source: google Ngrams.

A prominent example of the aggressive growth in recent years is the rise (and fall) of Greensill, a specialised finance company built around this type of financing.[63]

Like factoring, reverse factoring is a financing transaction. However, there are important differences between the two: reverse factoring often comes with an extension of the supplier's normal payment terms. At the same time, the supplier typically grants additional discounts. Reverse factoring has, in fact, been criticised for forcing smaller suppliers into accepting discounts or alternatively facing longer payment terms. Both the extension of terms and the discount make reverse factoring among the trickier structures to deal with properly in the completion mechanics. The reason is that it can be very difficult to disentangle the financing aspects of reverse factoring from the normal customer-supplier relationship.

For example, when analysing the financials of a potential target, it is necessary to establish a 'normal' level of working capital (discussed above in §2.01 [B]). This requires a pro-forma adjustments that remove the effects of reverse factoring from reported historical working capital (if that is the basis of the reference value). The adjustment also needs to consider any extension of the target's payment days – that is, if reverse factored trade payables are added to working capital on a pro-forma basis, the amount to be added may be less than the total payable as there is a financing component in the creditor with the financial institution, and that component belongs to financing liabilities (on a pro-forma basis). Moreover, reverse factoring requires adjusting historical P&Ls for any supplier discounts that have reduced cost of goods sold.[64] The discussion will return to this aspect of reverse factoring further below.

The effects of reverse factoring on the financial statements of the parties are as follows.

63. For example, *see* Duncan Mavin, *The Pyramid of Lies*, McMillan, 2022, 199.
64. If the target is the debtor in a reverse factoring arrangement.

For a supplier, the transaction accelerates the receipt of cash and leads to a derecognition of receivables. The cash added during the time between the receipt from the factor, and the time the debtor would have paid without the reverse factoring arrangement, is generated from an asset-based lending transaction. From the supplier's perspective, this is similar to non-recourse factoring.

From the perspective of the debtor (the corporate), reverse factoring replaces trade creditors with a liability to the factor. To the extent this liability exceeds what the trade payable with the supplier would have been (as a result of extended payable days), this represents a financing liability, although it is frequently not reported as such. Indeed, concerns over the reporting of reverse factoring liabilities have led to recent exposure drafts of the International Accounting Standards Board (IASB)[65] and FASB,[66] a response by standard-setters to cases such as Greensill, Carillion (a British construction group), Abengoa (a Spanish clean energy business) and NMC (a Middle Eastern healthcare group).[67]

Carillion, for example, went into liquidation in early 2018 after it collapsed under the burden of large, less-profitable-than-expected contracts (many related to public-private-partnerships) and a GBP 1.5 billion debt pile.[68]

In a report after its collapse, Moody's observed that Carillion's 2016 balance sheet and cash flows:

> failed to give a clear picture of the full scale of its liability to banks. While the balance sheet said the group's bank loans and overdrafts amounted to GBP 148 million, an additional amount – possibly as much as GBP 498 million – was owed to banks under the reverse factoring arrangement that started in 2013. This higher figure appears to have been reported within 'other creditors' and was consequently excluded from borrowings. Carillion reported group operating profit (excluding disposal gains) totalling GBP 501 million for the period from 2013 to 2016, an outcome seemingly corroborated by the cash flow statement, which showed cash generated from operations (before pension deficit recovery payments) of GBP 509 million over the same period.
>
> However, there was no disclosure that the cash inflow included bridging finance supplied by Carillion's banks under the reverse factoring arrangement. This would have contributed GBP 498 million (98%) of the GBP 509 million cash inflow if the facility had been fully utilised at the end of 2016.[69]

65. Exposure Draft 'Supplier Finance Arrangements (Proposed amendments to IAS 7 and IFRS 7)', 2 December 2021).
66. Proposed Accounting Standards Update, 'Liabilities – Supplier Finance Programmes (Subtopic 405-50)', 20 December 2021.
67. Carillion was one of the largest corporate failures in the UK, but by no means the only example of reverse factoring allegedly being used to conceal financial borrowings. *See* '*Greensill* case shows risks of supply chain finance', Financial Times, 4 March 2021, available at: https://www.ft.com/content/706203ec-4786-48f1-b859-ffe4c9171eee.
68. *See* 'Where Did It Go Wrong for Carillion?', BBC News, 15 January 2018. https://www.bbc.co.uk/news/business-42666275.
69. Moody's Investor Service, Announcement: Moody's: Carillion's Collapse Exposes Flaws in the Accounting for Supply-Chain Finance Arrangements, 13 March 2018, https://www.moodys.com/research/Moodys-Carillions-collapse-exposes-flaws-in-the-accounting-for-supply--PR_380769.

Another aspect that can make reverse factoring complex to deal with in transactions is that suppliers grant discounts as part of the arrangement. From the debtor's perspective, discounts in respect of input prices reduce the cost of purchasing, thereby increasing EBITDA and free cash flow. For the supplier, granting these discounts is, in effect, part of the cost of financing.

An acquisition where the buyer values the target on the basis of free cash flows or EBITDA which have benefited from such supplier discounts means enterprise value includes financial income that would not be there without the reverse factoring transaction. In theory, this requires pro-forma adjustments; these can be extremely difficult to quantify.

A buyer needs to restate working capital to reflect payment days at a 'normal' level (and the cash position at closing adjusted correspondingly), as if no reverse factoring had taken place. Doing so requires the buyer to know the precise extension of payables days that came with the supplier finance. This information is often difficult to obtain in an acquisition or a dispute.

[B] Leasing

[1] Introduction

Sir David Tweedie, former head of the IASB, once famously joked that one of his lifelong ambitions was to fly in an aircraft that was on the airline's balance sheet.[70] His comment reflected wider concerns over off-balance sheet financing around the time of the financial crisis of 2007 to 2009. By 2016, the IASB estimated that companies using IFRS or US GAAP had approximately USD 2.9 trillion of lease commitments that were off-balance sheet.[71] The recent fundamental changes to lease accounting can essentially be viewed as a reaction by standard setters to concerns over these off-balance sheet liabilities. These changes have brought many more lease liabilities on-balance sheet. Overall, these changes are among the most significant of the reforms introduced by the IASB since the financial crisis of 2007 to 2009.

Following a lengthy period of gestation, IFRS 16 'Leases' applied to accounting periods commencing on or after 1 January 2019, although early adoption was permitted if the entity had already implemented IFRS 15 'Revenue from Contracts with Customers'.

70. The Importance of International Accounting Standards, speech by Sir David Tweedie, the Empire Club of Canada, 25 April 2008. This section draws extensively on 'What Changes to Lease Accounting Mean for M&A Transactions' co-authored by Phil Hersey, Heiko Ziehms and Anna Hartley, World Accounting Report, October 2017, available at https://www.worldaccountingreport.com/accounting-issues/what-changes-to-lease-accounting-mean-for-ma-transactions-126889.htm.

71. http://www.ifrs.org/news-and-events/2016/01/iasb-shines-light-on-leases-by-bringing-them-onto-the-balance-sheet/.

Leases play an important role in transactions given the interaction of the target entity's accounting for leases with valuation and the equity bridge since lease liabilities are usually included in the definition of net debt. The above mentioned reforms give them even greater relevance.

Whichever airline Sir David chooses to travel with in the future, it is likely that the aircraft will be on the airline's balance sheet. Indeed, airlines are among those businesses most affected by the new standard, along with travel and leisure companies and businesses where property-related expenses represent a significant part of the cost base, such as retailers, financial services, legal services, and business consulting.

[2] IFRS 16 'Leases'

Under IAS 17, leases were classified as either 'finance leases' or 'operating leases'. The vastly different accounting treatments for these two types of financing arrangements meant that similar businesses operating in the same sector were not always readily comparable. In some sectors, leases are highly material and a key source of finance. Businesses were often able to structure leases in a way that they remained off-balance sheet.

The new standard, IFRS 16, removes the distinction between operating and finance leases for lessees and introduces a single approach that effectively moves almost all operating leases onto the lessee's balance sheet. The objective of the new standard is to provide users of financial statements with a fuller picture of a company's leverage – by bringing more of it onto the balance sheet – and aid the comparability of financial information across companies. The changes also affect key deal metrics and will be pertinent to M&A disputes.

The effect of bringing an operating lease onto the balance sheet means that an entity recognises an additional asset (termed 'right-of-use' asset) together with a lease liability, resulting in an increase in reported debt, in effect 'grossing up' the balance sheet. In the income statement the effect is a reduction in operating expenses (the lease charges, above EBITDA) partially or fully offset by increases in depreciation and interest (below EBITDA).

In the cash flow statement, the repayment of the principal component of the lease is recorded as a financing activity, rather than the single operating cash outflow of the lease payment; the interest element may, under IAS, be recorded as either a financing, operating, or an investing activity (IAS 7.31). When M&A practitioners use the cash flow statement to calculate free cash flow, it is important for them to consider whether interest is recorded as an operating, investing or financing cash flow. If necessary, it should be reassigned to the financing section of the cash flow statement in order to avoid an incorrect deduction of interest above free cash flow.

[3] US GAAP

The reform of lease accounting was an opportunity for closer convergence between US GAAP and IFRS standard-setters. In the event, they chose not to seize this opportunity. The recent changes to accounting for leases under US GAAP are not aligned with those under IFRS. While IFRS treats all leases under IFRS 16 as a form of financing for lessees, the Financial Accounting Standards Board (FASB) has gone another way. Its new lease accounting standard ASU 2016-02 'Leases' (Topic 842) also brings most leases on-balance sheet; however, the standard maintains the distinction between operating and financing leases. The distinction depends on whether the lessee effectively obtains control of the underlying asset rather than merely obtaining control over its use for the term of the lease. Operating leases continue to be recognised as a single operating expense in the income statement, on a straight-line basis over the life of the lease. EBITDA does not change relative to the previous accounting standards. This means that, in the equity bridge referred to in §2.01 [B] above, there is no upward effect on enterprise value as a result of 'converting' operating lease charges to depreciation and interest (and thus an increased EBITDA). However, this may result in an increase in debt if the definition in the SPA includes lease liabilities. Under an EBITDA-based valuation method, practitioners should therefore be aware that with US GAAP financials, the full lease payment should have already reduced EBITDA. Deducting the lease liability as net debt would mean double counting.

[4] Relevance to Transactions

[a] Effect on EBITDA-Based Valuations

The effects of the changes described above on the income statement and EBITDA-based valuations are shown in the example below (Figures 4.3 and 4.4). Under IFRS, bringing a lease onto the balance sheet effectively replaces the operating lease charge in the income statement with interest and depreciation expenses, which are below EBITDA, although the amounts in any period need not be identical. All else being equal (including the multiple used), this leads to a higher enterprise value.

Capitalising a lease also increases debt (by the amount of the lease liability), resulting in a higher net debt deduction in the equity bridge (again, if the definition of net debt in the SPA includes lease liabilities).

It would be a coincidence, however, if the two effects were to offset each other exactly, and in practice, they usually do not. Consequently, capitalising a lease (all else being equal) may impact the purchase price for the equity.

Figure 4.3 Lease Accounting and Valuation of the Target Business

IAS 17

Million GBP	2019
Revenue	100.0
Cost	30.0
Gross Profit	70.0
Operating expense	-50.0
Lease expense	-5.0
EBITDA	**15.0**
Depreciation	-3.0
EBIT	**12.0**
Interest	-0.5
EBT	**11.5**

IFRS 16

Million GBP	2019
Revenue	100.0
Cost	30.0
Gross Profit	70.0
Operating expense	-50.0
Lease expense	0.0
EBITDA	**20.0**
Depreciation	-3.0
Depreciation (lease)	-4.5
EBIT	**12.5**
Interest	-0.5
Interest (lease)	-0.8
EBT	**11.2**

2019 Purchase Price Impact

	IAS 17	IFRS 16
EBITDA 2019	15.0	20.0
EBITDA Multiple	8x	8x
Enterprise Value	**120.0**	**160.0**
Net debt	25.0	69.9
Equity Value	**95.0**	**90.1**

Figure 4.4 Effect of Lease Accounting Treatment on Equity Value

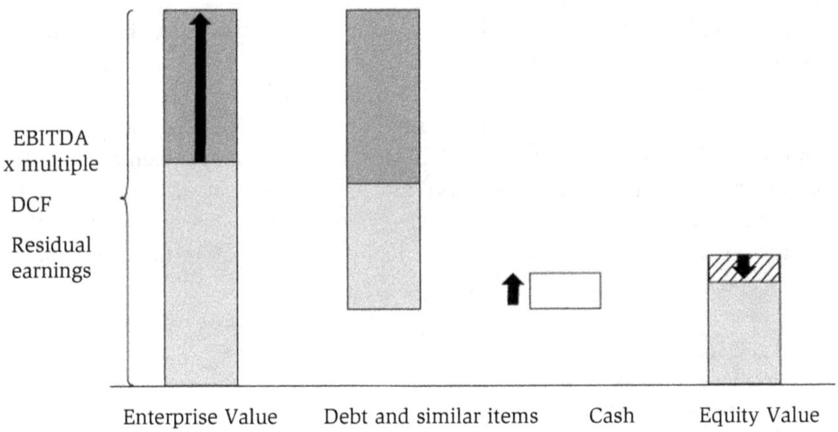

[b] Valuation Multiples and Effect on Net Purchase Price

One key determinant of whether the net purchase price will increase or decrease is the multiple used in the case of a multiple-based valuation. A higher multiple results in a correspondingly higher enterprise value, with a greater likelihood of it exceeding the revised debt amount (reflecting the change in lease debt).[72]

In theory, valuation multiples should adjust so that the effects of higher enterprise values and higher debt exactly offset each other and the only change to net purchase price reflects secondary effects (*see* below §4.04 [B] [5]). This logic is comparable to when observers of the stock market note that analysts are already 'pricing in' some factor or other in relation to leases regardless of the accounting.[73] In practice, such efficient price-setting in M&A transactions is far from being 'a given'. Consider that, when valuing a non-listed business the valuation multiple is often calculated with reference to comparable listed companies. As a result of the new standard, the comparable company multiples may also need to change. Even if the market priced leases correctly, historical multiples of the peer group would still reflect the previous off-balance sheet treatment and therefore need to be restated.

The higher the multiple, the greater the effect on enterprise value of moving the period's expenses associated with the lease from above to below EBITDA or vice versa. During times of high valuations, buyers who were able to introduce the accounting treatment into the negotiations over the proper valuation of the target company had an incentive to treat leases as operating; the same for deals involving high-growth sectors with high multiples (say, technology) where the adoption of IFRS 16 would have put further upward pressure on valuations in some cases. This has become less common under IFRS 16, however, at least for target companies that account under IFRS.

Conversely, in respect of lower multiples, it would be more likely that any change in enterprise value would amount to less than the associated change in debt. Thus, a significant downturn in the M&A market leading to lower valuations could be exacerbated in some cases by a net debt deduction for leases in excess of the benefit to enterprise value from a higher EBITDA.

The example given above can be viewed as a kind of arbitrage between a higher (or lower) EBITDA times a multiple, and a higher (or lower) net debt deduction. EBITDA is a measure of book return. It is the outcome of the application of accounting rules and conventions. Net debt, on the other hand, consists of cash and liabilities that are (typically) close to market values.[74] This kind of arbitrage, therefore, runs the risk of conflating accounting outcomes and market prices. An efficient market 'sees through' the accounting (*see* §11.01), however, in private M&A transactions this may not always be achievable/the case and the distortions of book returns due to accounting effects can be significant.[75]

72. In the example, a 'break-even' EBITDA multiple, i.e., a multiple that would make equity values identical (using alternatively IAS 17 or IFRS 16), would be 8.98.
73. *See, e.g.*, 'Accounting's Big Shake-up to Bring More Transparency', Financial Times, 20 January 2016, available at: https://www.ft.com/content/138fe994-bdd5-11e5-846f-79b0e3d20eaf.
74. This statement may not be strictly true for all liabilities but it is generally true for cash and most financial debt.
75. Book returns (such as EBITDA) not only convey information about economic profitability, but also about risk. *See* Stephen Penman and Xiao-Jun Zhang, *Connecting Book Rate of Return to Risk and Return: The Information Conveyed by Conservative Accounting*. Review of Accounting Studies 26, 391–423 (2021).

Another determinant of the purchase price calculation can be the timing of the transaction. Whereas the treatment as an operating lease usually meant straight-line expensing over the lease term, capitalising the lease under IFRS 16 means interest expense may be higher in the early years of the lease and decrease as the liability decreases. This can mean a front-loading effect on net income. While below EBITDA, it can be important to consider this effect, which in aggregate depends on the maturity of the lease portfolio, in multiple-based valuations that reference net earnings.

[c] Effect on Cash Flow-Based Valuations

The effects on a DCF valuation are different from those of multiple-based valuations. As discussed above, the repayment of the principal component of the lease instalment will be recorded as a financing activity, below free cash flow; the interest element may, under IAS, be recorded as either a financing, operating, or an investing activity. In the first case, it is below free cash flow, and in both alternatives, it is above free cash flow. In free cash flow-based valuation, if no adjustment is made, the enterprise value has already been reduced by interest in both these alternatives. It is, therefore, important for M&A practitioners using DCF models to avoid deducting interest from free cash flow when there is also a deduction for lease debt – a potential 'double dip'.

The effects on cash flow-based valuations are, however, not limited to cash flows above or below the free cash flow subtotal. Capitalising a lease may also change the calculation of the cost of capital if it is based on financial statements – both gearing and the weight of debt in the weighted average cost of capital (WACC). While in theory, there should be no effect on value (other than secondary effects from taxes), in reality, complex valuation models will often produce different outcomes.

[5] Secondary Effects

The changes to lease accounting may expose unpleasant truths about a target entity, for example, high levels of leverage. In the first instance, this is 'only the accounting'. But additional reported leverage can further result in real-world effects such as the non-compliance with loan covenants, potentially triggering additional regulatory capital requirements for companies in the financial sector. It is important to consider such secondary effects in the valuation.

[6] Leases and Post-M&A Disputes

Shafi v. Rutherford, discussed above in §3.04 [B], related to an error in the accounting treatment of a finance lease that had been incorrectly treated as an operating lease in the historical accounts. The 'binary' nature of the accounting treatment often means that the amounts involved in disputes over the classification of a lease contract are material relative to the purchase price. This is further complicated by the fact that a change in the accounting treatment of a lease, for example due to an error correction as in *Shafi v. Rutherford* that brings new debt into the completion accounts, is usually made at a time when there is no offsetting increase in enterprise value derived from a higher EBITDA or free cash flow. The missing interaction between the purchase price adjustment and valuing the enterprise is a common issue with GAAP overrides (*see* above §3.04 [B]). However, with the new lease accounting standard, fewer of these disputes can be expected.

This does not mean, however, that disputes over lease accounting will disappear. There continue to be areas of judgment in lease accounting over which it is easy to disagree. In addition, SPAs concluded prior to the introduction of IFRS 16 that did not foresee the consequences of the standard for the target's financial statements can result in earn-out disputes. For example, EBITDA-based earn-outs might not have foreseen that replacing operating lease costs with depreciation and interest increases EBITDA. Alternatively, earn-outs calculated with reference to net income may be by the front-loading effect on net income (*see* above §4.04 [B] [4] [b]). A disagreement over the earn-out basis may ensue.

IFRS 16 comes with judgmental accounting areas: Under the new accounting standard, right-of-use assets and accompanying liabilities are valued using a set of assumptions including interest rates, the exercise of options, inflation, future reinstatement costs, or residual value guarantee payments. Some of these key assumptions and potential areas of disputes are discussed below.

[a] Interest Rate Implicit in the Lease

The interest rate used to value the lease liability is the 'interest rate implicit in the lease' at its inception date. Where this cannot be established, the liability is estimated using the 'incremental cost of borrowing' for the lease. This will be the case for many leases. Determining the incremental cost of borrowing (the rate that an entity would borrow at to acquire the right-to-use asset over the lease term[76]) can be highly judgmental. The nature of NPV calculations used to value the liability is such that small changes in the discount rate can have a material impact on the valuation of the liability. In a corporate transaction, increasing the estimated incremental cost of borrowing would reduce net debt and, depending on the deal price mechanism, may increase the value of an entity - creating a potential area of dispute.

[b] The Lease Term

The lease term begins on the commencement date and comprises the non-cancellable period of the lease, together with:

76. The technical definition of a lessee's incremental cost of borrowing under IFRS is the rate of interest that a lessee would have to pay to borrow over a similar term, and with a similar security, the funds necessary to obtain an asset of a similar value to the right-of-use asset in a similar economic environment (Appendix A to IFRS 16).

- periods covered by an option to extend the lease if the lessee is reasonably certain to exercise that option; and
- periods covered by an option to terminate the lease if the lessee is reasonably certain not to exercise that option.[77]

Many lease agreements have options to extend the lease term. IFRS 16 generally requires reassessment of the lease term after the initial determination only when the company takes actions that could have a significant effect on the lease term.

With a net debt deduction, the timing for the exercise of options can be critical. If the lessee (the target company) exercises options to extend leases during the closing period, additional lease liabilities may be created and included within the net debt deduction. However, there may be no offsetting increase in the enterprise value derived from the EBITDA multiple at this stage. It is, therefore, important to consider the consequences to net debt and limit the ability of management to extend a lease during the closing period.

[c] Intangible Assets

There remains an inconsistency between the leasing of physical assets and intangible assets (licensing). A lessee can elect to apply IFRS 16 to leases of intangible assets, other than those items listed in IFRS 16.3 (licences, rights under licence agreements, and certain others), which are excluded from the scope of IFRS 16. As such, many intangible assets are not subject to the new leasing standard. For operating leases incorporating both physical assets and intellectual property, the allocation between the two elements is a potentially complex judgmental area. Whether a party has an incentive for a higher or lower share of physical assets will depend on the completion mechanics, the age of the assets, and so on. However, the effect can be material.

[C] Deferred Compensation: Pension Benefits

[1] Introduction

A feature of many transactions, defined benefit pension plans can be highly problematic. Pension liabilities are very sensitive to changes in actuarial assumptions, in particular interest rates. Until the reversal around 2020 of an almost forty-year trend of decreasing yields, the size of pension deficits, combined with the typical duration gap between assets and liabilities, created a major headache for dealmakers and in many cases still do. Despite the fact that many companies have taken action to address the problem by closing defined benefit plans to new entrants or amending scheme rules, many legacy schemes continue to exist. In some (occasionally high profile) cases, deals foundered because purchasers were unwilling to take on such large obligations. Alternatively, transactions were structured so as to ring-fence pension liabilities. Only

77. IFRS 16:B34.

recently have rising yields taken some weight off of deals. Nevertheless, defined benefit obligations remain an important topic in many transactions.

The reasoning behind pension obligations being treated as part of net debt in transactions has already been explained in §4.02 above. This section starts with a brief description of the two main types of pension plans, as well as the accounting rules and key actuarial assumptions underlying the valuation of pension obligations, before moving on to discuss examples of post-M&A disputes.

There are other types of deferred compensation – notably health care, insurance, and early retirement benefits – that can resemble pension benefits. However, the focus here is on pensions.

[2] Types of Pension Plans and Their Accounting Basis

Some background and knowledge of accounting are necessary to understand the treatment of pension liabilities in transactions. The discussion here is necessarily limited and based primarily on IFRS (IAS 19). While broadly comparable to US GAAP (ASC 715), there are important differences between the two, which are well documented elsewhere in accounting texts.

There are two principal ways an employer can sponsor retirement benefits for employees:

(1) Defined contribution plans: The employer and/or employee contributes a certain amount to a pension plan (often a fraction of an employee's salary), but without promising specific benefits on retirement. The pension the employee receives depends on the amounts contributed and the investment returns of the plan. 401(k) plans in the US are a type of defined contribution plan.
(2) Defined benefit plans: The employer promises specific benefits payable under certain conditions such as retirement, disability or death and a vesting period. These are often set as a fixed monthly amount or a fraction of an employee's average or final salary before retirement, weighted by the time of service (the formula can be complex). The employer can decide to set aside amounts to fund these pension promises fully, partially, or not at all.

Under IFRS, a plan is considered a defined contribution plan if an employer's legal or constructive obligation is limited to the amount it contributes to a separate entity. In principle, only the plan assets, namely the amount that has accumulated by the time the pension becomes payable, are available to the employee.

Let's turn to the net debt deduction in a transaction. The plans that play a key role here are, with few exceptions, defined benefit plans. The reason is that, with defined contribution plans, the sponsoring employer does not usually have a responsibility (beyond their share of the initial contributions while the employee was still working and the employer received the benefit of their work) to fund the obligations of the plan, including making good deficits. The liability of the defined contribution plan is equal to the plan assets.[78] The scheme is (by definition) fully funded. There is usually nothing to deduct as debt.

Defined benefit plans are very different. When quantifying the employer's obligation any underfunding should be treated as debt-like (except in the rare case that it is already reflected in enterprise value). Further, in transactions, pension liabilities should, in concept, be valued on a commercial, or fair value, basis[79] – that is to say, the net present value of the future cash flows required as funding of the defined benefit obligation, after deducting the value of any plan assets available for this purpose.[80] Any deficit that is deducted should therefore, in principle, be valued independently of the accounting (*see* above §4.02 [C]), although the book value is often a starting point in transactions.

The valuation process requires actuaries to use certain assumptions about financial and demographic variables, including:

- The discount rate (often determined by a yield curve and credit spread).
- Salary increases (if salary is part of the pension promise).
- Pension indexation.
- Longevity.

Salary increases and pension indexation are usually linked to inflation. The yield curve, credit spread, and inflation often have the greatest impact on the pension liability. Other assumptions include employee turnover and vesting periods of benefits.

The discount rate affects the balance sheet directly; inflation and longevity affect the cash flows for pension payments. As there is at least some degree of discretion in respect of many of these variables, actuaries can usually get to a range of acceptable values for the measurement of the defined benefit obligation under IFRS, US GAAP or other accounting rules. The application of some accounting standards can lead to book values for pension debt that are outside of a range of commercial values, for example, by requiring the use of a high discount rate or outdated mortality tables.

Agreeing the commercial value for a net debt deduction is what pension-related negotiations in M&A transactions are usually about.

[3] The Discount Rate

The discount rate is often the principal battleground in transactions since pension obligations (and hence the net debt deduction) can be sensitive to even minor changes

78. In fact, it can be more complicated. Some plans in some jurisdictions may be classified, for accounting purposes, as defined contribution plans even though there can be a residual risk that the sponsoring employer retains in the form if not of a legal, then a constructive obligation to make good deficits. Some hybrid plans that combine features of both may be accounted for as defined benefit or alternatively defined contribution.
79. Setting aside a buy-out valuation which is sometimes proposed by buyers and which will often lead to the highest valuation of the DBO.
80. It may be appropriate to consider in a transaction context whether any of the plan assets include operating assets of the firm, and implications for the valuation. This is an exception but can be the case with some Collateralised Trust Agreements (CTAs).

in this assumption. Under IAS 19, the discount rate used to value pension liabilities has to be determined by reference to the yield of 'high-quality' (often interpreted as AA-rated) corporate bonds.

To put things in perspective, consider that AA-rated bond yields for the Eurozone used by actuaries to value pension liabilities (assuming a duration that corresponds to a 'mixed population') under IAS 19 were approximately 3.6% on 31 December 2013, moved to 1.2% on 30 September 2016 and 2.0% on 30 September 2018.[81] US corporate 20-year AA-rated bond yields decreased from over 6% in 2007–2009 to 3.5% in July 2016, while 10-year AA-rated bond yields (another frequently used duration) decreased from around 6% to 2.35% in approximately ten years to July 2016.[82] In 2014 alone, average discount rates used for pension accounting purposes decreased from 4.84% to 4.05% in the US, and from 2.24% to 1.21% in Switzerland (a more than 50% decrease).[83]

More recently, yields have however risen significantly, taking pressure off deals: 10-year Treasury yields increased from 0.5% in early August 2020 to surpass 4% in October 2022 and remained there in August 2023.[84] 10-year Euro-denominated AA-rated bond yields increased from 1.1% at the beginning of February 2022 to 3.2% exactly one year later.

Pension liabilities have an inverse relationship to discount rates. The liability will increase when the discount rate decreases (and vice versa). Typical pension plans have a duration between fifteen and twenty years, and, as noted earlier, this makes pension liabilities very sensitive to changes in the drivers of the discount rates.

How sensitive? A rule of thumb is that for a typical term, a 0.25% change in the discount rate means a 3%–4% change in the defined benefit obligation. The author has found this to be a helpful rule of thumb to quickly and approximately understand sensitivities of discount rates in a transaction context.

Negotiations in M&A transactions often come down to where the parties are prepared to meet within an acceptable range of bond yields based on current market data (buyers argue for a value at the lower end of the range whereas sellers favour the upper end).

During the period of exceptionally low yields up to 2020, market participants responded with various tactics to soften the impact on transactions of high net debt deductions – essentially finding reasons to increase discount rates. These ranged from including lower (A-rated) bonds in addition to AA-rated bonds to simply adding a premium. The latter stance implies that prices in the bond market were arguably unsustainable (in fact, yields have since risen). While it is true that bond yields were extremely low, it was difficult to second-guess even bubbly market prices and to derive an 'appropriate' yield this way that is capable of being justified.

---

81. AON Eurozone Yield Curve, Development of Discount Rates for Sample Populations – last updated 30 September 2018, available here: http://www.aon.com/getmedia/9ce63b16-a135-477c-be84-f7b166b3c831/Rechnungszinsinformation_Eurozone_EN.pdf.aspx.
82. *See* bondsonline.com.
83. AON Global Report: Global Survey of Retirement Plan Accounting Assumptions, June 2015, p. 5. As highlighted in this report, the changes to discount rate assumptions may, in part, be due to changes in inflationary expectations.
84. Financial Times, US 10 year Treasury data.

There are ways to hedge exposure to interest rate changes (and other risks) in defined benefit obligations. In some transactions, this can be a way to reduce what is otherwise often significant scope for disagreement over the measurement of the DBO.

[4] Other Actuarial Assumptions

Pension liabilities are sensitive to the following actuarial assumptions other than the discount rate:

- Longevity: A broad rule of thumb is that a three-year increase in life expectancy can increase the pension liability by 10% to 20%. Mortality tables used by actuaries typically lag behind the significant improvements in life expectancy (even though these have more recently been levelling off). As a result, in negotiations, buyers occasionally propose adjustments to the tables to get to more realistic (higher) values (e.g., using life insurance data). More detailed longevity data can be available in the UK down to individual postal codes. However, adjustments to mortality tables are comparatively rare in practice. An argument against them (in particular if a business is sold to PE with a finite holding period) is that, as tables tend to lag life expectancy, the buyer can expect, when in due course they sell the business, to use life expectancies that are also outdated. However, this only works if life expectancy continues to increase at steady rates which is not necessarily the case. Note that longevity risk is a cash flow risk that buyers face even if they deduct the pension deficit. This risk can be hedged.[85]
- Projected salary and pension increases: Shrewd sellers who anticipate the dynamics of the negotiations in a disposal process may, when a target company draws up its accounts before a transaction, use assumptions that minimise the pension liability. Even if buyers see through this approach, this can anchor the negotiations in the seller's favour.

[5] Treatment in Transactions

Negotiations over the deduction of unfunded pension deficits are more often over their valuation than over the question of whether or not to deduct. In contrast to most other net debt items, pension liabilities tend not to be measured at closing but are agreed upon by the parties as a fixed value prior to signing (and specified as such in the SPA). Technically, a fixed amount deduction can be effected by defining it as a 'specific accounting rule' as referenced in the accounting hierarchy discussed above in §3.04 [A].

85. For example, Heineken, which acquired the UK business of Scottish & Newcastle in 2009, completed a longevity hedging and reinsurance transaction in 2015 in which it transferred GBP 2.4 billion of longevity risk related to around 19,000 pensioners in the defined benefit pension scheme of the Scottish & Newcastle Pension Plan. *See* Heineken in 2.4 billion pound longevity swap deal with Aviva, Reuters, available at: https://uk.reuters.com/article/uk-heineken-longevity-idUKKCN0RE0UD20150914.

The reason the use of a fixed deduction is often appropriate is that the value of pension obligations tends to be less influenced by day-to-day changes in the business than shorter-term liabilities.[86] Measuring the deficit at closing opens up the determination of the final purchase price to (usually unnecessary) uncertainty. In addition, measuring pension liabilities involves the use of significant assumptions. This affords the party that prepares the completion accounts discretion which may not be desired by the other party to the transaction. It is often more expedient (and safer) to agree with the value of a pension liability before signing than to have to set out the assumptions in the SPA so meticulously as to avoid ambiguity later.

Example: Measurement of Deficit at Closing (International Arbitration)

The case relates to an acquisition in which the seller had agreed to compensate the buyer for the deficit in a defined benefit pension scheme over a period after closing. The SPA included the provision that the pension obligation was to be measured at closing, using a methodology 'consistent with past practice'.

The actuaries for the target company had determined the discount rate by reference to AA-rated bonds (for the relevant term). This relationship in late June 2007, before signing, is shown in Figure 4.4. On the basis of data similar to this, the actuary had derived an appropriate discount rate for the relevant duration.

The financial crisis of 2007 to 2009 brought with it significant, unexpected volatility in bond yields, and market turbulence made prices difficult to establish. Yields at the end of November 2008 are displayed in Figure 4.5. Based on similar data, the buyer's actuaries derived a discount rate after closing. The disagreement related to whether the discount rate determined by the buyer's actuaries was on a basis that was 'consistent' with past practice.

Figure 4.5 AA-Bond Yields June 2007

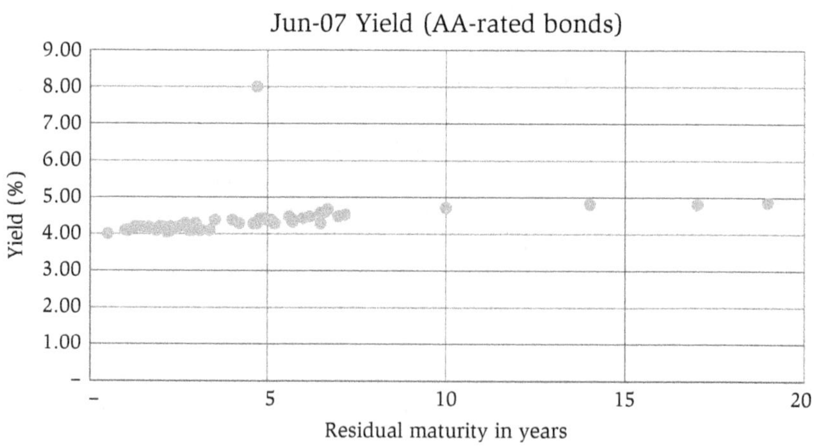

86. An important qualification is when employees, or groups of employees with vested benefits leave before closing.

Figure 4.6 AA-Bond Yields November 2008

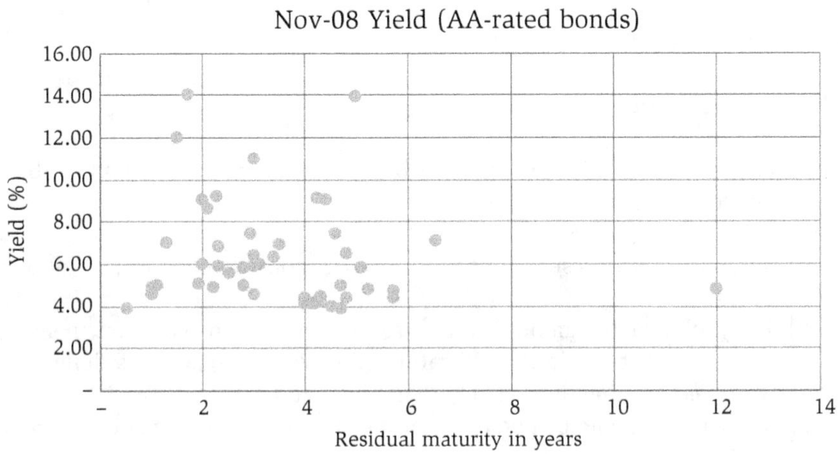

Had the turbulence in the credit markets been foreseeable, it could have been dealt with, for example, by setting a fixed bond yield in the SPA. The difficulty was in anticipating it at the time.

Legacy Plans

Another issue is that a sponsoring employer may be unaware of so-called legacy pension plans, perhaps because they were introduced years ago, may relate to relatively few employees and were subsequently closed – or a combination of these. Their existence may only come to light sometime after closing when retirement benefits are claimed. In such cases, a suitably worded warranty might provide a buyer with some protection (and encourage a prudent seller to take steps to satisfy themselves that they have uncovered all such plans).

Pensions in M&A-Related Disputes

Despite the importance of pension obligations in transactions and the complexity involved in their measurement, disputes in this area are not particularly common. This is likely because, as mentioned above, in many cases a fixed amount is agreed as a net debt deduction and, as a result, there is little scope for later disagreement. Having said that, when disputes do arise, the amounts involved can be significant relative to the size of the transaction.

The dispute discussed earlier in this section related to the measurement of the pension deficit. Another area where disputes can arise is over whether a particular obligation meets the SPA definition of net debt in the first place. One item in dispute in the sample of international arbitrations revolved around whether the term 'defined benefit obligation' in an SPA encompassed a French 'indemnité de fin de carrière' (a term used not only for pensions but for a variety of retirement benefits). The dispute could have been avoided had the definition of financial indebtedness covered the various types of deferred compensation.

[D] Provisions

[1] Introduction

A provision is defined by IASs as 'a liability of uncertain timing or amount' (IAS 37.10). It has to be recognised when:

(a) an entity has a present obligation (legal or constructive) as a result of a past event;
(b) it is probable that an outflow of resources embodying economic benefits will be required to settle the obligation (the word 'probable' is defined in IAS 37.23 as meaning 'more likely than not'); and
(c) a reliable estimate can be made of the amount of the obligation (IAS 37.14).

If all three criteria are met, then the amount recognised as a provision should be the best estimate of the expenditure required to settle the present obligation at the balance sheet date (IAS 37.36). Provisions for what are often one-off events (such as restructuring, environmental clean-up, or settlement of a lawsuit) are measured at the most likely amount (IAS 37.40). Provisions for large populations of events (warranties, customer refunds) are measured at a probability-weighted expected value (IAS 37.39).

US GAAP knows an 'estimated loss accrued for a loss contingency' (i.e., a contingent loss that is recognised as a liability). In US GAAP, ASC 450 and ASC 460 are the primary sources of guidance. A contingency is defined as:

> An existing condition, situation, or set of circumstances involving uncertainty as to possible gain (gain contingency) or loss (loss contingency) to an entity that will ultimately be resolved when one or more future events occur or fail to occur.[87]

There are important differences between provisions in IFRS and loss contingencies in US GAAP in terms of both recognition and measurement. Under US GAAP, a loss must be accrued if information is available before the financial statements are issued that indicate that it is probable that an asset had been impaired or a liability had been incurred at the date of the financial statements, and the loss can be reasonably estimated. 'Probable' is defined as likely, which is a higher threshold than 'more likely than not' under IFRS. All else being equal, this means that more contingencies qualify for recognition as liabilities under IFRSs than under US GAAP.

For a range of possible outcomes, if no amount in the range is more likely than any other amount in the range, the minimum amount in the range is used to measure the amount to be accrued for a loss contingency under US GAAP. Under IFRS, if no

87. The Master Glossary of the FASB Accounting Standards Codification.

amount in the range is more likely than any other amount in the range, the midpoint of the range is used to measure the provision.[88]

[2] Treatment in Transactions

Many provisions, including pensions already discussed above in §4.04 [C], as well as those relating to warranties, litigation, and restructuring, relate to operating, not financing activities. While defined benefit pension deficits are almost always treated as debt-like, for others, the treatment is less clear-cut.

The reason certain provisions can be treated as net debt even if they relate to operating activities was discussed above §4.02 [B]. It reflected a timing difference between incurring an expense (and receiving the benefit) and the (potentially much later) cash outflow. If closing occurs between the two, then the buyer has the burden of the (future) cash outflow, whereas the seller has had the economic benefit. The net debt deduction moves the present value of this cash burden from buyer to seller.

If a provision is recurring and constantly revolving, so that by the time it becomes cash-relevant it will have already been replaced by another provision, then there is an argument to treat it as working capital, not debt. Key considerations when negotiating the treatment as working capital or debt, therefore, usually include the length of time involved before the liability converts into cash, and whether it is recurring. Long-term provisions (like pensions) or one-off provisions (like litigation and restructuring costs) are more often debt-like unless already covered by indemnities. Things are less clear-cut where provisions relate to items that may or may not be considered 'a normal part of the business', for example, some types of warranty obligations.

Another aspect to consider is the interaction between a provision and an indemnity. An indemnity is a promise made by the seller to reimburse the buyer dollar-for-dollar for a specific liability if it arises.[89] For example, the outcome of litigation, or environmental clean-up requirements, may be better covered by an indemnity rather than a net debt deduction, especially if the amounts involved are difficult to estimate: indemnifying the buyer does not require an estimate to be agreed at signing or closing. In the case the seller has indemnified the buyer in full, there should not, in addition, be a net debt deduction for the same item.

Lastly, provisions that are treated as net debt in a transaction but are part of reported working capital in the monthly management accounts should not only be excluded from the definition of working capital at closing but also, on a pro-forma basis, from historical working capital when the reference value is determined.

---

88. RSM, *US. GAAP v. IFRS: Contingencies And Provisions At-A-Glance*, August 2014, p. 2, available at https://rsmus.com/content/dam/mcgladrey/pdf/contingencies-provisions-at-a-glance.pdf.
89. Below §12.01 [C].

[3] Provisions in Post-M&A Disputes

It is, perhaps, inevitable that provisions are often the subject of disputes since estimates involve a high degree of subjectivity and accounting rules give considerable discretion to the preparer of financial information. The sample of post-M&A disputes includes a number of different types of related disputes.

One type of dispute arises when one party claims that a particular item does or does not fall under the definition of net debt. A case in the sample of disputes is an International Chamber of Commerce (ICC) arbitration which related to an acquisition of a professional French sports team. The SPA definition of 'debt' included provisions for 'long- and medium-term bonus claims of players', but not short-term obligations. However, the SPA did not define precisely which obligations were short-, medium- or long-term. The dispute arose over whether bonus provisions that related to a player were correctly classified as 'medium-term'.

Another area of disagreement is the requirement to record a provision. As noted in the introduction to this section, IAS 37 requires the recognition of a provision if an outflow of resources is 'more likely than not' to occur (IAS 37.15). This usually means a probability of greater than 50%. Whether or not to record a provision, therefore, requires an assessment of probabilities. This links to the question of what information can be taken into account. As discussed above, a way to reduce the risk of a dispute in this regard is to limit in the SPA the period of time after closing for which new information can be taken into account (*see* §3.05).

Many disputes arise over the measurement of provisions, especially which costs to include. IAS requires the most likely outcome to be used as the provisioning amount (in case of a range of outcomes, the mid-point of that range). There is, however, limited guidance in the accounting standards as to which costs should be included in a provision. Not surprisingly, companies apply different practices. One dispute in the sample was over the inclusion of costs in a provision of an onerous contract. IAS 37.10 defines an onerous contract as:

> A contract in which the unavoidable costs of meeting the obligations under the contract exceed the economic benefits expected to be received under it.

IAS 37 requires a provision to be recorded for an onerous contract based on the unavoidable costs of meeting the entity's obligations under the contract. Unavoidable costs reflect the lower of the cost of fulfilling a contract and any compensation or penalties arising from failure to fulfil it (IAS 37.68). The dispute related to which costs were considered 'unavoidable' and therefore included in the provision.

There can be similar types of disagreements over the measurement of restructuring provisions. Costs of restructuring are deducted from the purchase price when the target is sold as a restructured business, but the restructuring measures have yet to be completed. With a net debt deduction, the parties intend to move the cash cost of these measures from the buyer (who pays for a restructured business) to the seller.

IAS 37 contains specific guidance for restructuring provisions. A provision is to be recognised when there is:

(a) a detailed, formal plan identifying the main aspects of the restructuring (IAS 37.72); and
(b) a valid expectation in those affected that the entity will carry out the restructuring by starting to implement the plan or by announcing its main features to those affected (IAS 37.10).

A restructuring provision should include only direct expenditures caused by the restructuring, not costs associated with the ongoing activities of the entity. As their measurement requires considerable judgment, it is not surprising that restructuring provisions are a prominent way to manage, or manipulate, earnings. An example is 'big bath' accounting that reduces a period's income significantly (often the first period under new management) by deliberately overestimating restructuring costs, only to 'bleed' those costs back to income and report earnings improvements in subsequent periods. There can be similar dynamics at work in a sales process. It is for the quality of earnings analysis to identify these manipulations.

A way to reduce the risk of a dispute is to agree a fixed amount as a net debt deduction for restructuring (before signing). Although this does not solve all problems as it requires estimates that can turn out to be incorrect - for example, a seller may decide to spend less than the agreed amount, increasing the cash position - this removes at least one area of potential disagreement. A fixed amount should generally be determined independently of the accounting basis of the liability. Further, it should be set on a basis consistent with the business plan on which the bid is based.

[E] Derivate Securities

[1] Introduction

The debt-like securities discussed above represent direct obligations to financial institutions (bank debt, leasing debt, factored receivables), former employees (deferred compensation), or government agencies (taxes). Companies can also enter into commitments that derive their value indirectly, from prices of underlying assets or from being linked to certain events. Such arrangements are derivatives.

Common types of derivatives are options, futures, forwards, and swaps. For example, the price of a call or put option on a stock depends, among other factors, on the price of the stock, to which it bears a (no-arbitrage) relation. Derivatives can be structured to depend on the prices of a variety of underlying variables, including share prices, commodity prices, debt securities, indices, weather events, emissions, electricity prices, and many others.[90]

The principal use of derivatives is to shift risk among investors. In the case of an interest rate swap, for example, a company may have borrowed at a variable interest rate and uses a swap to effectively convert variable into fixed interest rate payments. As a result, the borrower has effectively removed its exposure to interest rate volatility.

90. John C. Hull, *Options, Futures and Other Derivatives* (6th ed., Pearson 2006), p. 552.

Derivatives can relate to financing or operating activities. An interest rate swap that swaps variable against fixed interest payments can be considered an extension of the underlying loan agreement, and therefore a financing activity. On the other hand, a forward sale is a common way of selling commodities and can be viewed as an operating activity. The cost associated with derivatives used for hedging (whether or not charged to the income statement) is essentially the cost of removing exposure to volatility from everyday business activities, bringing the business to a less volatile state. Again, this cost could be an operating cost or a financing cost, depending on the underlying security or variable.

Accounting for derivative instruments, or hedge accounting, saw a significant reform with the recent introduction of IFRS 9, the new financial instruments standard that replaced IAS 39. The reform can be viewed in part as a response by the standard-setter to accounting issues that were highlighted by the global financial crisis of 2007 to 2009.

This section discusses the most common derivatives and then turns to their treatment in a transaction.

Financial Options

Options give their holder the right, but not the obligation, to buy or sell a fixed quantity of an asset either at some future date or during a specified time period in the future, and at a specific price. There are two basic types of options: 'call options' give the right to buy an asset at a certain price, and 'put options' give the right to sell an asset at a certain price. The most common type of financial option is stock options.

An option is considered a derivative security as its price depends on the price of the underlying share. The price at which an option can be exercised is called the 'exercise price' or 'strike price'. When the exercise price of a stock option is equal to the current price of the share, then the option is at-the-money. A call option with an exercise price below the current share price is in-the-money. The same is true for a put option with a strike price above the current share price. A call option with a strike price above the current share price and a put option with a strike price below the current share price are all out-of-the-money.[91]

Futures Contracts

A futures contract is an agreement to buy or sell an asset in a specified quantity, at a certain time in the future, and for an agreed price. It is a derivative instrument as its value depends on the price of an underlying asset. Futures contracts are usually standardised instruments and traded on exchanges at a publicly observable price, allowing the parties to buy or sell them at any time when the markets are open.

Forward Contracts

Like a futures contract, a forward contract is a contract that requires the holder to buy or sell an asset for a specified price at a specified future time. The difference between

91. *Ibid.*, n. 28, p. 657.

the two types of derivatives is that forward contracts are not normally traded on an exchange but in the over-the-counter market. Forward contracts are often used to hedge foreign exchange exposure.

Swaps

A swap is an agreement to exchange cash flows in the future at a certain formula. For example, an interest rate swap may exchange floating interest payments for fixed payments. At the inception of the swap, the total value of fixed interest rate cash flows over the life of the swap is typically equal to the expected value of floating interest rate cash flows. The swap is at-the-money. After some time, as the floating rate changes, the swap moves in-the-money or out-of-the-money. For a corporate, the purpose of a swap is usually to reduce or eliminate the risk posed by interest rate volatility.

[2] Treatment in Transactions

It is sometimes suggested in negotiations that all out-of-the money-derivatives should be treated as debt-like. This makes sense when their holder has an obligation to make a payment to a counterparty. This is the case, for example, for an interest rate swap where (from the target entity perspective of a fixed-rate payer) the fixed rate exceeds the variable rate. Such an obligation represents an economic burden at closing which a buyer acquires and which – if not already reflected in the carrying value of the loan – can be moved to the seller as a net debt deduction.

If a target company that is not a financial institution has entered into a currency swap which, for example, requires it to make up the difference in value of a weakening pound against US dollar, then it can also be argued that this commitment should be treated as debt.

However, out-of-the-money derivative securities do not necessarily represent an obligation to transfer value to a third party. For example, a call option that has a strike price above the share price is out-of-the-money. Similarly, a put option on a share with a strike price below the spot price is also out-of-the-money. These out-of-the-money derivative instruments represent only a right, not an obligation, to transfer value to a third party. If they remain out-of-the-money, the option will not be exercised, and their value will be zero at the time of expiration. However, even out-of-the-money options have a positive value. (While the intrinsic value of the option is zero, the time value is not zero.)

For most businesses that are not financial institutions, acquirers should value options separately and (even if out-of-the-money) add their fair value to enterprise value. This essentially treats them like cash (or other non-operating assets), reducing net debt.

Another case is the acquisition of a company that has issued share options (e.g., as employee remuneration). IFRS 2 requires a company to measure and recognise share-based payment awards (to employees or other parties) in its financial statements at the fair value of the goods and services received. They are expensed as vesting conditions are satisfied.[92] Expensing share options has been required since IFRS 2 was issued in 2004. US GAAP has similar provisions in ASC Topic 718, Compensation – Stock Compensation and in ASC Subtopic 505-50, Equity – Equity-Based Payments to Non-Employees.[93]

In general, once the awards have vested, they represent a reward for work already performed, similar to other kinds of deferred compensation.[94] At the time a share-based award is expensed, it reduces EBITDA; however, until an option is exercised, it has not yet diluted the existing shareholders (if equity-settled), or become cash-relevant (if cash-settled).

The first question when contemplating the treatment of stock options in an acquisition is whether or not they survive the transaction. The buyer may assume or substitute the target company's options; the options may alternatively be cashed out or cancelled. In some countries, an acquirer is required to make an appropriate offer for convertible securities in acquisitions (under certain circumstances).[95] A discussion of these alternatives is beyond the scope of this book. As a general rule, however, any cost of a target company's outstanding options to the shareholders of the acquiring company should be reflected in the purchase price at fair value. In cases of private M&A acquisitions in which stock options are assumed by the acquirer, a net debt deduction can be appropriate to reflect any cost of dilution to existing shareholders.

[F] Deferred Revenue

[1] Introduction

Deferred revenue is revenue that has not yet been earned although cash has been collected from customers in the form of a prepayment. It is usually (though not necessarily) reported in a company's balance sheet in current liabilities. Deferred revenue is one aspect of revenue recognition that can directly affect net debt (for a discussion of revenue recognition, *see* Chapter 9).

[2] Treatment in Transactions

Whether deferred revenue should be treated as debt or as working capital in a transaction is a frequent source of debate and negotiation.

The case for treating deferred revenue as debt (usually advanced by the buyer) is as follows: the target company has received cash from customers that is recorded in the balance sheet at closing. If there is no deduction in this respect, the buyer pays for the cash by way of a dollar-for-dollar increase in the purchase price. However, it is the buyer who will incur the cost associated with earning the deferred revenue after

92. Applying IFRS, Accounting for share-based payments under IFRS 2 – the essential guide, EY, April 2015, p. 2.
93. Expensing stock options was part of the reforms after the dot-com bubble of the late 1990s.
94. *See* §4.02.
95. For example, The UK Takeover Code, section D, Rule 15.

closing. The receipt of cash (in the form of prepayments received from customers) and the disbursement of cash (to suppliers or employees to fulfil the contract) do not match. A net debt deduction moves the economic burden of servicing the contract to the seller.

The counterargument for treating deferred revenue as working capital (usually advanced by the seller) is this: receiving prepayments from customers is a recurring part of the operations, and a constantly revolving level of prepayments exists at any given time. The target company will be able to fund the cash outflows to fulfil the contract out of future prepayments that will have been received by the time the costs become cash relevant.

As can be seen, the treatment of deferred revenue is by no means clear-cut and depends to a large extent on the nature of the target company's business and/or the prepayment. To illustrate, consider the following two extremes.

Example 1: Businesses Engaged in Large-Scale Construction

Two (almost) identical target companies are engaged in the construction of large power plants. They are about to commence the construction of one such plant. On the day before closing, Company A receives a prepayment from a customer of 30% of the contract value. It defers revenue. Company B receives a similar payment, but a day after closing.

At closing, should a buyer pay the same amount to acquire the shares of the two companies?

It seems clear that the amount of deferred revenue at closing (assuming no construction work takes place on the two dates in question) should be the difference in price. This suggests a net debt deduction is appropriate. If the seller insisted on customer prepayments falling into the definition of working capital, it would be reasonable for the buyer to argue that reference working capital should not include any such prepayments, so that, on closing, any prepayments over and above reference working capital are effectively treated as reductions to working capital and, hence, to the purchase price. This would achieve the same economic result as a net debt deduction. Nevertheless, as discussed above (*see* §4.03), a buyer may still prefer a net debt deduction.

Example 2: Business Engaged in High-Volume, Individually Low-Value Transactions

A newspaper publisher routinely receives payments on (prepaid) subscriptions from a large number of subscribers. The aggregate prepayments vary from day to day and may spike during the holiday season, but individual amounts are small, and it makes little if any difference when they are received. Whether any particular prepayment is received the day before or after closing is not material; there is always a level of prepayments in deferred revenue on any day of a month.

In this case, the prepayments meet the criteria of working capital: operating nature, short-term conversion into cash, and constantly revolving (*see* §5.03). The deferred item is more likely working capital.

The criteria that are discussed in Chapters 2 and 5 when considering the treatment as debt or alternatively working capital apply. When considering the treatment of deferred revenue, a question to ask is whether either the buyer or seller should be concerned about the exact closing (or locked box) date. If a party has reason to be concerned about the timing of a particular prepayment (as in example 1 above), then there is a case for a net debt adjustment. The more important the timing of payments to the final purchase price, the stronger the case to treat the item as debt. If, on the other hand, the timing is not important (as in example 2), then deferred revenue (if recurring) is more likely working capital. It is the cases in-between these two extremes that are often difficult to agree in negotiations.

An approach that is occasionally advocated is a net debt adjustment only for the future cost of fulfilling the contract to which the prepayment relates, not the entire prepayment received. The result is that, economically, the seller retains the profit margin on the contract while the buyer recovers the future cost of fulfilling their obligations under the contract, the reasoning being that the seller originated the contract and should therefore obtain the reward. There are two arguments against such an approach. First, it is not clear why the seller should retain the economic rewards relating to a particular contract only because cash has already been collected (as there would be no reallocation of the contract margin if cash had not been received and deferred). Second, agreeing an expected profit margin can be complex: the extent to which a seller should be entitled to retain profits by moving certain costs to the buyer is not at all clear, not even in concept.

[3] Deferred Revenue in Post-M&A Disputes

One reason deferred revenue is less common in disputes than other items is that the amount of cash received and deferred leaves relatively little discretion on the part of preparers of accounts.

Nevertheless, disputes can arise. In one case, the parties had agreed on a net debt deduction for the costs of fulfilling a contract for which the target company had received a prepayment. When the completion accounts were prepared, the parties disagreed on the extent to which overheads could be allocated to the contract. This shows that, if the method of measuring profit is not adequately defined in the SPA, the risk of a dispute is heightened. Even if defined, however, estimating contract costs can be complex. If the parties to a transaction wish to adopt this approach, it can be preferable in some cases to use a fixed percentage margin to avoid problems after closing.

[G] Capital Expenditure Creditors

[1] Introduction

Capital expenditure creditors are usually reported in a company's balance sheet in current liabilities within an aggregate figure for creditors, and not separately disclosed. Hence they tend to be regarded, prima facie, as part of working capital.

A net debt deduction for capital expenditure creditors is different from the capital expenditure purchase price adjustment discussed in §2.02 [D]. The purpose of the latter is to protect a buyer from a seller delaying capital spend in order to maximise the cash position at closing, and it achieves this by measuring actual (cumulative) capital spend against a target level, adjusting for any deficit. Spending that was deferred during the closing period is not necessarily captured by a net debt deduction for capital expenditure creditors at closing.

[2] Treatment in Transactions

The arguments for treating capital expenditure creditors as either working capital or alternatively net debt are similar to those discussed for deferred revenue earlier in this chapter. To the extent that the creditors relate to routine expenditure in the ordinary course of business, they would normally be included in working capital and taken into account in the computation of reference working capital. Exceptions to this would be:

- Where the target business is capital intensive and property, plant and equipment additions involve large sums which make it difficult to calculate accurately a reference working capital position at any given time (including the closing date).
- The target business incurs individual sums of capital expenditure from time to time which could result in actual working capital at closing not bearing comparison with reference working capital.

As mentioned elsewhere in this publication, it is important to ensure that balances are not double counted, for example, capital expenditure creditors are included in working capital and as a net debt adjustment.

[H] Non-controlling Interest (Or Minority Interest)

[1] Introduction

A non-controlling interest (called 'minority interest' before IFRS 3 was introduced; in this publication both terms are used interchangeably) is the interest in a subsidiary company not attributable to the parent that owns a controlling interest. This is depicted in Figure 4.7.

Figure 4.7 Non-controlling Interest in a Group Subsidiary

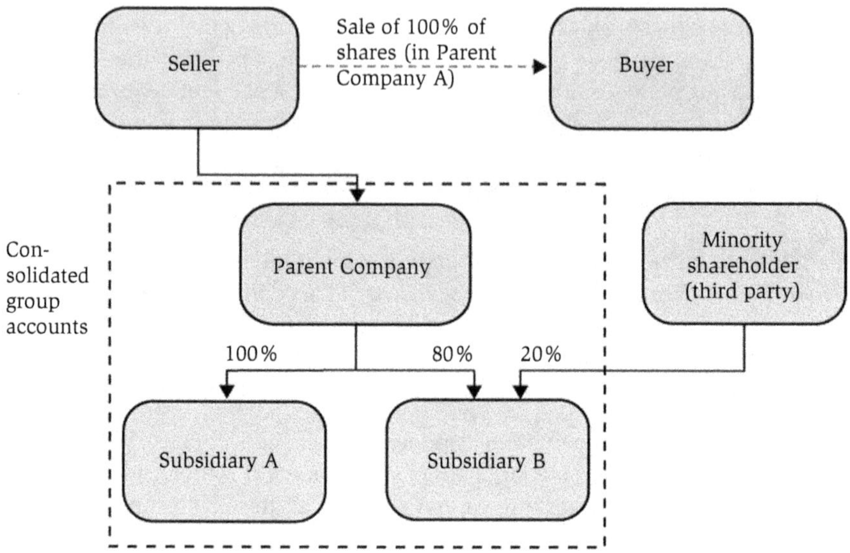

Parent Company holds an 80% interest and an unrelated third party holds a 20% interest in Subsidiary B –the minority interest. The minority interest may have come about for different reasons. For example, it may be held by the founder of a business who later sold their majority stake, or by management as a form of incentive after an acquisition.

In the consolidated financial statements according to IAS, Parent Company presents non-controlling interest within equity, separately from the equity of the owners (IFRS 10.22).

[2] *Treatment in Transactions*

[a] *Overview*

Continuing with the example above, let us assume that Seller intends to dispose of 100% of the share capital in Parent Company. The Buyer values the enterprise using both a DCF (on a free cash flow basis) and a multiple method, in each case based on consolidated financial information (which includes 100% of the results of Subsidiary B).

Subsidiary B's value is then, in a first step, included in full in the enterprise value attributed to the group. The enterprise value for the group as a whole does not reflect the fact that a minority owner is entitled to a share in the surpluses that Subsidiary B will generate in the future. For example, future dividend payments that correspond to the ownership proportions mean that the acquisition of 100% of the shares of Parent Company entitles Buyer to only 80% of Subsidiary B's dividends.

Without adjusting the valuation, the Buyer overpays. The purchase price for the common equity of Parent Company should, therefore, be reduced by the fair value of the minority interest in Subsidiary B. One way to achieve this in a DCF model is to remove from the valuation projected future dividends payable to the minority shareholder. However, it may be impractical to project cash flows for the subsidiary separately, especially for a subsidiary that is of minor importance. The DCF model is often prepared on the basis of consolidated group figures (i.e., 100% of the minority-owned subsidiary figures are entered) and not on the basis of the individual entities' respective projected cash flows. An alternative approach used more frequently is, therefore, to value the minority interest separately and deduct it from enterprise value as a debt-like item.

[b] Valuation Considerations

Valuing a minority interest, often a relatively small amount in the overall context of a transaction, can be unduly time-consuming. Because the fair value of a minority interest often differs from its book value, it is not necessarily appropriate to deduct the book value unless the amounts involved are immaterial.

Buyers also need to consider whether it is appropriate to apply the overall transaction multiple of the target group when valuing the subsidiary, since (among other things) the latter may operate in a different market or in a niche of the target group's market. For example, the subsidiary of a US Group that operates in an emerging market may be more adequately valued using a higher multiple. The reason is similar to that for considering different cost of capital assumptions for targets in different countries.

The fair value of a minority interest is also often different from the pro-rata value of the equity of the subsidiary in question, due to the value of control. Valuation practitioners sometimes associate control with a higher price, known as a 'control premium'. On the other hand, minority owners can have veto or other rights that can increase the value of the non-controlling interest.

Valuing a minority interest can be a time-consuming and complex exercise.[96] In view of the limited significance of the amounts in question, in many instances, a detailed valuation of the non-controlling interest is not merited. Instead, simple approximations can be used and this, in fact, is most frequently done in practice.

[c] Approaches in Practice

Fixed-Price Deduction

A common approach is for a minority to be valued separately from the rest of the target group, with a multiple- or a DCF-based valuation method (or a combination of the two), and a net debt/net working capital deduction based on the subsidiary's balance sheet at

96. Stephen H. Penman, *Financial Statement Analysis and Security Valuation* (4th ed., McGraw-Hill Education 2009), p. 370.

some date before the transaction, around the time of the valuation. The resulting value represents an equity value, which is then specified in the SPA as a (fixed value) net debt deduction. There is no further adjustment for the minority interest after closing.

Purchase price adjustments at group level are usually made on a 100% basis. This means that these adjustments include 100% of the minority-owned subsidiary's net debt and working capital items. As the minority-owned subsidiary's net debt and working capital positions will have changed to closing, whereas the net debt deduction for the subsidiary may be fixed, this could result in a discrepancy at closing. However, this is rarely a concern in practice. Otherwise, the parties can agree a separate net debt adjustment for the minority, or a correction to the overall group net debt adjustment as part of the true-up at closing.

Buyout Value

The minority interest is also sometimes determined as the (hypothetical) cost of buying out the minority owner. This is often a higher amount than a multiple- or DCF-based valuation of the subsidiary would suggest.

Valuation at Closing

Another approach is to specify in the SPA that a valuation using a multiple is to be performed at closing, along with a multiple to be used.[97] However, this can easily lead to disagreement over reported EBITDA of the subsidiary (if an EBITDA multiple is used). Protecting against this risk would require the SPA to identify all those components of EBITDA that should be excluded from the basis to which the multiple is applied, similar in this aspect to protections in earn-outs (*see* §8.03). This is often not a workable approach. As is the case with many other valuation matters in a transaction, the time to fix the amount of a deduction for a minority interest is generally before signing.

Book Value

A common starting point for the valuation of a minority share in transaction is its book value. However, if the minority is material to the overall purchase price, it is important to consider that, just as the book value of the group's consolidated equity is usually not its fair value, and hence not the appropriate basis of the purchase price for the shares (*see* the discussion in §11.01), the book value of the minority interest is usually not the appropriate basis for a net debt deduction either.

However, if the minority interest is not material, or if a book value for the minority is identical to or close to its fair value, then this may be a straightforward alternative. The book value should then be fixed in the SPA at the time of signing, as measuring it at completion would mean unnecessary complexity and expose the parties to unforeseen changes to the book value of equity at closing similar to those discussed above in §2.02 [F].

97. *See* Kiem, *Kaufpreisregelungen beim Unternehmenskauf* (2nd ed., C.H. Beck, 2018), p. 220.

[I] Deferred Taxes

[1] Introduction

Deferred taxes are hardly the first item to come to mind as a net debt deduction in a transaction. Indeed, the treatment as net debt is the exception rather than the rule. However, there is a rationale for deducting deferred tax liabilities, or for adding deferred tax assets in certain circumstances.

Under IFRS, deferred tax liabilities are recorded for income taxes payable in future periods in respect of taxable temporary differences (IAS 12.5). Deferred tax assets relate to income taxes recoverable in future periods in respect of deductible temporary differences but also to the carry forward of unused tax losses and unused tax credits.[98] Temporary differences can give rise to deferred taxes.[99]

Let's turn now to the treatment in transactions. Consider the following example.

Example: Deferred Tax

Two businesses are for sale. They are almost identical, except for the tax treatment of a particular operating asset. Both report the same carrying value for the asset in their financial accounts (both depreciating the asset over the same useful life). Their balance sheets are identical (except for a deferred tax item and equity). Company A, in the financial year prior to being sold, depreciated the asset in full in its tax accounts, reducing its taxable income for that year. Company B, on the other hand, elected to depreciate the asset over five years in its tax accounts, the same period that it applies for financial accounts purposes. It, therefore, reports the asset at the same carrying value in its financial and tax accounts.

Company B will benefit from lower taxes in the future. A reader of the companies' financial accounts alone might think each company has the same 'tax shield' (i.e., the same future depreciation expense). But a tax shield actually only exists for Company B. Do the two companies have the same value?

Clearly, the difference in value is the present value of the difference in future taxes that the two companies will pay (all else being equal). Undiscounted, this difference is the deferred tax liability in respect of the asset recorded in Company A's balance sheet (provided the deferred tax liability is valued correctly). As such, this should result in a difference in value.

If the difference in future tax payments of the two companies is built into the valuation model, no deduction for net debt is required. In practice, however, this is not always the case (*see* below §4.04 [I] [2] [a]). In Company A's valuation, therefore, there is a case for a net debt deduction; the buyer of Company A would otherwise overpay.

98. 'Taxable' and 'deductible' temporary differences are differences that, respectively, result in taxable amounts, or are deductible, in determining taxable profits of future periods when the carrying amount of an asset or liability is recovered or settled (IAS 12.5).
99. However, not all temporary differences result in deferred taxes. An exception is the initial recognition of goodwill – *see* IAS 12.15(a).

A possible objection to a net debt deduction might be where the temporary differences relate to short-lived balance sheet items that are constantly renewed so that they can be considered recurring. An example might be development expenditure – capitalised and amortised over a short period in the financial accounts but expensed immediately in the tax accounts. The deferred tax liabilities may meet the criteria for working capital.

[2] Interaction with the Valuation of the Target

[a] Income Approach

The income approach is discussed below usually in §11.04 [B]. The DCF method is the most commonly used form. A DCF model usually includes projections of future income tax payments. Many investors will model future income taxes of the target business separately. However, some use models that project income taxes on the basis of projected net financial (instead of taxable) income, thereby, in a first step at least, ignoring differences between the financial and tax accounts. If these differences are temporary and are not captured in the tax calculation in the DCF model, then they are effectively omitted from the model.[100] Since taxes on operating income are operating cash outflows (and therefore part of free cash flow), this, in turn, will result in an incorrect enterprise value. Setting aside discounting, the valuation error is the same amount as the deferred tax asset or liability.[101] So an adjustment for the deferred tax asset or liability effectively corrects for using the financial income as the basis of calculating taxes instead of taxable income.

[b] Market Approach

This approach is discussed below in §11.04 [C]. It includes multiple-based valuations that often relate price to pre-tax earnings (e.g., EBIT or EBITDA). Such an approach effectively ignores income taxes in the earnings measure. Tax effects are instead incorporated in the valuation multiple (at least in concept). What does this mean for deferred taxes in transactions? It might be assumed that a normal level of deferred taxes is implicit in the multiple, and further that the target company's future tax burden will ultimately revert to the mean of the peer group of comparator companies. However, this assumption is not necessarily correct. Taxes can be managed (similar to other operating expenses that are also not generally expected in valuations to revert to the mean).

100. The same applies if these differences relate to tax-loss carry forwards available to be set against future taxable profits subject to meeting the criteria of IAS 12.
101. International Accounting Standards do not permit the discounting of deferred tax assets or liabilities (IAS 12.53).

[c] Deferred Tax Assets

Treating a deferred tax asset as net debt means adding the carrying value to the purchase price, similar to a cash equivalent. One case where this is common relates to pension deficits where the tax base can be substantially lower than the carrying value in the financial accounts. As for deferred tax assets related to tax loss carryforwards, the question is usually whether the carry forward will be available to a buyer after a transaction to offset future profits; as such they are often considered and priced separately, in which case the value of the deferred tax asset is not added to the purchase price as a cash-like item.

[3] Deferred Taxes in Post-M&A Disputes

Most disputes that relate to deferred taxes are not over the deferred tax asset or liability in the first place, but the underlying asset or liability that has given rise to deferred tax. A change in that underlying asset or liability impacts the deferred tax. This is often relevant in accounting warranty breaches, where corrections of deferred taxes are secondary effects of other breaches. Another area of dispute can be over the valuation allowance against (gross) deferred tax assets, or if there is uncertainty over future taxable income.

[J] Overdue Trade Payables

A business may be unable or unwilling to pay its trade debts when due. For example, a distressed business may have an explicit or tacit understanding with a large supplier that allows it to extend payment terms. The extension of terms in such a case is a mutual financing decision. Another example is when related parties settle intercompany payables only periodically, for example at the end of a reporting period. From a group perspective, stretched and technically overdue creditors may not matter. However, if the acquisition target is a group entity, its working capital may be materially distorted.

These examples illustrate that stretched or overdue trade payables can, to some extent, lose their normal, short-term, constantly revolving operating characteristics which usually make them part of working capital. Instead, 'stretched' payables have a financing element that, if material, should be considered in net debt.

[K] Cash and Cash Equivalents

As indicated in the equity bridge in §2.01, cash and cash equivalents increase the equity value. The principal idea is that the buyer can extract the cash after closing and should, therefore, pay for it dollar-for-dollar. This assumes of course that the buyer can extract such cash, that is, the cash is unrestricted or 'free'.

'Free' cash is cash that is not needed to operate the business and for which there are no legal, regulatory, or other restrictions preventing it from being extracted from the business in full. Cash and cash equivalents that are not 'free' in this sense should not form part of cash for purposes of the net debt definition. On close examination, most (though by no means all) businesses require a certain minimum level of cash for day-to-day operations; this cash is, effectively, working capital. It is sometimes referred to as 'working cash'.[102] Examples are cash floats in tills at retailers or intra-month cash needs (to the extent they are not already reflected in the working capital reference value).

Other than cash needed for the day-to-day operations, some markets have exchange controls or minimum capitalisation requirements (for financial institutions) that can also tie up cash. There can also be cases where cash is held in entities with negative net assets for which extracting cash in the form of dividends or other payouts to shareholders or related parties may be restricted. (It is important when reviewing these cases to consider net assets under a local legal framework and local GAAP and as it is those that may restrict dividend payouts).

There are numerous reasons why firms hold more cash and cash equivalents than they need in their operations: the cash may be intended for payout as a dividend, or for future investments, or it may be held simply as a precaution. Further, the repatriation of earnings of foreign corporate subsidiaries may trigger taxes that could have been deferred, leading to large amounts of untaxed offshore earnings (not all of which are however cash).[103] In many transactions, the question of precisely which component of cash is not restricted can be difficult to analyse.

One approach some buyers take is to propose that the seller take all cash out of the target business before closing, so that the business is transferred, ostensibly, cash-free. This is the safest way for the buyer to obtain certainty that he or she is not paying for trapped cash, and the best test of whether it is, in fact, cash that can be taken out of the business at will because it is not needed for operating the business. However, in complex transactions with multiple subsidiaries, each with its own cash position, it is cumbersome to extract all cash, and rarely if ever done.

Another aspect to consider is the definition of cash and cash equivalents. The term 'cash at bank' may not be sufficiently precise, as it may not encompass items within the bank reconciliation which may reduce cash, such as deposits in transit or outstanding (or bounced) checks. Cash and equivalents may also include items that are really receivables (such as credit card receivables) and which the external auditors may have considered to be immaterial.

Which part of the cash balance is considered to be 'free' and which is subject to restrictions or required in the operations of the business should be defined in the SPA, either as a fixed amount or by specifying a measurement method (such as a percentage of total cash or a percentage of sales).

---

102. For example, Stephen H. Penman, *Financial Statement Analysis and Security Valuation* (4th ed., McGraw-Hill Education 2009), p. 292.
103. According to an estimate by the US Congress Joint Committee on Taxation, in September 2016, US companies had USD 2.6 trillion in untaxed offshore earnings. *See* Untaxed offshore earnings of US companies rises to USD 2.6 trillion, The Washington Examiner, 29 September 2016.

CHAPTER 5

Working Capital

§5.01 INTRODUCTION

Working capital is the part of the balance sheet where many types of volatile 'real world' events often most prominently find their way into transactions. It was within working capital that the financial crisis of 2007 to 2009 and the covid pandemic left some of their most visible traces in balance sheets - impaired trade receivables, unsellable inventories (or no inventories), stretched payables. Given the areas of subjectivity in accounting for working capital and the many estimates it requires, it is perhaps no surprise that this is the balance sheet category where the largest number of disputes originate.

As discussed in Chapter 2, indicative offers at the early stages of a transaction often refer to a 'headline' or 'cash- and debt-free' price. This refers to enterprise value, the present value of the target's operating activities. Enterprise value is determined on the basis that all the assets and liabilities needed by the target business in order to operate are transferred to the buyer as part of the transaction, including an appropriate level of working capital. A shortfall in working capital at closing means that the target business is not transferred with all assets and liabilities that are normally needed to operate the business and that are intrinsic to the determination of the headline price. The seller transfers a deficit in value to the buyer. Conversely, a surplus of working capital means that the seller transfers more value than is assumed in the valuation.

Most businesses require a certain positive level of working capital as part of their normal operations. Much like a car requires at least some petrol in its tank, and that petrol ties up cash that the owner could use for other purposes, working capital (if positive) ties up cash that would otherwise be available for alternative uses. Why do businesses require working capital? Sales do not convert into cash immediately, resulting in trade receivables; many companies need inventories of raw materials and finished goods, an investment in current assets. Both are examples of positive working capital. Other components of working capital are negative: suppliers are not usually paid immediately upon delivery of goods or services, hence companies record trade payables.

For some businesses, overall net working capital is negative. Rather than tying up liquidity, negative working capital generates it (from operating activities). This is the case when a company takes credit from suppliers, turns inventory quickly and is paid by its customers in cash. For example, Amazon reports negative working capital.[104]

It is very common for non-binding offer letters to specify that the headline price presupposes that the target business will be transferred with an 'appropriate', 'normal', or 'adequate' level of working capital without quantifying at this stage what the appropriate level is. The buyer expects the seller to run the business properly and, in particular, that there will be no deficiency of working capital as a result of the seller being overzealous in his or her desire to reduce net debt (by maximising the cash position). Such wording paves the way for a working capital adjustment in transactions involving completion accounts as well as locked boxes. In the latter case, it is (or should be) understood that the same rationale entails a normal level of working capital at the date of economic transfer, and any deficit or surplus is reflected in the fixed purchase price.

A normal level of working capital – 'the reference value' – is specified in the SPA as part of the working capital price adjustment mechanism, along with the basis of measurement. The actual level of working capital is subsequently measured at closing. If closing working capital exceeds the reference value, this means an upward (usually dollar-for-dollar) adjustment to the purchase price. Conversely, a deficit results in a reduction in the purchase price.

The rationale is that, if at closing the business has more working capital than it needs to operate, then the buyer pays for the excess dollar-for-dollar as the buyer could extract the surplus working capital from the business. If, however, there is a working capital deficit, then the purchase price is correspondingly reduced because the buyer will have to bring working capital back up to a 'normal' level, requiring additional funding (which is deducted from the purchase price).

§5.02 INTERACTION WITH NET DEBT

For the working capital adjustment to work properly, a 'clean interaction with the definition of net debt is essential. This means that no item should be captured by both definitions (working capital and net debt), and no relevant item omitted. If the ultimate purchase price does not properly reflect the actual value of the net assets that are

104. In the year ended 31 December 2017, Amazon reported average Days Sales Outstanding (DSO) of 22.1, average Days Inventory Outstanding (DIO) of 44.8, average Days Payable Outstanding (DPO) of 93.9, and an average cash conversion cycle of minus 26.9 days. Trade working capital continued to be negative in 2022. (*Source*: CapitalIQ, differences due to rounding).

transferred, this can be a cause of discontent for whichever side overpaid and can lead to disputes.

To understand this interaction, consider the way in which the cash (and cash equivalents) position interacts with individual components of working capital as demonstrated by simple day-to-day transactions: the receipt of funds from customers means that the cash position increases and trade receivables decrease. The effects offset each other: net debt decreases (as cash increases), and working capital decreases (as receivables decrease). Conversely, when a company pays a supplier, net debt increases (as cash decreases) and net working capital increases (trade payables decrease).

Every increase in net debt leads to a dollar-for-dollar reduction in the net purchase price. Every increase in working capital results in a dollar-for-dollar increase in the net purchase price (as long as the working capital adjustment is measured against the reference value). If the net debt and the working capital mechanisms interact as they should, then there is an exact offsetting effect. It does not matter if a particular receivable has been turned into cash or a creditor has been paid on a particular date, because the effects on the purchase price of the changes in net debt and working capital offset each other. Accelerating collections from customers, deferring payment to creditors, liquidating inventories prematurely: none of these will have an impact on the net purchase price if the working capital and net debt adjustments interact correctly.

If the interaction functions properly, and an appropriate working capital reference value is agreed, the parties should, in terms of the purchase price alone, be indifferent to the precise level of working capital and cash (or debt) at closing. In this regard, working capital in excess of the reference value counts just like cash in the determination of the final purchase price, which makes sense as long as all of its components are genuinely as good as cash. This is a matter of clarity as to what working capital encompasses and the approach to its measurement. Both should be specified in the SPA. They are discussed in the following sections.

§5.03 DEFINING WORKING CAPITAL

There is no standard definition of working capital in the transaction context. What is treated as working capital and how it is measured (i.e., the precise basis of accounting) needs to be agreed between the parties and set out clearly in the SPA.

A convention is that, at a minimum, working capital includes trade receivables, trade payables, and inventory. This is often called 'core' or 'trade' working capital. However, these three components usually do not capture all items that are working capital in nature, and the definition of core working capital in SPAs therefore almost always needs to encompass other items in order to ensure a 'clean' interaction with net debt.

As to which other items to include, there are no hard-and-fast rules. However, when considering whether a balance sheet item should be part of working capital, it is appropriate to consider the nature of operating items and contrast them to financing items (*see* above §2.01 [B]): a normal level of working capital is part of enterprise value, the value of the operations. Against this background, the following criteria can therefore be useful in determining whether and to what extent individual assets or liabilities are working capital:

- working capital consists of operating assets or liabilities;
- these assets or liabilities convert into cash in a short period of time; and
- they are constantly revolving.

These criteria are discussed below. If all three are met, then there is usually a good argument to consider the item to be part of working capital

[A] Operating Nature

As discussed in Chapter 2, enterprise value is the present value of future returns of the operations. It includes only operating assets and liabilities (as opposed to financing assets and liabilities).

The distinction between operating and financing activities has been established in the literature since Modigliani-Miller.[105] Operating assets and liabilities arise from operating activities, i.e., activities associated with the production of goods or services: making sales to customers who do not pay immediately, procurement of goods or services needed for production, or managing stocks to be able to react to customer orders are all operating activities usually directly associated with the core purpose of the enterprise. They give rise to trade receivables, trade payables and inventory, respectively, each operating assets or liabilities, and core components of working capital.

Financing activities, on the other hand, have to do with the distribution of surpluses generated by the operations (e.g., paying dividends or servicing debt) or perhaps, funding operating cash shortfalls (e.g., raising liquidity in the capital markets). When considering whether a balance sheet item should be treated as working capital, the first question is therefore whether the item relates to an operating activity or alternatively serves to finance the operations.

[B] Conversion to Cash in the Short Term

Being part of the operating activities is a necessary condition for an item to be categorised as working capital, but not a sufficient condition. That is, not all operating items are working capital. Working capital also converts into cash in the

105. *See* above §2.01.

short term: trade receivables are settled by customers, suppliers are paid, and inventory is sold, normally within a few days, weeks, or months. This timing aspect brings working capital close to cash.[106]

According to accounting convention, balance sheet items are classified as 'current' if they convert to cash in no more than one year.[107] The treatment in transactions usually follows this convention since financial accounts readily provide the requisite information. However, in some cases, buyers may consider a year to be comparatively long for current assets to convert into cash in the context of the analysis of working capital (which they pay for dollar-for-dollar): a trade receivable that is almost a year old, or slow-moving inventory, may give rise to concerns over recoverability. Allowances and write-downs that reflect such concerns require judgment on the part of the preparer of financial information. However, the issue with current assets is more often their net carrying value rather than the classification as working capital or something else. For creditors, questions over the classification as working capital are not uncommon, for example, when stretched trade payables turn into financing items (*see* §4.04 [J]).

[C] Constantly Revolving/Recurring Nature

A further criterion is that working capital items are constantly revolving. As these items convert into cash, they are replaced by new short-term assets and liabilities (though not necessarily at the same time and of the same amount). At any given point in time, a business has a certain level of short-term operating assets and liabilities. The net position changes constantly and may follow cycles, seasons, or long-term trends (such as growth or inflation).

If working capital never changed, it would be straightforward to set a reference value against which closing working capital is to be measured. Indeed, if the level never changed, no working capital adjustment would be necessary. In reality, working capital changes constantly, and this is what presents the challenge – especially when significant swings are involved – when setting a reference value against which closing working capital is to be measured.

[D] 'Core' and 'Wider' Working Capital

There are many potential balance sheet items that meet these criteria beyond the three included in the definition of 'core' or 'trade' working capital. In order to help the reader with the problem of how to deal with specific working capital items, below is a list of balance sheet items and an explanation of how they may be handled (Figure 5.1).

106. Fixed assets or pension liabilities, for example, usually do not convert into cash in the short term, and these items are therefore usually not considered to be working capital.

107. Strictly speaking IAS 1.66 sets out criteria that do not necessarily require cash conversion within one year.

Figure 5.1 Components of Working Capital

- Trade receivables
- Inventory
- Trade Payables

Core/trade working capital

- Prepaid expenses
- Goods received not invoiced
- Short-term personnel-related accruals
- Employee withholding taxes
- Value added or sales taxes
- Other short-term tax assets or liabilities

Other items often treated as working capital

- Prepayments received/deferred revenue
- Provisions (different types) (see above §4.[D])
- Deferred tax (see above in §4.[I])
- Rent deposits
- Insurance claim receivable (typically not part or ordinary activities)

Items that may be classified as working capital or net debt

The last category in the list in Figure 5.1, in particular, includes items which can be either working capital or net debt. For further discussion, please refer to Chapter 4.

It is important to review each element of the target business's balance sheet during the financial due diligence and to consider whether it should be treated as working capital or net debt. A technique that is frequently used is to allocate each item of the balance sheet into one of four categories: working capital, net debt, infrastructure (that may indicate the need for a capital expenditure adjustment) and 'other' (for which no adjustment may be required). Such an analysis is sometimes called the preparation of a 'functional balance sheet', or the 'bucket approach'. Its purpose is to ensure that no balance sheet item is omitted from SPA definitions unless it has been considered and found not to require an adjustment. To be useful, the balance sheet analysis must be sufficiently granular to identify subcategories of line items that differ from the allocation to working capital or net debt of the broader category they are included in.

An example of a potential omission in the definition of working capital is the line item 'goods received not invoiced'. Unless it is included in the definition of working capital, the seller could theoretically increase working capital at closing by requesting a key supplier to withhold invoices just before closing.

An example of a functional balance sheet analysis is in Table 5.1 (note that the allocation into 'buckets' may differ depending on the circumstances).

Table 5.1 Example of a Balance Sheet as of 31 May 2018

	Working Capital	*Net Debt*	*Infrastructure*	*Other*	*Total*
USD thousand					
ASSETS					
Cash And Equivalents (gross)		3,091			3,091
Restricted Cash		–210			–210
Short Term Investments		2,111			2,111
Total Cash & ST Investments	**0**	**4,992**	**0**	**0**	**4,992**
Accounts Receivable	2,397				2,397
Accounts Receivable – related parties	14				14
Other Receivables – taxes	79				79
Other Receivables – VAT	83				83
Other Receivables – Insurance claim				42	42
Other receivables – employees		7			7
Total Receivables	**2,573**	7	**0**	**42**	**2,622**
Inventory	4,981				4,981
Restricted Cash	210				210

	Working Capital	*Net Debt*	*Infrastructure*	*Other*	*Total*
Other Current Assets – Deferred tax					–
Other Current Assets – Deposits	17				17
Other	9				9
Total Other Current Assets	**5,217**	**0**	**0**	**0**	**5,217**
Gross Property, Plant & Equipment			1,720		1,720
Accumulated Depreciation			–761		–761
Net Property, Plant & Equipment	**0**	**0**	**959**	**0**	**959**
Long-term Investments – fair value of warrants		36			36
Goodwill				2,121	2,121
Other Intangibles				237	237
Other Long-Term Assets				339	339
Total Other Non-Current Assets	**0**	**36**	**0**	**2,697**	**2,733**
Total Assets	**7,790**	**5,035**	**959**	**2,739**	**16,523**

	Working Capital	*Net Debt*	*Infrastructure*	*Other*	*Total*
LIABILITIES					
Accounts Payable	2,532				2,532
Accrued Exp.	465				465
Curr. Port. of LT Debt		12			12
Curr. Port. of Cap. Leases		87			87
Unearned Revenue, Current	355				355
Other Current Liabilities – Deferred Tax (Current)				8	8
Other Current Liabilities – VAT	21				21
Other Current Liabilities – Tax Audit		12			12
Other Current Liabilities	82				82
Total Current Liabilities		111	0	8	3,574
Long-Term Debt – Unsecured Senior Notes		717			717
Capital Leases		831			831
Unearned Revenue, Non-Current		445			445

	Working Capital	*Net Debt*	*Infrastructure*	*Other*	*Total*
Def. Tax Liability, Non-Current				190	190
Construction liabilities				451	451
Pensions		1,229			1,229
Employee Loans		503			503
Other Non-Current Liabilities				856	856
Total Non-Current Liabilities	0	3,725	0	1,497	5,222
Total Liabilities	3,455	3,836	0	1,505	**8,796**
Common Stock				5	5
Additional Paid In Capital				292	292
Retained Earnings				7,553	7,553
Treasury Stock				–97	–97
Accumulated Currency Loss				–19	–19
Other Comprehensive Income		–7			–7
Total Common Equity	**0**	–7	**0**	**7,734**	**7,727**
Total Liabilities and Equity	**3,455**	**3,829**	**0**	**9,239**	**16,523**
Net Working Capital	**4,335**				

	Working Capital	*Net Debt*	*Infrastructure*	*Other*	*Total*
Net Debt		**1,206**			
Net Infrastructure Assets			**959**		
Other				**–6,500**	

§5.04 THE REFERENCE VALUE

[A] Introduction

As working capital constantly changes, often significantly, determining an appropriate reference value is usually not straightforward. M&A practitioners typically develop an average value by examining month-by-month figures for the target business for twelve, twenty-four or (less often) thirty-six months. (The average should cover at least one full seasonal cycle to be representative of the normal working capital needs of the business.) According to a recent survey, the most commonly used reference is the average reported working capital of the last twelve months.[108]

Determining the reference value using historical averages is the most common approach. An alternative is to use the working capital ratios (such as DSO, DIO, and DPO) of a peer group, and to apply these ratios to revenues and cost of sales, respectively, of the target business, in order to determine a normal working capital level. This approach can be relevant when the working capital development of the target has been significantly affected by non-recurring events (such as events during the covid pandemic) that mean that the average is not representative of the target business's 'true' working capital needs going forward. However, these cases are less common.

All else equal, a buyer inevitably seeks a high reference value against which actual working capital is measured: the higher the reference value, the greater any deficit (or lower any surplus) when actual working capital at closing is measured against it. A seller, on the other hand, will argue for a low reference value. It is a zero-sum game, the outcome of which will typically depend significantly on the relative strengths of the parties' negotiating positions.

A similar dynamic applies in locked box transactions, the difference being that working capital is measured at the locked box date rather than at closing. The difference between actual working capital and the reference value at the locked box date is then included in the fixed purchase (or at least it should be). The conflicting

108. Grant Thornton, *A Smarter Way to Get Deals Done, International Survey: Identifying International Market Practice for Equity Value Adjustments and Sale and Purchase Agreements*, November 2017, p. 10. According to this survey, 63 % of respondents reported that the 'Last 12 Months' (LTM) period before the completion date was the typical reference period for assessing the working capital target.

incentives for buyer and seller are the same as in a purchase price adjustment. Actual working capital at closing is, of course, irrelevant in a locked box transaction, at least in this context.

Some factors which commonly influence the determination of an appropriate reference value are discussed below.

[B] Seasonality

[1] Non-seasonal Businesses

Developing a reference working capital figure for a business not affected by seasonality is relatively straightforward. Figure 5.2 shows the monthly working capital profile of such a business over twelve months.

Figure 5.2 Working Capital Profile: Non-seasonal Business

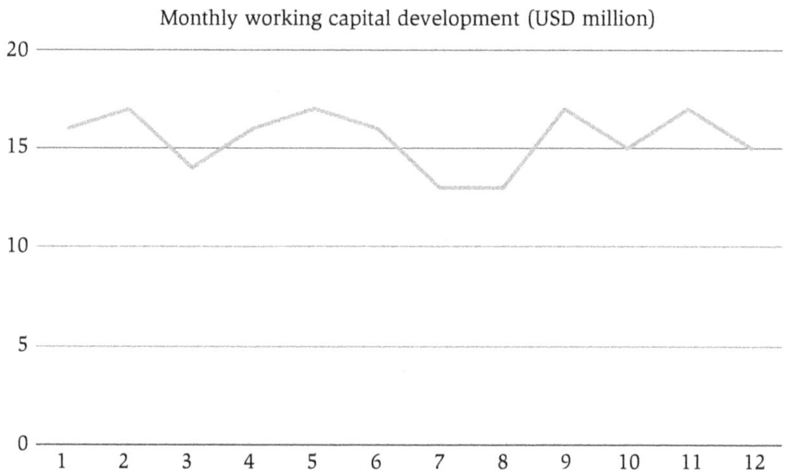

Assuming these twelve months are representative of the business at closing and of its overall working capital needs, including intra-month levels, then simply averaging the twelve months would form a reasonable basis for a reference value.

[2] Seasonal Businesses and the Notion of Different Reference Dates Depending on the Closing Date

In Figure 5.3, working capital fluctuates significantly: it is over three times higher during the summer months than in the seasonally lowest months. Prima facie, no single level of working capital could be considered to be representative of the overall working capital needs of the business.

Figure 5.3 Working Capital Profile: Seasonal Business

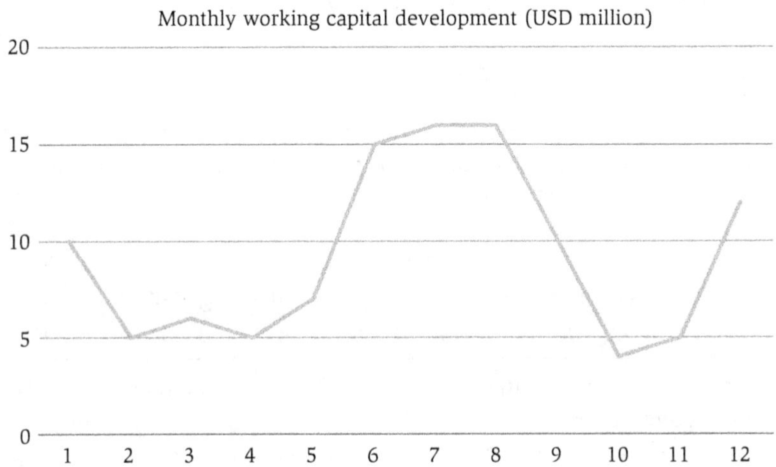

For seasonal businesses, some argue that a simple average over twelve months (or a longer period) is not appropriate and that the working capital reference value should depend on whether working capital is at a seasonal high or low: in this example, if closing is expected during one of the summer months, or at the end of the year, the argument goes, the reference value should be based not on an average of the twelve months but on an average across the seasonally strongest months only. Equally, for a closing in a period of less activity a correspondingly lower value would come into play. Does this make sense?

It should be pointed out here that, because of its interaction with the cash position, working capital should not be viewed in isolation: a peak in working capital typically mirrors a trough in the cash position. A peak in working capital may be explained, for example, by high sales and, hence, receivables (before sales turn into cash), or an inventory build-up. Conversely, a low level of working capital typically signifies a higher cash balance.

The example below sets out the two alternative approaches. Closing is on either 30 April or 31 August of the year. The business is subject to significant seasonality, with net working capital in August over three times the level in April. Table 5.2 shows the net working capital position at month-ends and net debt (reflecting the change in the cash position due to the working capital change). The average net working capital over the twelve-month period is 9. Net working capital on 30 April is 5 and on 31 August it is 16.

Table 5.2 Monthly Working Capital

	Jan	*Feb*	*Mar*	*Apr*	*May*	*Jun*	*Jul*	*Aug*	*Sep*	*Oct*	*Nov*	*Dec*	*Avg. (Twelve Months)*
Working capital	8	5	6	5	7	15	16	16	10	4	5	11	9.00
Net debt	500	500	497	498	497	499	507	508	508	502	496	497	
Cash change from WC	n/a	–3	1	–1	2	8	1	0	–6	–6	1	6	
Net debt	500	497	498	497	499	507	508	508	502	496	497	503	

Scenarios A and B show two alternative approaches to the reference value: in scenario A, the parties have agreed a reference value, 9, against which actual working capital is measured at any closing date in the year. In scenario B, there are two different reference values, depending on the closing date. Arguments in scenario B are set out below, provided by seller and buyer, respectively, for an adjusted reference value:

For closing on 30 April: Reference value of 5 (the level of working capital in April)	Seller argues that working capital reflects seasonality and buyer is assuming less debt, hence equity price is higher.
For closing on 31 August: Reference value of 16 (the level of working capital in August)	Buyer argues that working capital reflects seasonality (i.e., if seller does not provide that level working capital buyer is being shortchanged), hence buyer pays a lower equity price.

It is assumed in this example that actual working capital (at closing) is the same as in the period over which the reference value was computed. This is a simplifying assumption. Tables 5.3 and 5.4 set out the calculation of the purchase price adjustments and equity value in each of the two scenarios.

Table 5.3 Scenario A: Constant Reference Value

Closing Date	*30 April*	*31 August*
Reference value	9	9
EV	1,000	1,000
Less net debt	–497	–508
Actual WC less Reference WC	–4	7
Equity value	499	499

Table 5.4 Scenario B: Reference Value Adjusted to Reflect Seasonality

Closing Date	*30 April*	*31 August*
Reference value	5	16
EV	1,000	1,000
Less net debt	–497	–508
Actual WC less Reference WC (5 (low) and 16 (high))	–	–
Equity value	503	492

A constant reference value (scenario A) results in the same equity value, independent of the closing date. Different reference values (scenario B) result in different equity values, depending on the closing date, whereas, under the assumptions given above, the value transferred from seller to buyer is unchanged.

In the example discussed above, with seasonality (Table 5.2), liquidity was simply moved between net debt and working capital and never left the two categories. The system was 'closed'. In reality, the cash or net debt position does not always move in step with changes in working capital. A perfect link between working capital and cash usually applies in real life only for very short periods during which it is true that day-to-day working capital movements can be linked directly to cash (every dollar collected from a customer leads to a dollar increase in cash). Another way to look at this is to plot the cash position against the working capital line in Figure 5.3. While cash and working capital are directly linked at the moment when working capital converts into cash, this relationship would not necessarily be visible in an imaginary cash line. The reason is that once received, cash can be spent on things that are accounted for outside the definitions of working capital or net debt. When a company acquires fixed assets, for example, cash disappears from the categories of working capital and net debt. However, spending cash does not usually mean that value disappears – it is merely put to other uses or converted into other assets or reduces other liabilities. These assets and liabilities may be outside the definition of working capital or net debt. It does not matter where precisely the cash goes, it is not replaced with nothing.[109]

109. Unless it was wasted.

The fair approach (which results in a constant equity value) is to agree on a single reference value regardless of the closing date, provided the business is not growing (or shrinking) significantly. After all, all other things being equal, the underlying value of the business has not changed.

[C] High-Growth Businesses

High-growth businesses present a different challenge. Figure 5.4 depicts the working capital profile of a rapidly expanding company that requires an increasing level of working capital to support its growth. What should the reference value be in this case?

Figure 5.4 Working Capital Profile: High-Growth Business

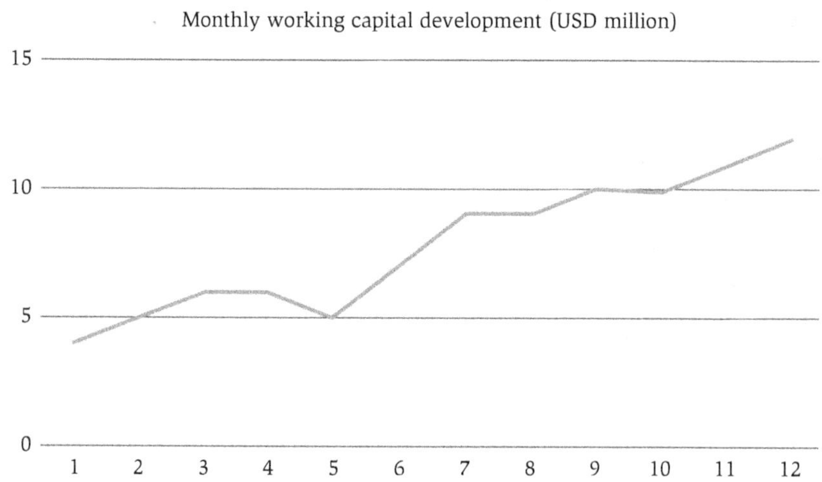

As indicated earlier, the reference value should represent a normal working capital level *at closing*. An average across historical working capital figures before closing would understate the working capital the business requires at closing when it will have outgrown its past average levels.

One issue when determining a normal working capital value for a high-growth business is that the exact closing date is usually not known ahead of time. If the uncertainty covers a significant time period, it will require critical estimates in respect of when the closing date is due to fall. And, if closing were delayed for some reason, it might be necessary to revisit the reference value that had been originally agreed for an earlier closing date.

One approach, usually favoured by the buyer, is to use projected working capital, or a combination of historical and projected figures, to determine the working capital reference value. According to a recent survey, 24% of respondents used some combination of historical and forecast results or an entirely forecast period.[110]

For a growth company, the working capital level after closing will be higher than in the pre-closing period. A reference value that is solely based on a post-closing projection of working capital would therefore usually overstate the working capital needs of the business at closing. In effect, such a reference value would mean that the seller is being asked - by way of the working capital adjustment - to fund working capital growth after closing. This approach is not consistent with the notion that the buyer, not the seller, should fund the growth of the business it has acquired.

[D] High Growth and Seasonality

Figure 5.5 depicts the working capital development of a business that is not only rapidly expanding but also subject to seasonal influences.

Figure 5.5 Working Capital Profile: High-Growth Seasonal Business

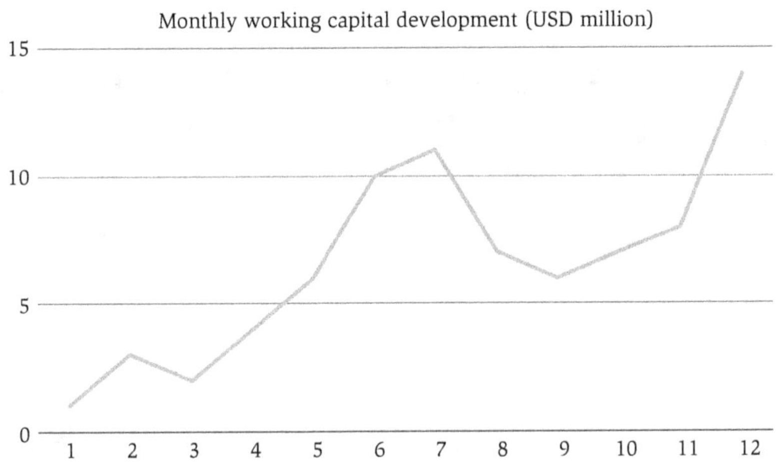

In this situation, it is necessary to separate the growth aspects from the seasonality. One approach is to: (a) project working capital at the planned closing date using the business plan on which the valuation is based; and (b) analyse historical seasonality and, by overlaying those data, adjust the projected working capital for any seasonal influence. In these circumstances, the suggested approach is to project an agreed reference working capital for a series of possible closing dates.

110. Grant Thornton, *A Smarter Way to Get Deals Done, International Survey: Identifying International Market Practice for Equity Value Adjustments and Sale and Purchase Agreements*, November 2017, p. 10.

[E] Intra-Monthly Movements

The discussion of monthly working capital figures above concerned end-of-month balances. However, working capital may be subject to significant swings during the month, and a discussion of working capital would be incomplete without considering these intra-monthly movements. For example, a company may pay a major supplier on the second day of each month, which means that at month-ends, trade payables are close to their peak and, as a result, net working capital near its lowest point. Intra-monthly working capital levels are much higher in this example than an analysis limited to month-end data would suggest.

Alternatively, a company may have significant creditor payment runs on the last days of each month, so that net working capital is at its peak at month-ends. This is depicted below in Figure 5.6.

Figure 5.6 Intra-Month Working Capital Profile

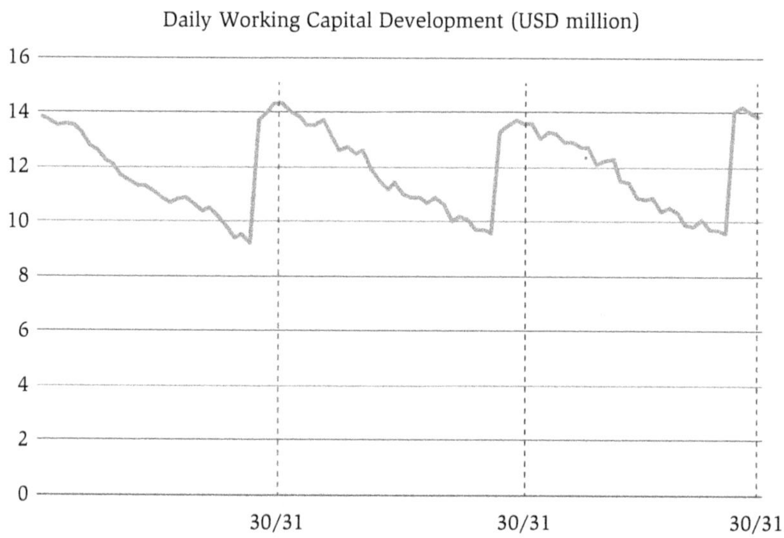

Further, many companies manage their cash and working capital positions at specific reporting dates, for example, to meet covenants in credit agreements, or for interim or annual reporting purposes. In addition, significant cash outflows may occur on the same day of each month, making working capital 'lumpy' during the month.

As a result, month-, quarter- or year-end working capital figures may not be representative of the everyday working capital position of a business. In fact, they can be the least representative dates from which to gain an understanding of the true working capital needs of the business.

It is often necessary, therefore, to consider using averages not only at month-ends but also to use other data points, such as weekly or even daily figures.

[F] Switching Between a Completion Accounts Process and a Locked Box

In some negotiations, the parties may switch from a purchase price adjustment contemplated at an early stage of the transaction process to a locked box or vice versa. For example, an indicative offer may include a completion accounts process. Then, during the negotiations, the parties settle on a fixed purchase price.

As discussed above, the reference value of a working capital adjustment should represent the normal working capital position at closing; for a locked box transaction, it should represent the normal working capital position at the locked box date. The two need to be the same. Consider a fast-growing business where the level of normal working capital changes between the two dates (*see* §5.04 [C]). In case of a switch during the negotiations from a locked box to a purchase price adjustment (or vice versa), the parties should therefore revisit what the normal level of working capital at the relevant date is.

[G] Normalising Working Capital

Historical working capital often includes one-off or non-recurring assets or liabilities. It is necessary to eliminate these from the reported figures in order to obtain an average that is representative of the business's underlying working capital requirements. Normalising working capital can be a complex process that requires access to trial balances and detailed explanations of the movements of individual assets or liabilities and whether they are recurring. This can be time-consuming, especially for items outside the definition of core working capital. A similar problem arises when the definition of working capital references assets or liabilities that include items that should be excluded from working capital at closing (even though they may not be considered exceptional). These items should then be eliminated from the historical figures as well.

The following are examples of items that might be normalised:

- Non-recurring receivables, for example, from an insurance claim/awards related to legal action.
- Capital expenditure creditors (frequently recorded in trade payables).
- Movements in foreign exchange rates that have had an impact on figures denominated in a company's functional currency (even though the underlying foreign currency-denominated balances were unchanged).
- Short-term payables for financial leases (§4.04 [B]).
- Balances owed to financial institutions in reverse factoring (*see* the example under §4.04 [A] [5]).
- Intercompany items that may continue albeit move to a third party or to arm's length terms with the vendor.
- Accrued interest reported within trade payables.

In addition to these adjustments, it may be appropriate to eliminate the effect of commodity price movements on historical working capital figures that are the basis of the reference value, that is, to restate these figures, on a pro-forma basis, using (for example) spot prices at the time of the analysis. Otherwise, part of the purchase price adjustment would be due to differences between historical commodity price levels and the spot price which may make no commercial sense. In economies with high inflation, a similar pro-forma restatement may be useful to eliminate the effect of general price increases.

Pro-forma adjustments may also be necessary for one-off events during the historical period that lead to a sustained change in the level of working capital the target business needs going forward. For example, in case of a (permanent) change in payment terms with a key customer or supplier during the historical period, the historical working capital figures should be restated as if the new policy had been in place throughout the historical period over which the average is derived.

Lastly (although not primarily a matter of normalising working capital), buyers should also consider whether they need contractual protection from sellers pushing sales before closing (whether by discounting or other means) in order to increase trade receivables at closing.

[H] Accounting Choices and Changes in Estimates

Additional considerations when determining the working capital reference value include the consistent application of accounting policies and practices and the reliability of estimates used over the historical period from which the reference value is derived. The following are (by no means exhaustive) examples of items to be considered in this regard:

- Changes in the bad debt allowance. The effect of any changes (in particular arbitrary ones) in the method of calculating the allowance should be eliminated where possible in order to arrive at accurate figures that reflect bad debt experience consistently. In order to protect against bias in accounting estimates, it can be appropriate to replace management judgment with a formula-driven accounting policy for the bad debt allowance in the completion accounts.
- Long-term contracting balances, including receivables recognised under the percentage of completion (POC) method. Estimates of the stage of completion and costs to complete as well as provisions for losses directly affect the carrying value of these items are discussed further in Chapter 9.
- Factored receivables that have been derecognised. This understates working capital, as discussed in §4.04 [A] (relative to the underlying working capital needs of the business). Factored receivables (and the associated debt) should be grossed up for purposes of a working capital reference value.
- Inventory valuation – cost capitalisation. It should be ensured that the capitalisation of costs, including the level of overhead absorption, has been done consistently. This is one of the most difficult accounting areas to address

in the SPA and requires careful consideration of any discretion available to the preparer of the completion accounts. If there is an increase at closing, buyers should be clear on whether they are willing to pay dollar-for-dollar for an increase in capitalised internal costs of the target entity.

- Inventory valuation – net realisable value. Net realisable value brings market prices into the completion mechanism. In volatile markets where prices can be difficult to establish, there may be ambiguity or uncertainty, for example, over which sources to use for market prices. This figures in post-deal disputes, for example, in fast-moving markets such as renewable energy or natural gas. It may again be appropriate to use a formula-based approach to inventory valuation in the completion accounts in these cases.

[I] Adjusting the Average to Reflect Different Rates for Borrowing and Lending

The discussion in §5.04 [B] above considered seasonality and concluded that, even for seasonal (no growth) businesses, it is appropriate to use an average reference working capital figure, derived over a historical period. Another facet in this regard concerns the cost of capital connected with variances in working capital from the average figure in either direction.

Seasonally strong months tie up more liquidity in working capital. This liquidity has to come from somewhere, and this is associated with a cost. A company uses cash (or a working capital facility) to fund the additional working capital needs during periods when these exceed the average. Conversely, in periods when working capital is below the average, the additional freed-up liquidity can be used to another end and may generate a return.

Treating these funding surpluses and deficits in the same way would be appropriate if the cost of capital for short-term investments and short-term funding needs of the business were the same. But they are usually not.

If the working capital reference value is determined as the simple arithmetic mean across historical net working capital figures, then differences between borrowing costs and investment returns are not reflected. To rectify this, in some deals parties propose that the average should be weighted by the difference in the cost of capital.

As discussed, the working capital reference value should be set in a way that will not cause the parties concern if the closing date shifts. In concept, for the parties to be indifferent, an incremental cost of funding working capital deficits should be added to the average, and the reference value should therefore be slightly higher than the average.

While this somewhat arcane principle gets an occasional airing, it has become very rare possibly because interest rates decreased for many years and borrowing rates and short-term returns alike were very low.

[J] Intercompany Balances

Intercompany balances should be categorised according to whether they are working capital, debt, or to be settled before or at closing:

- Working capital balances with related parties may move to a third party after closing, or remain but at arm's length terms.
- It is not uncommon for intercompany items reported within working capital to be unpaid for longer terms than between third parties. Consider that these balances may have a financing nature. *See* §4.04 [J].
- It is often appropriate to agree to settle intercompany balances before closing where possible in order to avoid credit risk with the other party after the transaction and the possibility that the counterparty may offset amounts owed with other claims post-closing.

§5.05 THE COLLAR APPROACH

One fairly common approach to working capital adjustments is that an adjustment is made only if the difference between actual and reference working capital (in either or only one direction) exceeds a de minimis amount. This is known as a 'collar'. No adjustment is made if actual working capital is within the collar, i.e., the de minimis amount is not exceeded. In case the de minimis amount is exceeded, the adjustment may be limited to the excess (the amount outside the collar) or it may be for the entire amount including the collar. This needs to be clearly set out in the SPA.

The collar is invariably a comparatively low amount. One of its purposes is to remove potential disagreements over small amounts that are, in aggregate, clearly within the collar: if an individual item over which there could be disagreement between the parties does not cause the aggregate to exceed the collar amount, this may reduce the probability of a dispute over such small items.

It is also sometimes argued that it saves time not to have to calculate exact amounts. However, this is true only if it is certain that the difference between actual and reference working capital is within the collar without having performed calculations; more typically, in order to establish whether the collar is exceeded, it is necessary to perform the same analysis as without a collar.

The potential drawbacks or risks of using a collar are often clearer than the advantages. While a collar is relatively common for the working capital reference value, the same approach is very rarely (if ever) used in relation to the net debt adjustment. However, the working capital adjustment should complement the net debt adjustment: a collar around one but not the other means the interaction between the two adjustments is no longer seamless. It is easy to leave money on the table here from the perspective of the buyer who is exposed to the seller's desire to manage down working capital (but to remain within the collar) and maximise the cash position. In the presence of a sophisticated, aggressive seller this represents a real risk, even if limited to the collar amount. It should be avoided where possible.

CHAPTER 6

Capital Expenditure

§6.01 OVERVIEW

Capital expenditure is the use of funds to acquire or improve a long-term asset. As the use of funds can be either a cash outflow or involve taking on additional debt, the level of capital expenditure before closing impacts the level of net debt at closing. With a net debt adjustment, a seller who slows down capital expenditure prior to closing increases the cash position at closing. The buyer not only pays for an inflated cash position (as part of net debt) but also obtains a business with a capital expenditure backlog.[111]

The principal idea behind the capital expenditure adjustment is to protect the buyer from this type of seller manipulation. It does this by reducing the purchase price for any shortfall against a target value in the cumulative level of capital expenditures in the closing period. The adjustment effectively offsets a cash position that, at closing, is higher than it should be only because capital investments were delayed or cancelled.

Capital expenditure adjustments may be one- or two-sided. A one-sided adjustment can only lead to a reduction in the purchase price. A two-sided adjustment means that the purchase price can also increase if cumulative capital expenditure between signing and closing is higher than the agreed level. In effect, the two-sided adjustment reimburses the seller if the target spends more than planned on capital goods during the period up to closing (which means that it has less cash than otherwise). In the case of higher-than-planned capital expenditure, a two-sided adjustment can mean that the buyer pays for excessive investment over which it has no control, something to avoid.

111. For maintenance spending (one type of capital expenditure), it has been argued that prevention is cheaper than cure. *See* https://www.ft.com/content/cf700fad-6e87-3b32-867c-8686853c76f1. 'Catching up' an investment backlog can require greater expenditure than was originally deferred. This means in practical terms that a capital expenditure adjustment may be more effective in removing the incentive from a seller to slow down capital spending than it is at putting the buyer in the same position as if the seller had spent as planned.

The SPA may also include provisions that give the buyer the ability to influence significant investment decisions during the closing period. For example, it may specify which investments should be made before closing or give the buyer approval rights for individual capital expenditure items above certain thresholds. Depending on the jurisdiction, these types of provisions in the SPA will need to avoid a situation in which a buyer is considered to already exercise control over strategic business decisions of the target before closing, something called 'gun jumping'.[112] This has been a recent focus of competition authorities both in the US and Europe.[113] However, these are legal considerations outside the scope of this book.

To work properly, the capital expenditure adjustment must be based on a planned level of spending over a period of time up to the expected closing date (and beyond if there is a risk that the transaction closes later than expected). The target level of capital expenditure over this period should be consistent with the business plan on which the business was valued. Similar to the working capital reference value, which represents a 'normal' working capital level of the business, the capital expenditure target often assumes the continuation of a 'normal' level of capital expenditure over time. The difference is that a working capital adjustment is measured against a single reference value, whereas the capital expenditure adjustment is measured against an accumulating reference level that increases over the closing period and therefore depends on the closing date.

As the capital expenditure adjustment requires a continuously increasing reference level over the (expected) closing period, annual or quarterly capital expenditure budgets may need to be phased into monthly or more frequent capital expenditure targets. Whether to plan on a monthly, weekly, or even daily basis will essentially depend on how 'lumpy' capital spending is. For a large group with capital expenditure comprised of many comparatively small individual items which are fairly evenly distributed across the working days of a month, monthly targets will be sufficient. If individual purchases of fixed assets are significant relative to the overall level of spend, then planning capital spend can involve detailed projections.

Another area of complexity is the definition of capital expenditure. A particular concern can arise when the definition includes overheads (which can be eligible for capitalisation under GAAP). The result is the capitalisation of cash outflows that would have been incurred regardless. Buyers need to be careful that such internal costs do not displace external capital expenditure, especially in situations where a seller has the ability to slow down external spending prior to closing. The risk is that a buyer receives an under-invested business at closing with no corresponding purchase price adjustment to make up for the shortfall.

---

112. For example: *Altice v. European Commission*, case T-425/18, judgment of the General Court, 22 September 2021; *United States v. Smithfield Foods and Premium Standard Farms* 1:10-CV00120 (DDC 21 January 2010).

113. *See Gun jumping*, Lexis Nexis produced in partnership with Stéphane Dionnet and Pauline Giroux of Skadden Arps Slate Meagher & Flom LLP, available at https://www.skadden.com/-/media/files/publications/2017/01/gun_jumping.

Take, as an example, accounting for development costs. IAS 38.57 sets out the criteria for when these costs can be capitalised, including the technical feasibility of completing the asset, the ability to use or sell the asset, and that the asset will generate probable future economic benefits. Applying these criteria often requires significant judgment on the part of those preparing the financial statements and can consequently afford sellers significant scope to influence the amount of capital expenditure that goes into an adjustment. A seller who slows down the (external) acquisition of investment goods prior to closing and instead increases the amount of capitalised internal costs will increase the cash position at closing (assuming internal development staff are paid anyway). This will reduce net debt at closing but, unless the buyer is contractually protected, it will not result in an offsetting capital expenditure adjustment. In addition to overpaying for the cash position at closing, the buyer obtains an under-invested business.

§6.02 DISPUTES RELATED TO CAPITAL EXPENDITURES

Disputes over capitalising costs are very common. The chapter discusses two examples. The first relates to the costs included in a capital expenditure adjustment, the second to the adequacy of disclosures in addition to disagreement over the capitalisations themselves.

Most capital expenditure-related disputes are over alleged breaches of financial statements warranties or disclosures (*see* the second example). Damage claims are frequently based on alleged misrepresentations where the financials affected by the misrepresentations represent the 'base year' on which a buyer's EBITDA-based valuation was based. The dynamic at work in these cases is that capitalising costs effectively converts operating expenses (which are deducted in EBITDA) from one period into depreciation (which is not deducted in EBITDA) in future periods. This effectively increases EBITDA in the period in which the costs are capitalised. In this way, sellers can shift operating expenses, especially internal costs, into future years' depreciation below EBITDA.

Such (aggressive) accounting may be within or outside the confines of GAAP. However, even if a buyer can show in a dispute that the accounting was incorrect, sellers occasionally respond that this merely means that expenditures were shifted from investing to operating cash flow (both above free cash flow) and that this can have no relevance to 'value' (and, by extension, cannot give rise to damages). This runs into the observation that operating expenditure is of a different nature from capital expenditure: the former is short-term, whereas the latter represents an investment in long-term assets, that is, economic benefits of future periods. The accounting information reflects that difference (or is meant to). This can give rise to complex arguments over the valuation-relevance of capitalising expenditures, sometimes further complicated by questions over the adequacy of disclosure beyond the capitalisation itself.

Example of a Dispute over Capitalised Expenditure Adjustment (International Arbitration)

A recent arbitration dispute arose from the acquisition of a European automotive supplier, a capital-intensive business, by a US corporate. The SPA contained a capital expenditure adjustment that set out capital expenditure targets up to the expected closing date and an adjustment for any shortfall against the target.

After closing, the buyer alleged that development costs had been aggressively capitalised during the closing period, including internal costs that did not meet the criteria for capitalisation. Had these costs been expensed instead, this would have led to a shortfall against the capital expenditure targets and a purchase price adjustment. (The parties settled).

Example of a Dispute over Capitalisation of Costs and Breach of Disclosure Requirements (International Arbitration)

The target company was under pressure to achieve ambitious earnings targets and had capitalised significant internal and external costs in the period leading up to signing. These included costs of research and development. In the cash flow statement for the last financial year prior to signing, the target only reported those capital expenditures within investment cash flows that had become cash-relevant by the end of the reporting period. That is, unpaid capital expenditure creditors were reported among trade payables and entered the cash flow statement as part of the change in working capital. The part of working capital changes that related to capital expenditure was not identified in the cash flow statement.

The buyer considered the capitalisation of costs to be excessive. The buyer was also not able to identify total capital investment in the period – paid or unpaid – from the cash flow statement. To add to the complexity, the target had engaged in reverse factoring (*see* section §4.04 [A] [5]) as part of which it transferred almost all trade creditors, including capital expenditure creditors, to a financial institution. It had reclassified these trade creditors from working capital into financial debt, again without disclosing the nature of the transferred creditors. It was therefore difficult for the buyer to understand either the normal working capital needs of the business or the historical level of capital expenditure. The buyer claimed that, as a result, it had overpaid for the business and that the business was under-invested at closing. The claim gave rise to complex damages questions.

CHAPTER 7

Locked Box Transactions

§7.01 OVERVIEW

The principal idea behind the locked box mechanism was introduced above in §2.03. As discussed there, in a locked box transaction, the fixed purchase price reflects the levels of cash, debt, and working capital at a historical reference date, the locked box date. The transaction can be viewed as economically (though not legally) backdated to the locked box date. The timeline for this type of transaction is shown below in Figure 7.1.

Figure 7.1 The Locked Box Timeline

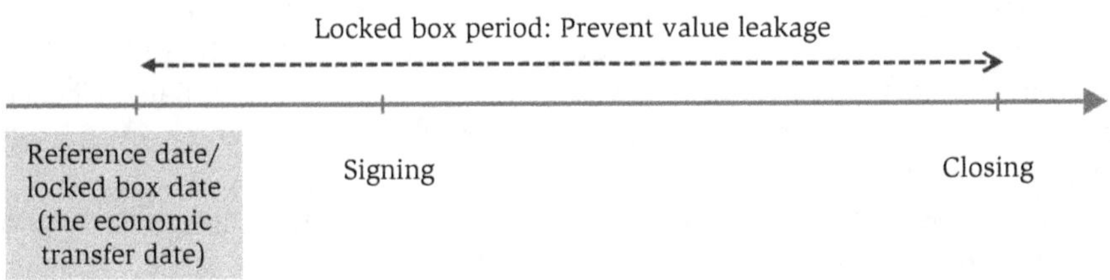

The time between the locked box date and closing, the 'locked box period', can be divided into two parts: the period from the historical reference date to signing, and the closing period. The distinction matters as the length of the first period is known at signing (which is when it ends), whereas the length of the closing period is very often unknown. The locked box mechanism therefore needs to accommodate uncertainty as to the length of the closing period and must ensure that the parties each receive at closing the value that they bargained for: the buyer needs to be protected from 'value leakage' (over an unknown period), and the seller compensated for cash surpluses that are generated up to closing and transferred to the buyer in the cash position, without a price adjustment.

The locked box is generally considered a seller-friendly mechanism (although that is not necessarily always the case). As discussed above in §2.03, its popularity is typically linked to the relative strengths of the parties during the negotiations. These strengths can shift significantly over the M&A cycle. For example, an analysis of the period 2007 to 2011 by PwC found that a decrease in the number of deals during the global financial crisis from 2007 to 2009 corresponded with an increase in the use of the completion accounts mechanism.[114] Correspondingly, when deal numbers picked up from late 2009 onwards, the use of completion accounts fell sharply, and that of locked box mechanisms increased. And the study suggested rapid and pronounced market responses: around November 2009, the analysis shows a peak at which approximately 80% of all analysed deals featured completion accounts; both a year earlier, and a year later, fewer than 50% did.

This chapter first discusses the reference date and length of the locked box period. It then addresses the problem of potential 'value leakage' and goes on to discuss different approaches to the value accrual (or locked box interest rate) that is frequently agreed for the period up to closing.

§7.02 THE REFERENCE DATE AND THE LOCKED BOX PERIOD

The historical reference date is frequently the date of the last available audited financial statements. As many companies use the calendar year, the most common locked box date is 31 December. It is generally desirable to keep the locked box period short, which means that there are typically more locked box transactions in the first half of the calendar year than in the second: if too much time has passed since the last financial year-end, then the parties can alternatively agree on a more recent locked box date than the preceding year-end (often a half-year or quarter-end), or move to a purchase price adjustment. Using interim dates, however, makes it more likely that the locked box date financials are unaudited. In any event, it is generally important that the locked box accounts have been subject to some level of external review at signing, even if a lower level of review than an audit.

Given that there is no 'true-up' at closing, the financial due diligence on the locked box date financial statements takes on even greater importance than in a completion accounts transaction: it represents the only opportunity for the buyer to identify items that should be reflected in price, and that opportunity ends with signing.

It is generally important to keep the locked box period comparatively short. The more time that passes between the locked box date and closing, the more the business will change, and the more opportunity there will be for value to be extracted (intentionally or otherwise), or for the business to develop in unforeseen ways so that

114. *Pricing mechanisms: Locked box v. completion accounts*, *PLC Magazine*, Ronan O'Sullivan and Ross McNaughton, February 2012, 2. https://webstorage.paulhastings.com/Documents/PDFs/2110.pdf.

the value transferred at closing may no longer be what the parties bargained for. More specifically, the longer the locked box period, the more difficult it is to avoid leakage – to keep the box 'locked'. Consider, as a thought experiment, a locked box period of fifty years, and the unsolvable problems associated with ensuring that a buyer would receive the value then that correspondes to the fixed price agreed today. Most locked box periods, therefore, do not exceed a few months, although occasionally they can be significantly longer.

§7.03 VALUE LEAKAGE

It is a central concern for the buyer that no value is extracted from the target entity during the locked box period prior to closing, other than what has been agreed between the parties (called 'permitted leakage'). To ensure this, the SPA should contain 'no leakage' provisions. The buyer's concern in this regard usually relates to transactions between the target entity and the seller, or parties related to the seller. A straightforward example of leakage is the payment of a dividend by the target company just prior to closing. Potential leakage is, however, not limited to dividend payments or even transactions between the target business and the seller.

Below are some of the ways by which sellers or related parties can extract value before closing, and where buyers may therefore require contractual protection:

- Dividend payments by the target to the seller.
- Share buybacks.
- The accelerated repayment of shareholder loans.
- Transactions between the target and the seller or related parties that are not at arm's length, for example, due to a change in intercompany prices. This is one reason why locked box mechanisms are often less suitable for carve-out transactions.[115]
- Changes in intercompany charges or cost allocations between the target and the seller or related parties.
- Advisory fees in connection with the transactions.
- Waivers by the target of claims against the seller or related parties.
- Management compensation in excess of normal payments.
- Capital expenditure in excess of predetermined levels, or the acquisition of unusual or unnecessary capital goods.
- Disposals of subsidiaries or ownership interests in other companies.
- Loan guarantees and any other securities issued by the target on behalf of the seller or related parties.
- Out-of-court settlements of disputes.

The list above is not exhaustive, and buyers and their advisors should consider any other potential ways by which value can be extracted during the locked box period. The parties also often agree on specific transactions that represent 'permitted leakage',

115. Another is that there is often no stand-alone trading history for the carve-out asset.

which are then specified in the SPA and reflected in the fixed price. This is discussed further below in this section.

No purchase price adjustment at closing means there is no interaction between leakage provisions in the SPA and any 'true-up' for net debt or other balance sheet item. It is therefore usually important to use SPA definitions of 'leakage' in a way that captures items regardless of whether they will have been cash-settled at closing when the seller transfers the economic burden that is associated with any leakage. Leakage is different in this respect from merely a shift between cash and debt that a net debt adjustment is concerned with (see §5.02).

Some types of leakage are known before signing and permitted – that is, before signing, the parties may agree on certain types of extractions of value during the closing period, known as 'permitted leakage'. Examples of permitted leakage include pre-agreed dividends, bonus payments, or the repayment of a shareholder loan. Such permitted leakage is, or should be, reflected in the fixed purchase price.

It can be exceedingly difficult for a buyer to identify leakage (outside of permitted leakage). This is especially the case where leakage is not recorded in the target's accounts, or where it is not recorded where it should be or where it has been recorded historically, sometimes deliberate acts used by a seller to conceal value extraction. For example, if an unusually high intercompany charge in the locked box period is not debited to 'intercompany' accounts, finding it can turn into a difficult forensic exercise. Buyers will often not initiate this search unless red flags have already been raised and they suspect that leakage has occurred.

§7.04 LOCKED BOX-RELATED DISPUTES

Locked box transactions are less likely to end up in disputes overall compared to completion accounts transactions (given that there is no purchase price adjustment), but disputes do exist. This section discusses some locked box-specific aspects of M&A disputes.

One type of dispute starts from the problem discussed above at §7.02 that, the longer the locked box period, the more the target business is subject to change, and the more difficult it becomes to foresee all potential areas of leakage. To protect buyers, SPAs include leakage protections, including 'ordinary course' clauses.[116] The parties can disagree over the interpretation of the term 'ordinary course'. This is however primarily a legal matter (although it may be informed by knowledge of ordinary business practices), and outside the scope of this book.

Another locked box-specific aspect that ends up in disputes relates to the concept of economic backdating of locked box transactions. The idea is that the seller in effect manages the target business during the locked box period on behalf of the buyer, and for the buyer's benefit. Any profits generated between the effective date and closing accrue to the buyer (as cash and working capital are transferred at closing without a

116. Often a warranty in respect of the historical period to signing and a covenant in respect of the period to closing.

price adjustment). Correspondingly, under this concept, a buyer would carry the economic burden of any losses during the locked box period. Disputes can arise over unforeseen events that result in such losses that are not reflected in price and that the buyer effectively finances, although it had no control over the event that caused them, and (often) no contractual protection under which such losses can be recovered. The following case is an example.

Example of a Dispute over Locked Box Transaction (International Arbitration)

The seller warranted that the monthly management accounts for the locked box period (of several months) gave a 'true and fair view' of the target's financial situation. During the locked box period, the target incurred significant losses when an accident damaged a manufacturing facility. The target did not account for these losses in the management accounts, even though management had by then obtained quotes for repair which showed that the costs involved were significant.

After closing, the buyer alleged breach of the management accounts warranty. The seller argued that in choosing a locked box mechanism, it had been the parties' intention to transfer the risks and rewards of ownership at the locked box date, which meant, in the seller's view, that any profits and losses after the locked box date, whether or not foreseeable, would be on account of the buyer. That is, if the target had failed to account for the expected cost of repair, that accounting error could not give rise to any damages.

The buyer argued that the value accrual, or 'daily profit charge' for the closing period (see below §7.05) had been calculated on the basis of the expected average daily cash returns in the period to closing. This meant in its view that the expected returns of the closing period effectively transferred to the seller, and that the buyer had therefore not agreed to bear the commercial risk associated with the target's trading over this period (given that it did not receive the returns).[117] At the time of writing, the case was pending.

Example of a Dispute over Locked Box Transaction (*Aras & Others v. National Bank of Greece*, High Court of England and Wales)[118]

Another example of a dispute over a locked box transaction is the case of the National Bank of Greece which was sued in the UK over its EUR 2.7 billion sale of QNB Finansbank AS ('Finansbank') shares.

The claimants were senior executives of Finansbank, a large Turkish bank. The case related to claimants' entitlement to a fee which they contended became payable by the Defendant, National Bank of Greece SA ('NBG') under certain incentive fee agreements. The agreements entitled the executives to a fee in the event of the disposal by NBG of more than 5% of its shares in Finansbank (defined as an 'Exit Event'). On 21 December 2015, NBG entered into an SPA under which it agreed to sell its shares in

117. The argument would not have been available if the locked box interest had been a risk-free rate.
118. *Aras & Others v. National Bank of Greece S.A.* [2018] EWHC.

Finansbank to Qatar National Bank SAQ ('QNB'). The transaction closed on 15 June 2016. QNB paid an amount of EUR 2.711 billion to NBG.

The subsequent dispute related (among other matters) to the question whether the 'Exit Event' had taken place at signing (21 December 2015) or alternatively closing (15 June 2016). The date was relevant to the determination of the last book value of equity before the date which, in turn, was the basis of the calculation of the incentive fees. The equity book values were significantly different on 30 March 2016 and 30 September 2015 (the date of the locked box accounts), the two-quarter ends preceding closing and signing, respectively.

The court held that the Exit Event date was signing, the date the fixed price was agreed with QNB (subject only to 'Leakage') and that the relevant equity book value was, therefore, the value at 30 September 2015, the preceding quarter-end. This value had been known to the parties when they negotiated the fixed price. After the SPA was signed, the Claimants were in no position to influence the achievement of a higher 'Exit Value'. The court considered that the purchase price based on the locked box date (30 September 2015) was fixed and that any additional surpluses or deficits would effectively accrue to the acquirer.

§7.05 THE VALUE ACCRUAL

[A] Introduction

It is common for the parties to agree a value accrual, or interest charge, that is intended to compensate the seller for the economic returns of the target between the (backdated) economic transfer date (the locked box date) and the payment date of the purchase price (closing). This type of compensation is alternatively known as 'value accrual', 'daily profit charge', 'locked box interest', 'ticker rate' or 'ticker adjustment'. This publication uses the terms 'value accrual' or 'locked box interest'.

Any positive returns that the target generates during the locked box period increase the value of the net operating assets that are transferred at closing (provided no leakage occurs). Until then, owning the target company ties up the seller's capital, whereas the seller only receives the purchase price at closing.[119] Sellers want to be compensated for the value generated during this period, and there is no purchase price adjustment to do this. SPAs therefore usually specify amounts that accrue over each day of the closing period, similar to an interest charge applied to the (fixed) purchase price. This interest, or value accrual, is usually calculated for the entire (expected) locked box period.

However, in some transactions, the interest or value accrual only applies to a fraction of the closing period. This is called a 'ticker', as it only starts at an agreed date after the locked box date (but during the closing period), for example, an originally

119. Even if the returns were foreseeable and priced into the bid, once realised, they convert from expected, risky cash flows to lower risk or near zero-beta assets, such as cash or working capital.

expected closing date. One purpose of a 'ticker' in these cases is to compensate the seller for the period that capital is tied up only if that period is longer than expected. This can protect the seller from a buyer who deliberately delays closing in cases where it has the ability to do so.

In some deals with long locked box periods or comparatively significant daily accrued amounts, the aggregate value accrual can be a substantial fraction of the total consideration. It is therefore worth considering the conceptual basis on which this charge should be set. There is, perhaps surprisingly, no general consensus on this conceptual basis and the market uses several alternative approaches, each with different outcomes that sometimes reflect more the relative bargaining positions of the parties than any conceptual considerations. The more common alternatives are discussed in the following section.[120]

[B] Approaches to the Value Accrual

[1] Overview

As indicated earlier, the accrual can be viewed as compensation to the seller whose capital is tied up until closing and who does not otherwise share in the returns of the target entity over the locked box period. Another way to view the value accrual that can be helpful to consider is as a mechanism to put the seller in the same position as if the transaction had not only been (economically) backdated, but had in fact closed on the locked box date, instead of the later actual closing date.

The discussion below is premised on two assumptions: (1) The parties have access to liquid capital markets; and (2) the purchase price is payable at closing in a single payment; therefore, in the rare event that a signed transaction does not close, the buyer would not pay the purchase price.[121]

[2] Seller's Return on Capital Employed

One approach is to use the rate of return on total capital employed in relation to the seller's business over the locked box period. The deferral of the purchase price until closing deprives the seller of the opportunity to invest the proceeds in its own business. Such an investment would have generated a return that may be approximated, in percentage terms, as the average return of the seller's other operating activities over this period.

---

120. *See* also, Grant Thornton, *A Smarter Way to Get Deals Done International Survey: Identifying International Market Practice for Equity Value Adjustments and Sale and Purchase Agreements*, November 2017, p. 7.
121. This resembles a secured lending transaction in which the lender (the seller) is entitled to repossess the collateral in the event of a default by the borrower (the buyer). The discussion further below will return to this idea.

This approach can however run into the following objections: First, an incremental return is not necessarily the same as an average return, and it is the former that the approach requires, at least in concept. Second, a seller who believes it was deprived of an opportunity to generate a return in excess of its cost of capital could have raised funds in the capital markets in order to take advantage of these investment opportunities - had these opportunities been available. To the extent it chose not to take advantage of them, this suggests that they were not available. This can make the use of the seller's return on capital employed - at least to the extent it exceeds its cost of capital - difficult to justify.

[3] Seller's Weighted Average Cost of Capital

An alternative approach is to use the seller's Weighted Average Cost of Capital ('WACC'). This is the assumed cost to the seller of replacing the liquidity that was tied up during the locked box period.

This approach assumes that the seller could have obtained additional liquidity at its existing WACC, i.e., that the incremental cost of equity and debt financing would have been equal to the average cost of the seller's existing financing, which suggests no change to the weights in WACC. Again, this need not be the case.

Buyers might also argue against this approach by highlighting that locked box interest should depend not on the seller's cost of capital but on the cost of financing the asset in question, the target entity. Using a seller's high WACC would penalise a buyer who has no influence over the seller's cost of capital.

[4] The Buyer's Incremental Cost of Borrowing

Another alternative is to view the purchase price as a loan from the seller to the buyer. An appropriate price of the loan, or rate of interest, would be the buyer's incremental cost of borrowing. As closing requires payment of the purchase price, the arrangement is similar in some ways to a secured lending transaction. The value accrual would, therefore, be determined on a similar basis as the incremental cost of a secured loan.

This approach is generally difficult to implement, for (at least) two reasons. First, the seller is unlikely to know the borrowing cost to the buyer of this specific type of secured debt instrument (even the buyer may not know). The analysis required to estimate a rate may not be worth the time and effort. Second, the approach may lead to different locked box interest rates for each bidder (if the secured cost of borrowing varies between bidders). This would mean different final purchase prices even in situations where each bidder places an identical underlying value on the target entity. This would penalise bidders with higher borrowing costs, including young, high-growth companies, companies with more aggressive leverage, or emerging markets investors.

[5] The Risk-Free Rate

The use of a risk-free rate starts from the idea that the buyer takes on the (economic) risks and rewards of ownership of the target from the locked box date. If the buyer assumes this risk, and is compensated for it with the returns generated up to closing, it follows that the seller cannot also be entitled to compensation for the same risk. The seller can, therefore, only be entitled to a risk-free interest rate.

However, even if the locked box date is considered to be the time at which the risks and rewards of ownership transfer in economic terms, this does not make the subsequent period to closing entirely risk-free to the seller. Consider, for example, MAC or similar clauses that mean that certain major adverse events cause the transaction not to close. This leaves some of the most fundamental risks associated with the target firm with the seller.

[6] Daily Profit Charge

Among the more common approaches to the value accrual is to forecast the profit the target is expected to generate over the locked box period (or some other recent period), and then to calculate an average daily profit that is added to the purchase price for each day up to closing. This is called a 'daily profit charge' or 'daily profit rate'.

The idea behind a daily profit charge is to reimburse the seller for the returns that accrue to the buyer during the locked box period when the seller continues to manage the target. If profits during the locked box period translate into cash or working capital at closing (as the box is locked), then does this not produce a similar outcome to a purchase price adjustment?

Other than that, estimates of future profits are not the same as the measurement of actual cash and working capital at closing, there is another important difference: the valuation date of a locked box transaction is, or generally should be, the locked box date, and profits of the locked box period are included in enterprise value (at least in theory). For a completion accounts transaction, the valuation date is, or should be, closing, and enterprise value therefore reflects only returns from that date onwards. A daily profit charge that reimburses a seller for profits in the locked box period would therefore mean that he or she receives these profits in addition to a purchase price that already includes their expected present value at the locked box date. That would be double counting. The problem can be addressed by adjusting the locked box valuation date.

While in practice the daily profit charge approach is a common approach, it can therefore be difficult to justify in theory to the extent the profits are, in fact, already 'priced into' enterprise value.

Another important aspect of setting a daily profit charge is the definition of 'profit': Should the charge be based on net earnings, EBIT, EBITDA, cash flow, or something else? Since locked box interest relates to the purchase price for the equity, not enterprise value, the daily profit charge should, in concept, correspond to the earnings to which the equity holders are entitled, i.e., net profits after interest, taxes, and any other expenses that reduce the return on the target's equity. Earnings measures such as EBITDA or EBIT are not appropriate as a basis of the daily profit charge, as they overstate the return on equity: they are used as a basis of enterprise value, not equity value.

Further, since the purpose of the daily profit charge is to capture and compensate for economic value created during the (finite) locked box period, it is usually not appropriate to use cash flows instead of earnings as a basis for measuring this value (contrary to what is sometimes proposed as cash flow is less affected by accounting choices): there is no reason to omit from the basis of the daily profit charge any value that has not yet turned into cash at closing. The appropriate basis to measure the accrual of value is accrual accounting.

Another complication arises if the target entity is loss making in the closing period. In concept, the daily profit charge should then be negative: the seller effectively compensates the buyer for each day of losses that accrue to the buyer. Negative daily profit rates are, however, rare.

Lastly, a practical problem with the determination of the daily profit charge is that sellers typically have significantly more information about the target entity than buyers. Due to this information asymmetry, the daily profit charge is frequently set at the higher end of the range of profits that can be reasonably expected during the locked period. This information asymmetry underpins the general seller-friendliness of locked box transactions. The buyer needs to ensure, at a minimum, that the prospective financial information on which the profitability during the locked box period is based is consistent with the business plan that it used to value the business and on which it has based its bid.

CHAPTER 8

Earn-Outs

§8.01 OVERVIEW

An earn-out is an arrangement under which the seller of a business receives payouts, in addition to the basic purchase price, that are contingent upon the achievement of agreed performance targets over a period of time after closing (known as the 'earn-out period'). Earn-out targets can be financial or non-financial.

Earn-outs are often used when the price expectations of buyer and seller are significantly apart. They can provide an effective means of bridging the gap. However, earn-outs can be problematic: what was an inability to agree on the target entity's value before signing can all too easily turn into a dispute – in other words, the can is merely kicked down the road.

This aspect of earn-outs was expressed by the Delaware Court of Chancery, which, commenting on the characteristics of earn-outs, noted that they typically reflect:

> disagreement over the value of the business that is bridged when the seller trades the certainty of less cash at closing for the prospect of more cash over time ... But since value is frequently debatable and the causes of underperformance equally so, an earn-out often converts today's disagreement over price into tomorrow's litigation over the outcome ... .[122]

Similarly, in *Starbev GP Ltd v. Interbrew Central European Holdings BV*, the judge, commenting on the issues that gave rise to the dispute, noted:

> The parties had clinched their deal, and the question as to how the deferred consideration would work in practice was pushed off into the indefinite future.[123]

---

122. *Airborne Health, Inc. v. Squid Soap, LP*, 984 A.2d 126, 132 (Del. Ch. 2009), quoted in Kevin R. Shannon and Michael K. Reilly, *Post-Closing Earnouts in M&A Transactions: Avoiding Common Disputes*, 2011.
123. *Starbev GP Ltd v. Interbrew Central European Holdings BV* [2014] EWHC 1311 (Comm), para. 57.

This dispute is discussed in §8.03.

Earn-out disputes usually relate the measurement basis on which the earn-out is calculated. Fundamentally, the issue is very often the (necessarily imperfect) connection between the metric used and the value it is supposed to measure. This connection can only ever be an approximation. The buyer, who is in control of the business during the earn-out period, usually has an incentive to manage the earn-out basis (downwards), exercising judgment when preparing the accounts in order to minimise the earn-out payment or to just miss earn-out targets. Further, earnings measures on which earn-outs are based often include one-off or non-recurring elements, and there can easily be disagreement whether to include these in the measurement basis. These factors make earn-outs prone to disputes. Some examples are discussed further below in §8.03.

§8.02 THE PURPOSE AND ROLE OF EARN-OUTS

While a principal purpose of an earn-out is to facilitate a transaction by bridging the price expectation gap between buyer and seller, there are other important functions. These are discussed further below.

[A] Bridging the Price Expectation Gap

An earn-out measures part of the target entity's value that is dependent upon one or more unknown future events after closing.[124] If the expectations of buyer and seller as to developments after closing (and therefore value of the target entity) are significantly apart and cannot be reconciled, an earn-out is a mechanism to bridge the gap.

Examples of uncertainty that can be difficult to deal with in a transaction context are binary outcomes that are linked to the target's value. Consider a regulator's approval decision of a new drug that, if successful, would become an important driver of future profits. The parties may disagree over the probability of the approval.[125] An earn-out that is linked to such an event with an uncertain outcome is a mechanism to measure value subsequently when the uncertainty is resolved, and only then fix the price. The reasoning suggests that the metrics underlying the earn-out measurement should be closely associated with 'value'. The earn-out basis is discussed below in §8.03.

[B] Allocation of Risk

It is normal for a buyer to take on the risks and rewards of ownership at closing. An earn-out re-allocates part of this risk to the seller: if the target's performance falls short

124. Note that it is always the case that events after closing are uncertain, and an earn-out therefore shifts some of that uncertainty from buyer to seller. *See* below [B].

125. The use of the term 'probability' is not precise in this context. Many earn-out payments correspond to the pay-offs of (European) call options. Strictly speaking, probabilities do not enter into their valuation (instead, it is volatility and other parameters that determine the value of options).

of targets agreed as part of the earn-out, then the buyer will owe a lower, or no, earn-out payment. The buyer will also have received a business that is worth less than otherwise, provided the earn-out target is linked to value. If actual developments exceed expectations, then the buyer will pay more but will also have received more in value (this simplified example assumes symmetry in the earn-out payoffs). Part of the effect on the valuation of the target business of exceeding or falling short of projected trading is moved to the seller.

[C] Incentivisation of the Seller

Earn-outs are often used as a mechanism to incentivise an owner-manager or entrepreneur who is selling a majority stake in his or her business, but who will stay on managing or otherwise contributing to its performance after closing. The earn-out can create an important incentive to maximise their efforts as they continue to share in the rewards after closing.

[D] A Source of Acquisition Financing

An earn-out can also be viewed as a source of acquisition financing. The earn-out component of the total consideration is deferred until uncertainty over the target's trading in the relevant period after closing is resolved, and it is clear that earn-out targets have been met. The deferred component of the purchase price, if based on a measure of profit such as EBITDA, is effectively paid out of the target entity's profits after closing if these profits are actually achieved. If these profits translate into cash flow, then this part of the consideration does not need to be financed by the buyer.

This aspect of earn-outs was particularly relevant during and just after the financial crisis of 2007 to 2009, when acquisition finance was difficult to obtain. At the time, many deals deferred a significant part of the total consideration into the earn-out period. An example is *Starbev GP Ltd v. Interbrew Central European Holdings BV*, where an earn-out helped bridge the gap in the PE sponsor's acquisition financing.[126] This dispute is discussed in the following section.

§8.03 THE EARN-OUT BASIS

[A] Earn-Out Metrics

Earn-outs can be linked to financial or non-financial metrics, or a combination of the two. Each type is discussed below.

126. *Ibid.*, para. 16.

[1] Financial Metrics

Financial metrics typically relate to sales, sales growth, or measures of profit such as EBITDA, EBIT, or net profit. They can also occasionally relate to variables such as prices charged by a supplier in respect of a specific product.

It is essential that the SPA define precisely the basis on which the relevant performance measure underlying the earn-out is to be calculated. In the case of an earn-out linked to measures of profits (however defined), the SPA should, among other things, ensure that the target entity's accounts are drawn up on a basis consistent with that applied before closing. By way of illustration, items to be specifically addressed here might include changes in accounting policies and practices (e.g., adopting a more conservative revenue recognition policy), one-off asset write-downs, changes as a result of new intercompany arrangements (e.g., where the buyer's group begins to supply certain products or services at higher prices than hitherto), or the charging of management and similar fees by the new owner. A single recharge of a group service, for example, could extinguish profits that would have otherwise triggered a significant earn-out payment. Equally, the parties will often limit the scope for discretion in the preparation of the earn-out statement and attempt to ensure that profits of the earn-out period are not affected by items that have nothing to do with value. Sales or profits that enter the measurement basis of an earn-out should usually be recurring and cash-relevant.

Capturing all possible adjustments to future income *ex ante*, at the time the earn-out is agreed, can be like attempting to normalise future periods' earnings (when it is difficult enough to normalise historical earnings). Even where an SPA contains comprehensive rules for the calculation of the earn-out basis, these can prove to be impractical or difficult to implement. Despite apparent (hard-fought) agreement before signing, there can easily be scope for disputes later. For example, wording that requires the exclusion of 'one-off' or 'non-recurring' items can easily be subject to disagreement. This is what happened in *Comet Systems, Inc. Shareholders' Agent v. MIVA, Inc.* which is discussed further below in this section.

Where possible, the earn-out calculation should be based on financial information that is validated by an external party, ideally audited financial statements (before the application of more specific rules in the SPA that govern the earn-out basis). The following example highlights this.

***Treatt plc v. Barratt and others* (England and Wales Court of Appeal)**[127]

This dispute related to an earn-out that was based on audited accounts for certain calendar years ending on 31 December. The buyer's own year-end was 30 September. After the acquisition, the buyer changed the year-ends of certain companies it had acquired to 30 September to bring them in line with its own accounting year-end and thereby facilitate the preparation of consolidated group accounts. The buyer did not, in

127. *Treatt plc v. Barratt and others* [2015] EWCA Civ 116. There was an unsuccessful appeal: [2015] EWCA Civ 116 (18 February 2015).

addition, prepare audited accounts with 31 December year-ends for the relevant companies after closing.

As a result, when the time came for the buyer to prepare an earn-out notice, it had no audited accounts of the acquired companies for the calendar year with which to do so. Instead, the buyer prepared the earn-out notice by reference to the audited consolidated accounts for the group (ending 30 September 2010), subtracting management account figures for the preceding three months (1 October 2009 to 31 December 2009) and then adding figures (taken from other management accounts) for the three-month period following 30 September (1 October to 31 December).[128] The dispute was over whether the notice prepared by the buyer on this basis was a valid earn-out notice pursuant to the relevant clause in the SPA.

The requirement in the SPA for the parties to use the audited accounts rather than management accounts was considered by the judge to be an important safeguard and designed to improve the reliability of the figures in the accounts.[129] The notice that was based on the management accounts was not considered a valid earn-out notice. The dispute over the amount of the earn-out payment was referred to an independent expert determination in accordance with a process set out in the SPA.

The following case returns to the problem of excluding unusual, 'one-off' or 'non-recurring' items from the earn-out basis. In this case, the parties disagreed over whether a change-of-control bonus paid to the employees of the target company prior to closing was a 'one-time, non-recurring expense', in which case it would have been excluded from the earn-out basis.

Example of a Dispute over Non-recurring Elements in Earn-Out Basis (*Comet Systems Shareholders' Agent v. MIVA*, US Court of Chancery of Delaware)[130]

The earn-out in *Comet Systems, Inc. Shareholders' Agent v. MIVA, Inc.* consisted of a combination of two financial and one non-financial earn-out targets of the acquisition target, Comet, a connected desktop software company: a 'Revenue Goal', a 'Cost Goal', and a 'Specified Software User Base Goal'. As a threshold condition to any payout on the Revenue Goal, revenue per user had to exceed the cost per user in the relevant year (defined in the SPA as operating costs excluding amortisation and one-time, non-recurring expenses). As a threshold condition to any payout on the Cost Goal, the profit per user had to be over a threshold amount in the relevant period.

A central issue was whether a change-of-control bonus paid to the employees of the target company was a 'one-time, non-recurring expense' that should be excluded from the cost basis when calculating the earn-out.

MIVA, the buyer, prepared the earn-out calculation. It calculated an earn-out payment for the year 2004 that resulted entirely from achieving the 2004 User Base Goal. For the 2004 Revenue Goal and Cost Goal, MIVA's calculation showed profit per

128. *Barratt and others v. Treatt plc* [2013] EWHC 3561 (Ch), para. 45.
129. *Ibid.*
130. *Comet Systems, Inc. Shareholders' Agent v. MIVA, Inc.* C.A. No. 2793-VCL Court of Chancery of Delaware. Decided 22 October 2008.

user below the relevant thresholds. In the underlying calculations, MIVA included a USD 800,000 bonus to Comet's employees under the merger bonus plan.

In Comet's view, the bonus payment should have been excluded from the cost per user calculation as it was a 'one-time, non-recurring expense'. MIVA argued that the bonus payment was an ordinary cost of business, as acquisition bonuses contribute to employee retention during the sale process and thus revenue generation. Further, MIVA argued that Comet had paid bonuses in the past, had treated prior bonuses as normal operating costs, and further that bonuses were common in the technology industry.

The court found that the merger bonus was a one-time, non-recurring expense to be excluded from the earn-out basis.[131]

The following case relates to a PE investor that expected to hold the target firm for a comparatively short time and agreed to share with the seller part of any excess returns that would be realised as part of the PE investor's exit.

Example of a Dispute over Excess Return Payments (*Starbev v. Interbrew*, High Court of England and Wales)[132]

In 2009, CVC Capital Partners (CVC) acquired the Dutch subsidiary of brewer Anheuser Busch (and with it the Central and Eastern European brewing businesses of Anheuser Busch) for EUR 1.5 billion, a multiple of 6.7 times EBITDA. Part of the consideration was deferred. The earn-out clause in the SPA stipulated that, on a future on-sale of the business, Anheuser Bush would receive a share of 40% of CVC's return above certain threshold levels. The thresholds were to apply in step changes over time, with increases over a four-year period after the sale. As the excess return payment, a type of earn-out, depended on the return upon a re-sale of the business, both the amount of the (initial) investment and the exit price were relevant to its calculation.

It is interesting to note how far apart the parties' perceptions of the value of the deferred part of the compensation were: the buyer considered the earn-out to be a 'low-value give', whereas the seller's investment bankers valued it between USD 200 million and USD 400 million.[133]

Soon after closing, CVC started investigating potential exit opportunities. Its efforts were successful when, at the end of 2011, a North American brewer approached CVC with an indicative bid for the business of 11 times 2011 EBITDA. CVC was looking at a successful exit opportunity. The transaction with the North American bidder closed in June 2012. The price was reported to be EUR 2.65 billion. Part of the overall consideration in this exit transaction was a convertible note of EUR 500 million.

Shortly after closing, CVC notified Anheuser Busch, the original seller, that the investment threshold (a multiple times the invested amount, where the multiple depended on the divestment date) had not been surpassed, and no excess return payment had been triggered. This led to a swift response on the part of Anheuser

131. *Comet Systems, Inc. Shareholders' Agent v. MIVA, Inc.*, http://caselaw.findlaw.com/de-court-of-chancery/1267797.html.
132. *Starbev GP Limited v. Interbrew Central European Holdings BV* [2014] EWHC 1311 (Comm).
133. *Ibid.*, paras 23 and 24.

Busch, which had assumed it would be in for a windfall. It appointed independent accountants to verify and report on the PE firm's calculations and subsequently asserted that the investment amount as stated by CVC was not correct.

In August 2013, CVC exercised its option under the convertible note and received additional consideration of EUR 500 million (less certain deductions). It paid an amount of EUR 32 million of deferred consideration. In the original seller's view, however, it was owed a total deferred consideration of approximately EUR 200 million.[134] Among the matters in dispute was whether the convertible note had been structured in a way so that the earn-out payment would be reduced (as certain thresholds would not be reached). The Court of Appeal confirmed that the dominant purpose of the convertible note transaction was to reduce the payments due to the seller.

The following is an example of an earn-out dispute over foreign currency conversion. It shows how comparatively easy it can be to avoid some earn-out disputes: had the SPA specified the date for foreign currency conversion, or a specific exchange rate, there would not have been disagreement, at least over this aspect of the earn-out.

Example of an Earn-Out Dispute over Foreign Exchange Conversion (ICC Arbitration)[135]

Two US and two Brazilian companies (the Buyers) acquired shares in a Brazilian subsidiary from two Brazilian companies and a German company (the Sellers). Part of the consideration was deferred, however the Buyers paid a USD 7 million advance on the earn-out. After closing, a dispute developed that consisted of several claims and counterclaims.

One of the counterclaims related to the exchange rate to be used to convert the USD advance into Brazilian reals, the currency in which the earn-out would ultimately be payable. The buyers argued that the exchange rate at closing should be used, whereas the sellers argued that the exchange rate should be the rate at the time the earn-out was paid (two years after the advance payment was made). The tribunal found that the appropriate exchange rate was the one at the time the earn-out payment became due, not the time of the advance payment.[136]

[2] Non-financial Metrics

Earn-outs can alternatively be linked to non-financial metrics, such as market share, regulatory approvals, clicks on a website, a product launch, the number of units sold of certain products, project or product development milestones, customer retention, or the receipt of subsidies, to name only a few. These are frequently combined with financial metrics.

134. *Ibid.*, para. 54.
135. ICC Case 14691 Final Award, in: ICC International Court of Arbitration Bulletin Vol. 24/No. 1 - 2013, p. 132. ICC 14691.
136. *Ibid.*, p. 132.

As with financial metrics, it is important to base non-financial earn-outs on metrics that cannot be easily 'managed', or manipulated. For example, once in control of the target company, a buyer may be able to influence the timing of regulatory approvals, thereby affecting an earn-out target that is linked to them. Likewise, sales volumes (units) might be distorted by 'channel stuffing', the practice of inflating sales of a period by supplying retailers with more products than they can sell, at the expense of volumes in subsequent periods that may be relevant to the earn-out.

The following example relates to the development of a project that was relocated after closing.

Example: *Deere & Company v. Exelon Generation Acquisitions* (US Superior Court of Delaware)

In 2010, Deere sold its wind energy business to Exelon for USD 860 million.[137] The assets sold included both wind farms that were already operating and wind farms in development. The SPA included total potential earn-out payments of USD 40 million, contingent upon the successful completion of certain milestones on three new projects, among them the Blissfield Wind Project which involved a USD 14 million earn-out provision.

The Blissfield Wind Project was originally intended to be developed in Lenawee County, Michigan. However, Exelon subsequently determined that, due to regulatory changes in the township, it would not be possible to develop it there. After exploring alternative sites, Exelon negotiated the relocation of the project to Gratiot County, Michigan, where it successfully developed the Beebe Wind Farm.

Exelon argued that the project in Gratiot County was a new project. It pointed out that the SPA did not provide for the relocation of the project and argued that the Blissfield Wind Project had been abandoned because it could not be completed in Lenawee County. Deere, on the other hand, argued that the Blissfield Wind Project had only been relocated, that it was not required to be built in a specific location, and that the milestones under the SPA had been met, which triggered an earn-out payment.

The court found that the project had been relocated, not abandoned, and that Deere was entitled to the earn-out payment.

[B] The Earn-Out Period

Earn-out periods are often between one and three years, occasionally up to five years, and in rare cases, even longer. In general, the longer the period, the more opportunity there is for disagreement to emerge: a long earn-out period means more changes to the business which will often increasingly less resemble the asset for which the parties originally defined the earn-out basis. As time passes, the seller will also bear increasingly less responsibility for the developments after closing.

137. *Deere & Company v. Exelon Generation Acquisitions, LLC*, C.A. No. N13C07-330 JTV CCLD https://www.casemine.com/judgement/us/5914e5d4add7b04934909070.

Changes to a business in the earn-out period can also affect the ability to measure and report earn-out metrics in a way that is consistent with what the parties intended. The following are examples of changes that may affect the earn-out basis and lead to disagreement:

- A strategic buyer integrates the target business into its group operations to achieve synergies.
- A PE sponsor merges the target business with another portfolio company's operations for similar reasons.
- A target business shares overhead functions and cost allocations with those of other companies.

Any of the circumstances above can mean that the target's basis of reporting financial information is no longer consistent with the basis before the transaction. It is important in that case to agree on a consistent pro-forma basis and define it in the SPA.

Earn-outs can be less problematic for financial (PE) buyers who do not plan to merge operations than for many strategic buyers. For strategic buyers, successful earn-outs are frequently linked to metrics that are not affected by the integration of the target entity into the new owner's operations – examples are prices charged by a specific supplier or non-financial metrics that are key drivers of the business plan.

[C] Preparation of the Earn-Out Statement

The process for the (annual) preparation of the earn-out statement and calculation has some similarities with the preparation of the completion accounts. Once the buyer (who is usually responsible for the preparation) delivers the draft earn-out statement to the seller, the seller has the opportunity to review it. The preparation and review periods need to be specified in the SPA. As the buyer is in control of the business during this time, the seller should also secure access rights to the accounting records of the target company to be able to review the earn-out statement.

If the seller agrees with the draft earn-out statement, it becomes final. If the seller takes the view that the earn-out statement has not been prepared in accordance with the terms of the SPA, then it prepares a written objection notice. Following the objection notice is a period for negotiations during which the parties attempt to reconcile their differences on the items in dispute. If they cannot reach agreement, the dispute may be submitted to an independent expert if this is the dispute resolution mechanism stipulated in the SPA (or otherwise agreed between the parties).

[D] Purchaser's Covenants

The SPA can include seller protections for the earn-out period, frequently a combination including the following: the target company will not engage in M&A activity, enter into new lines of business not related to its business activities at closing, alter its financing structure, voluntarily be dissolved or liquidated, or deviate from specified business plan measures.

[E] Conclusions

The analysis of earn-out disputes above offers some lessons as to how disputes might be avoided. For one, clear and unambiguous SPA definitions in respect of the earn-out basis remove ambiguity and areas of potential disagreement. Specific dates for foreign currency conversion, clearly defined exchange rates or clear definitions of the terms 'consideration' and 'investment projects' would have made the disputes above much less likely.

Below are further considerations that can reduce the likelihood of an earn-out dispute:

- A comparatively simple structure is generally advantageous. Complexity increases the ability to manipulate the earn-out basis. The simpler it is to measure, the less scope there is for disagreement.
- A short earn-out period is generally preferable.
- Earn-out metrics should be linked to the 'value' (of the target) that they intend to measure. Even if metrics do not correlate with value perfectly, it can be useful to think about the earn-out in such a way that its purpose is to ensure that any *incremental* change of the earn-out metric is directly and proportionately linked to a change in the value, or in purchase price.
- Another general observation is that the higher up in the income statement the earn-out performance is measured (moving from sales at the top to net income at the bottom), the fewer opportunities there are for the preparer of the financials to 'manage' the earn-out basis. Sales (or volumes sold, or prices) tend to be less dispute-prone than net profit.
- It is advisable to require the use of consistent accounting policies and to ensure access rights for the seller.
- The use of example calculations in the SPA exhibits frequently reduces ambiguity.
- Lastly, sellers should consider how best to leave as little as possible to the buyer's discretion when preparing the earn-out figures.

CHAPTER 9
Revenue Recognition

§9.01 OVERVIEW

Revenue recognition is a central theme in post-M&A disputes for two reasons.

First, it is an important link between a target company's accounting information and its valuation: additional (profitable) sales increase a period's reported earnings, and historical earnings are often the basis, or at least the starting point, of the target's valuation. In transactions where the purchase price is determined as a multiple of a measure of earnings (such as EBITDA), the incentive to overstate earnings is magnified, possibly by as much as the multiplier. Even when a buyer values the target using a DCF method, inflated historical revenues may mean expectations of future revenue are too high and, in turn, affect the buyer's valuation.

The second reason that revenue recognition often gives rise to disputes is that accounting rules require important estimates and assumptions, and this can offer the preparer of the financial statements significant discretion.

When to recognise revenue is typically associated with two key uncertainties: whether a product or service has in fact been provided and whether cash will be collected. For many years, the criteria for recognising revenue could be expressed as follows: revenue should only be recognised when (a) it is earned and (b) it is realised or realisable. This may still be useful general guidance for thinking about the issues associated with recognising revenue, although recently introduced substantially new accounting standards use different terminology (*see* below §9.02). In any event, revenue recognition continues to be a judgmental area of accounting. This creates scope for disagreement both over the timing and measurement of revenue.

Both the IASB and the FASB have recently issued new revenue recognition standards. IFRS 15 replaced almost all existing revenue recognition rules in IAS (in particular, IAS 18 and IAS 11). IFRS 15 came into effect on 1 January 2018. The new

IFRS and US GAAP revenue recognition standards are very similar. They are discussed further below in §9.02.

The basic principle in IFRS 15 is that an entity recognises revenue to depict the transfer of promised goods or services to customers in an amount that reflects the consideration to which the entity expects to be entitled in exchange for those goods or services. The standard applies to revenue recognised both at a point in time and over a period of time.

Revenue recognition over a period of time includes revenues in relation to long-term contracts. For these, management judgment and estimates can play a key role if revenue is recognised with the degree of completion (which requires judgment in respect of the extent to which the earnings process is complete). The accounting for long-term contracts and related disputes is discussed in §9.03.

Revenue recognition does not necessarily give direct rise to purchase price adjustments (with the exception of trade receivables or a net debt deduction for deferred revenue (*see* §4.04 [F])). Disputes involving revenue recognition, therefore, more often relate to warranty breach claims or intentional misrepresentation. One such dispute is *Sycamore Bidco Ltd v. Breslin & Dawson.*[138]

Example of a Dispute over Revenue Recognition (*Sycamore Bidco Limited v. Sean Breslin/Andrew Dawson*, High Court of England and Wales)

The central accounting figure in this case was 'total revenue'.[139] The buyer, and claimant, Sycamore Bidco, PE-owned, acquired Gissings Advisory Services Ltd from two sellers and later claimed damages for misrepresentation. The claim related to the erroneous inclusion of a monthly reduction in the charges by an IT supplier (granted as compensation for previous problems with the supplier's services) in the target company's reported revenue. Net income and cash flow in the relevant period were not affected by this error. However, the buyer argued - successfully - that its valuation model meant that the inflated historical revenue figure led to an overstated valuation. The SPA included the following accounts warranty:

> 4.1: The Accounts:
> 4.1.1 show a true and fair view of:
> (a) the state of affairs;
> (b) the assets and liabilities; and
> (c) the profit or losses
> of each Group Company to which they relate and the Group (on a consolidated basis) as at the Accounts Date;
> 4.1.2 have been prepared in accordance with relevant generally accepted accounting practice ... .

138. *Sycamore Bidco Limited v. Sean Breslin/Andrew Dawson* [2012] EWHC 3443 (Ch).
139. *Ibid.*, para. 116.

The relevant accounting standard was UK GAAP. The relevant definition of 'turnover' was defined as:

> The revenue resulting from exchange transactions under which a seller supplies to customers the goods or services that it is in business to provide.[140]

The judge found that the reduction should not have been included in turnover as there was no evidence that there was any un-recouped expenditure or any unremunerated provision of services at the date of the agreement, and it could not be treated as compensation in respect of such matters. Accordingly, the turnover figure was overstated. Further, the judge found that the compensation should probably have been treated as 'other income', and that including the compensation in turnover failed in a material way to present a true and fair view of the state of affairs of the company or its profit and losses.

An interesting aspect of the case is the links between historical accounting error and the correct counterfactual, on which damages are based. The discussion returns to this case below in §12.02 [B] [2].

§9.02 RECENTLY INTRODUCED REVENUE RECOGNITION STANDARDS

IFRS 15, applicable to accounting periods beginning on or after 1 January 2018, was developed in parallel with equivalent changes to US GAAP.[141] The purpose was to remove inconsistencies in revenue recognition practice, provide a more robust framework for addressing revenue issues, and improve comparability of revenue reporting across sectors and jurisdictions. The new standard continues to have important areas of judgment. For example, IFRS 15 has the following requirements:

- For long-term contracts where revenue may be recognised over time, the percentage of the performance obligation satisfied is subject to estimates, including appraisals of results achieved, surveys of work completed, milestones reached, units produced, costs incurred, or labour hours expended. Appraisals, surveys of work completed and estimates of total hours or costs of a project involve technical knowledge and often require significant judgment.
- Contracts with variable consideration or where some goods are expected to be returned by customers also require important estimates. Estimates of probabilities or amounts can be biased or simply turn out to be incorrect.

The past three years have shown that, as before, revenue recognition continues to play a prominent role in M&A-related disputes.

140. *Ibid.*, para. 216.
141. This section draws significantly from 'This is How IFRS 15 will Impact M&As', Financial Director, 32 May 2017, Phil Hersey, Heiko Ziehms and Anna Hartley.

§9.03 REVENUE RECOGNITION FOR LONG-TERM CONTRACTS

[A] Relevant Accounting Guidance

When a performance obligation is satisfied over time, a firm may, under certain conditions, recognise revenue before the obligation has been performed in full, by measuring the progress towards completion (IFRS 15.39). The degree of completion may be assessed using an 'output method' or alternatively an 'input method'.

Output methods measure revenue based on direct measurements of the value to the customer of goods or services transferred to date relative to the remaining goods or services promised under a contract. Input methods recognise revenue based on the entity's efforts or inputs to the satisfaction of a performance obligation, for example, costs incurred relative to the total expected costs for the satisfaction of that performance obligation. In both cases, the firm recognises a profit along with revenue. Two key estimates enter into reported profitability when reporting earnings: the degree of completion, and the overall contract profit (of which a fraction is realised). If these estimates are aggressive, then the recognition of revenues and profits is accelerated, a key area of disputes.

IFRS 15.4 requires a company to update its estimates continuously. In case long-term contracts are expected to be loss-making, IAS 37 requires the immediate recognition of losses.

[B] The Degree of Completion and Cost to Complete

Estimating the *degree of completion* of a large project and the remaining *costs to complete* often both require technical expertise and judgment. It is easy for bias to creep into resulting accounting estimates, especially if much depends on the reported profitability. It is easy to overestimate the degree of completion or an entire contract's expected profitability before it has been completed, only to find at its end that actual profits are much less (or that the contract was loss-making).

The unbiased exercise of judgment would mean that new information that comes to light during long-term contracts would increase or decrease contract profitability in an approximately equal number of cases (all else equal). As IFRS requires the immediate recognition of expected losses in full, a typical pattern would be one were an entity recognises losses early. In reality, the opposite may be more often the case. To illustrate, Figure 9.1 sets out cumulative profits (reported under the previous standard, IAS 11) over the lifetime of a portfolio of four long-term contracts for a target company. The analysis was performed in a subsequent warranty breach dispute that related to revenue recognition. (While each of the contracts had a different term, they are compressed (or expanded) here to show them on one timeline.)

Figure 9.1 Evolution of Reported Contract Profitability over Time

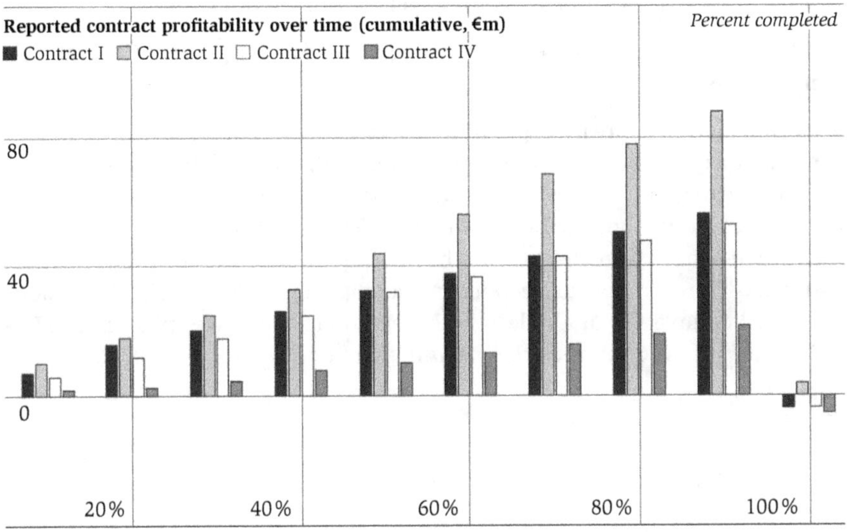

Over the terms of all four contracts, management estimates of total contract profitability were consistently too optimistic. This led to overstated profits in all periods except the last, in which the contracts were completed. Only at the end of each contract term, with no future periods available to defer losses to, did the company finally 'come clean' and report them. In three out of four cases, cumulative losses reported in that ultimate period exceeded all previously (incorrectly) reported profits.

Under the previous rules (IAS 11), earnings of long-term contracts could generally be overstated in two ways:

(1) Underestimating the costs to complete work under the contract. In this case, the 'real costs' were only reflected in the accounts when the contract had been completed; total costs turned out to be much higher than the previous estimate suggested.
(2) Overstating the degree of completion in the periods up until the last reporting period. Overestimating the degree of completion accelerates the recognition of contract profitability and can be used to move it into a financial year on which the valuation is based, even if management's estimate of overall profitability is correct (which it often is not).

Accelerated revenue recognition also means the accelerated recognition of earnings. Such earnings are not necessarily recurring, and in case they are not, they should not be extrapolated into future periods or included in the basis of valuation of a business if the basis is a historical EBITDA figure (or another measure of profitability that includes them). Identifying bias in the revenue recognition process is an important step towards removing such non-recurring elements from the basis of valuation. The type of analysis shown above is a financial due diligence tool that can serve to identify aggressive accounting in historical periods, and from there quantify appropriate adjustments to EBITDA for acquisition targets with long-term contracts.

Example of a Dispute over Revenue Recognition for Long-Term Contracts (International Arbitration)

A buyer acquired a company engaged in the construction of power plants. The buyer was in the process of building numerous plants at the time of the acquisition, and the average construction period was well over one year. The buyer valued the business using the income method (a DCF valuation). The projected cash flows used in the valuation were based on the target's business plan to which the buyer had made adjustments. The cash flow projections included a cash receipt of GBP 15 million upon the expected completion of a milestone in relation to the power plant in 2017, which would be the second year after closing at the end of 2015.

Figure 9.2 Valuation Model and Working Capital Adjustment

Enterprise Valuation

In GBP million	**2016**	**2017**	**2018**	**2019**	**2020**	**2012**	**Terminal value**
	Plan	Plan	Plan	Plan	Plan	Plan	Plan
EBIT	70	74	77	80	82	85	
Depreciation	12	12	13	14	15	15	
Change in working capital	−2	−5	−9	0	−8	−8	
Change in POC receivables	−12	(15)	−8	−8	0	0	
Change in other net operating assets	5	−12	3	−6	−2	2	
Operating cash flow	73	84	76	80	87	94	
Capital expenditure	−20	−23	−20	−20	−20	−22	
Free cash flow	53	61	56	60	67	72	78
WACC	10%	10%	10%	10%	10%	10%	10%
TV growth rate							3%
Terminal value (undiscounted)							1,114.29
Discount factor	1.00	0.91	0.83	0.75	0.68	0.62	0.56
Present value of free cash flow	53.00	55.45	46.28	45.08	45.76	44.71	628.99
Enterprise value	**919.27**						

Working Capital Adjustment

In GBP million	**Reference value**	**Closing date**	**Difference**
		Actual	
Trade receivables	70	64	−6
POC receivables	11	25	(14)
Inventory	50	57	7
Trade payables	−80	−84	−4
Net working capital	50	62	12

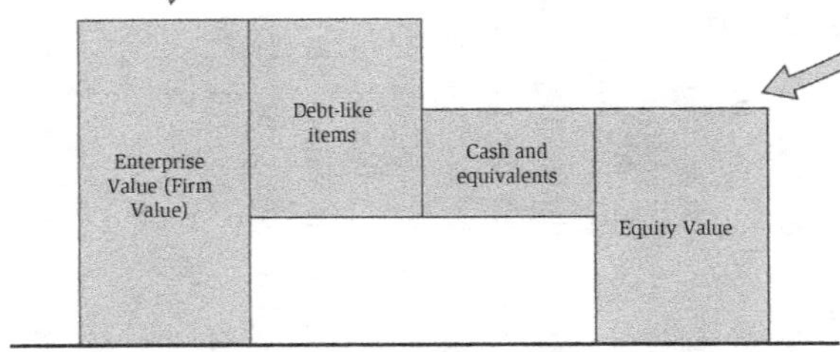

The expected cash receipt of GBP 15 million is visible in the cash flow statement in Figure 9.2 above as a reduction of the percentage of completion (POC) receivable (a credit) in 2017. This cash inflow, discounted, was therefore included in enterprise value. Further, the definition of working capital in this transaction included POC receivables. The POC receivable was included in working capital at closing (it had not yet been invoiced at that time). The expected cash inflow and the working capital item therefore related to the same underlying transaction.

Figure 9.2 shows that the POC receivable had increased the working capital at closing by GBP 14 million, which meant that closing date working capital exceeded the reference value (which did not reflect a POC receivable of this magnitude). All else being equal, this led to an additional working capital adjustment of almost GBP 14 million – however, the same amount (though discounted) was already included in enterprise value. The buyer argued (unsuccessfully) that it had not been aware that the POC receivable related to the same project for which the cash inflow had been included in the seller's projections.

The problem of double counting illustrated in the example above may appear to be a rare occurrence at first sight, but it is really not limited to POC accounting. Consider work in progress (WIP) inventory, far more common than POC receivables and similar except that WIP inventory usually does not include expected profits. In principle, the kind of double counting in the example above could occur with WIP inventory instead of a POC receivable (the difference being the profit margin). The reason this problem does not surface more frequently in disputes is that individual components of inventory are often less significant in value relative to overall working capital, and the average time for WIP to convert into cash is usually shorter. However, large construction projects that are accounted for using the (more conservative) 'completed contract' method of revenue recognition in which all revenue and profit are recognised only upon completion can mean similar risks of double counting.

In this transaction, as in many, different teams, including external advisors, had worked on the valuation and on the completion mechanism. They had not communicated sufficiently and were not aware of the risk that an item in working capital may already have been reflected in enterprise value.

CHAPTER 10

Fraud

§10.01 INTRODUCTION

Fraud can have many different meanings, depending on the context and the law that governs it. One court observed that:

> [the] law does not define fraud; it needs no definition; it is as old as falsehood and as versatile as human ingenuity.[142]

In the US alone, fraud has been described as 'infinite in variety'.[143] Fraud is defined by *Black's Law Dictionary* as:

> A knowing misrepresentation of the truth or concealment of a material fact to induce another to act to his or her detriment.[144]

The definition of the Association of Certified Fraud Examiners (ACFE) is as follows:

> any intentional or deliberate act to deprive another of property or money by guile, deception, or other unfair means.[145]

142. *Weiss v. United States*, 122 F.2d 675, 681 (5th Cir. 1941), cert. denied, 314 U.S. 687 (1941). Evolutionary biologists have suggested that the human brain evolved as a mechanism of ever more elaborate cheating on the one hand, and an ever greater ability to detect cheating by others on the other. *See, e.g.*, Richard Dawkins, *The Selfish Gene*, 40th Anniversary Edition 2016, 244.
143. *Reddaway v. Banham*, [1896] A.C. 199 (H.L.) 221 (Eng.)., cited in: That Pesky Little Thing Called Fraud: An Examination of Buyers' Insistence Upon (and Sellers' Too Ready Acceptance of) Undefined 'Fraud Carve-Outs' in Acquisition Agreements by Glenn D. West, The Business Lawyer; Vol. 69, August 2014, p. 1054.
144. Bryan Garner, ed., *Black's Law Dictionary*, 8th ed. (2004), s.v., 'fraud.'.
145. Association of Certified Fraud Examiners, What is Fraud? Fraud 101. Available at https://www.acfe.com/fraud-101.aspx.

This is a broad definition. It encompasses corruption, asset misappropriation and financial statement fraud (each with numerous subcategories).[146] In the context of M&A, financial statement fraud and corruption are perhaps the most likely to cause issues that lead to disputes.

The deliberate nature of a misrepresentation, or intent, is what distinguishes fraud from other wrongful acts.

[A] Financial Statement Fraud

The ACFE defines financial statement fraud as:

> the deliberate misrepresentation of the financial condition of an enterprise accomplished through the intentional misstatement or omission of amounts or disclosures in the financial statements to deceive financial statement users. Note that financial statement fraud, much like all types of fraud, is an intentional act.[147]

Fraud cases are frequently among the most high-profile M&A disputes, even though they are not the most common source of claims: an analysis of the cases in the sample of disputes (*see* §1.04) (though not representative of all M&A disputes) suggests that fraud was among the claims in approximately 10% of cases. According to one survey from 2017, 'seller misrepresentation' was identified as the most common area of dispute by 17% of respondents, well behind earn-out clauses and completion accounts disputes (33% each).[148]

The authors of another recent study estimated that, on average, 10% of large publicly traded firms are committing securities fraud every year(with a 95% confidence interval of 7% to 14%), and further that in normal times only one-third of corporate frauds are detected.[149]

A sample of recent cases demonstrates a variety of ways in which financial statement fraud can occur in a transaction:

(1) The acquisition of Autonomy by Hewlett-Packard (HP) in 2011. This was the second-largest acquisition in HP's history. HP executives alleged that they were misled by Autonomy and that those actions accounted for the majority of a USD 8.8 billion write-down after the transaction.[150] In a public statement, HP announced that:

146. The Fraud Tree, ACFE, https://www.acfe.com/-/media/files/acfe/pdfs/2022-rttn-fraud-tree.ashx.
147. ACFE's 2015 Fraud Examiner's Manual.
148. Grant Thornton, *A Smarter Way to Get Deals Done International Survey: Identifying International Market Practice for Equity Value Adjustments and Sale and Purchase Agreements*, November 2017, p. 18. Although the survey does not specify, 'misrepresentation' may include cases of unintentional misrepresentation, so that the share of disputes involving intentional misrepresentation is likely less than 17%.
149. Dyck, A., Morse, A. and Zingales, L. *How Pervasive Is Corporate Fraud?* Review of Accounting Studies, 2023.
150. Autonomy deal is a lesson for managers, Financial Times, 2 December 2012.

> some former members of Autonomy's management team used accounting improprieties, misrepresentations and disclosure failures to inflate the underlying financial metrics of the company, prior to Autonomy's acquisition by HP. These efforts appear to have been a wilful effort to mislead investors and potential buyers, and severely impacted HP management's ability to fairly value Autonomy at the time of the deal.[151]

In early 2018, Autonomy's former CFO was convicted of fraud in the US after being found guilty of artificially inflating the firm's financial position before it was sold. Although he appealed against the judgment, he was ultimately unsuccessful.[152]

In 2022, the English High Court held that HP had substantially succeeded in its claims against the former CEO and CFO. At the time of writing, the amount had not been communicated by the High Court, but the judge has indicated that damages will be 'substantial', though 'substantially less' than the USD 5 billion claimed by HP.[153]

In 2023, Autonomy's former CEO was extradited to the US to face criminal fraud charges relating to HP's acquisition of Autonomy.[154]

(2) The acquisition of mobile operator EE by BT from Deutsche Telekom and Orange, the French telecoms group. The transaction closed in early 2016. Part of the consideration of GBP 12.5 billion was paid in BT shares. Orange and Deutsche Telekom became shareholders of BT in 2016 as a result (Deutsche Telekom owned 12%). In early 2017, BT issued a profit warning after discovering a complex fraud in its Italian business unit that led to a GBP 530 million write-down at BT. This triggered a decline in BT's share price in the first half of 2017 by almost 25%.[155] Deutsche Telekom wrote down its share in BT by EUR 2.2 billion and subsequently by a further EUR 1.1 billion. BT subsequently struck a GBP 225 million settlement that ruled out further legal disputes with Orange and Deutsche Telekom.[156]

The case is similar in at least one aspect to The *Hut Group Ltd v. Nobahar-Cookson*[157] (discussed further below): in both cases, the consideration consisted (in part) of shares in the buyer's group, and the sellers alleged after closing that financial statement fraud had occurred (but that the fraud

151. HP Issues Statement Regarding Autonomy Impairment Charge, HP, 20 Nov. 2012, https://mondovisione.com/news/hp-issues-statement-regarding-autonomy-impairment-charge-hp-internal-investiga/.
152. Bloomberg 27 August 2020, Autonomy's Ex-CFO Loses Appeal over Wire Fraud Convictions, https://news.bloomberglaw.com/white-collar-and-criminal-law/autonomys-ex-cfo-loses-appeal-over-wire-fraud-convictions.
153. [White and Case, 27 May 2022, *HP v. Autonomy: The 'fake it' 'till we make it' start-up culture on trial*, https://www.whitecase.com/publications/alert/hp-v-autonomy-fake-it-till-we-make-it-start-culture-trial].
154. *Autonomy founder Mike Lynch extradited to US*, Financial Times, 23 May 2023, available at https://www.ft.com/content/4c933c58-b129-4b80-80e7-b198a9d9d5b5.
155. Financial Times, Deutsche Telekom takes further EUR 1.1 billion hit from BT stake, 3 August 2017.
156. *Ibid.*
157. *The Hut Group Ltd v. Nobahar-Cookson and another* [2016] EWCA Civ 128, discussed in §10.03.

dated back to before the transaction). In both cases, this meant that the consideration shares – the acquisition currency – were worth less than the seller had expected.

(3) The acquisition of ERA Mining Machinery Ltd by Caterpillar Inc in 2012 for USD 677 million. ERA Mining Machinery Ltd was the holding company for Zhengzhou Siwei Mechanical & Electrical Equipment Manufacturing Co Ltd, one of China's biggest makers of hydraulic coal-mine roof supports. The purchase was billed as a coup for Caterpillar whose advisors received an award for 'cross-border deal of the year'.[158] Shortly after closing, Caterpillar announced that it had discovered 'deliberate, multi-year, coordinated accounting misconduct' at Siwei, and wrote down goodwill by USD 580 million, or 86% of the value of the deal.[159]

(4) The Special Purpose Acquisition Company (SPAC) boom of 2020 came with significant scrutiny by regulators and numerous high-profile lawsuits. SPACs were used as a way of taking early-stage companies public. Among the first charged by the SEC were a Russian-founded space start-up, Momentus Inc (the acquisition target), Stable Road Acquisition Company (the SPAC), and two executives. The charges related to misleading claims about Momentus' technology ahead of the acquisition. Momentus allegedly falsely told potential investors that it had successfully tested its propulsion technology in space and made other misleading statements in public filings.[160] Stable Road Acquisition Company was also charged on the basis that it had failed its due diligence obligations to its investors. Total penalties amounted to more than USD 8 million, alongside other conditions on Momentus and the transaction.

Financial statement fraud often relates to intentional misrepresentations by the seller or by the management of the target, although misrepresentations can also be made by the buyer (*see* the discussion of *The Hut Group Ltd v. Nobahar-Cookson* below). As a consequence of a seller's misrepresentations, a buyer may discover after closing that the target business has a lower earnings potential than the information the buyer received prior to signing suggested, or that there are previously unknown liabilities that the buyer would have reflected in the price had they been disclosed.

[B] Corruption

Corruption is another type of occupational fraud which can be relevant in M&A. The ACFE distinguishes four major categories: bribery, conflicts of interest, illegal gratuities, and economic extortion. Of these, bribery has received significant recent coverage

158. The M&A Atlas Awards Asia Pacific Middle Markets, 8 November 2012, Category: Asia Pacific Deal Award Winnder Cross-Border Deal of the Year – Large.
159. Special Report: How Caterpillar got bulldozed in China, Reuters World News, 23 Jan. 2014, https://www.reuters.com/article/us-caterpillar-china-special-report/special-report-how-caterpillar-got-bulldozed-in-china-idUSBREA0M03720140123.
160. https://www.sec.gov/news/press-release/2021-124.

in the media as enforcement of anti-foreign corruption statutes has been stepped up in many jurisdictions.

Penalties for bribery and corruption can be severe under the Foreign Corrupt Practices Act in the US, the UK Bribery Act, or other anti-corruption legislation. An example is the acquisition of Amec Foster Wheeler by Wood Group in October 2017, both multinational engineering and project management groups. In March 2017, it was announced that Wood Group would acquire Amec Foster Wheeler for USD 2.2 billion.[161] On 11 July 2017, the UK Serious Fraud Office announced it was investigating Amec Foster Wheeler and its predecessor companies for suspected historical offences of bribery, corruption and related offences.[162] The case was settled in July 2021 with a Deferred Prosecution Agreement, which included financial penalties and costs of USD 177 million globally.

§10.02 THE FRAUD TRIANGLE

[A] Introduction

The research cited above[163] suggested that, on average, 10% of large publicly traded firms are committing securities fraud every year – even without the pressures of a transaction. The same research indicates that in normal times only about one-third of frauds in public companies are detected.[164] This makes it likely that many dealmakers underestimate the risk of fraud, or, in in Bayesian terminology, the 'base rate' of fraud cases. It is therefore important for acquirers to be vigilant to potential fraud, and efforts to increase the detection probability during the due diligence phase are usually a good investment of time. They start with an understanding of the conditions in which fraud is more likely to occur.

The fraud triangle is a framework that can help structure the analysis of fraud risk. It was first introduced by the American sociologist Donald Cressey.[165] Cressey's original hypothesis from which the fraud triangle originated is as follows:

> Trusted persons become trust violators when they conceive of themselves as having a financial problem which is non-shareable, are aware this problem can be secretly resolved by violation of the position of financial trust, and are able to apply to their own conduct in that situation verbalizations which enable them to adjust their conceptions of themselves as trusted persons with their conceptions of themselves as users of the entrusted funds or property.[166]

The factors identified by Cressey that cause someone to commit this type of fraud are depicted in Figure 10.1.

161. https://www.bbc.co.uk/news/business-39253416.
162. https://www.sfo.gov.uk/2017/07/11/sfo-confirms-investigation-amec-foster-wheeler/.
163. *See supra* n 11.
164. *Ibid.*
165. Donald R. Cressey, *Other People's Money*, 30 (Montclair: Patterson Smith, 1973).
166. *Ibid.*

Figure 10.1 The Fraud Triangle

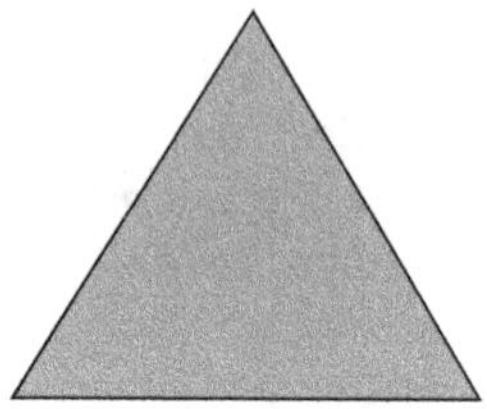

Each of these factors, and how it might arise in an M&A context, is explored further below.

[B] Pressure

The first element of the fraud triangle is pressure. Anyone who has worked on M&A transactions knows that the parties are subject to a variety of pressures: sellers will generally be motivated to present the target in the best possible light. As the transaction progresses, this motivation can turn into pressure to go beyond 'gilding the lily', especially when new information suggests a downward trend in trading (relative to the bidder's expectations). Disappointing earnings numbers, or the unexpected loss of a key customer, can threaten the deal or at a minimum change the dynamics in negotiations.

Experienced sellers (and their advisers) will think carefully about the way to set expectations and the release of news during the negotiations – honestly, in real time, but in a way that allows them, to the extent possible, to maintain momentum. However, sellers who do not manage the process thoughtfully may feel there is never a good time to 'come clean' and disclose adverse developments, and a downward spiral can begin in which a seller continues to fail to provide important information, thereby misrepresenting the target's trading in order to push the deal over the line. This is a risk even where a seller does not originally start out with an intention to deceive.

This dynamic features in many M&A deals where buyers subsequently claim damages for fraudulent misrepresentation. For example, in *Erlson Precision Holdings Ltd v. Hampson Industries plc*, the buyer learned on the day following the sale that a key customer was terminating all business with the target.[167] This meant that various forecasts which the seller had provided to Erlson over a period of ten months prior to the transaction were over-optimistic. The seller's CEO had been made aware of the customer's decision much earlier. The seller was found guilty of fraudulent misrepresentation.

167. *Erlson Precision Holdings Limited (formerly GG132 Ltd) v. Hampson Industries plc* [2011] EWHC 1137 (Comm), 20 April 2011.

Pressures can also build from investment deadlines. SPACs, for example, generally have two years to complete a transaction or face liquidation (though some have opted for shorter periods). As the deadline to invest approaches, intense pressure to identify targets can build.[168] Similarly, private equity firms can come under pressure to deploy funds within limited fund terms.

The principals working on a transaction may be the first to feel these and other pressures during a disposal process. However, pressure can be passed on to the target management, and down to the seller's or the target's accountants, or outside advisors who prepare financial information or assist in the sale process. Exit bonuses, success fees or the chance of repeat work may all depend on achieving a successful disposal.

In some acquisitions, the buyer's shares are used as the 'acquisition currency'. This can lead to pressure on the buyer to keep the value of their shares up. For example, in *The Hut Group Ltd v. Nobahar-Cookson*, discussed below at §10.03, the sellers received consideration shares valued on the basis of the buyer's financials (which later turned out to be misstated). The buyer's senior management allegedly put its finance team under pressure to report figures that were consistent with the 'growth story' the buyer wished to present to the outside world (whether or not it reflected reality).[169]

[C] Opportunity

The second element of the fraud triangle is opportunity. The opportunity for a seller to commit fraud in an M&A process often arises from information asymmetry: it is usually the seller who knows far more about the business, who decides what to disclose and when, and who can influence the accounting choices of the target company before closing.

Buyers attempt to level the playing field by conducting due diligence, but there are always limits to access to information before signing. Access is usually more restricted in competitive auction processes in seller-friendly markets. In addition, sellers who intend to deceive typically make every effort to ensure that access is even more restricted than necessary. Overly restrictive access, aggressive responses when faced with legitimate information requests, or an exaggerated sense of urgency can be 'red flags' for fraud, *see* below at [§10.03]).

For example, in *Erlson Precision Holdings Ltd v. Hampson Industries plc*, the seller not only withheld information about a customer loss but, in fact, actively tried to keep the buyer from learning of this development, asking the customer to keep the information confidential.[170]

168. The 'merge or lose' dilemma has led aggrieved investors to claim that sponsors rushed due diligence, inflated forecasts and failed to disclose important risks. *See* the Financial Times, FT Alphaville, *The special purpose acquisition company fallout is going to be spac-tacular*, 11 January 2023.
169. *See* below §10.03.
170. *David v. Goliath*, New Law Journal, 22.7.2011, Available at https://www.russell-cooke.co.uk/media/1898/seller-beware-the-dangers-of-withholding-information-july-2011.pdf.

[D] Rationalisation

The third element of the fraud triangle is rationalisation. This is the ability of the person who commits fraud to convince him- or herself that their actions are acceptable or justifiable.

In transactions, rationalisation can develop from a (tacit) understanding that sellers are expected to 'dress up the bride', or that all sellers 'manage earnings' and that the onus is on the buyer to ask the relevant questions to identify aggressive accounting. Sellers also tell themselves that the sums involved are immaterial or that a customer who announces its intention to leave does not really mean it.[171]

It is generally true that sellers do their best to present the target company in the best possible light, and purchasers in most situations accept that the lily is often gilded. In *The Hut Group Ltd v. Nobahar-Cookson and another*, the buyer submitted that 'there is nothing wrong in principle with presenting your numbers in the best possible way, though of course you must do so honestly rather than dishonestly'.[172] However, intentional misstatements are a different matter.

§10.03 RED FLAGS

The detection of fraud is not part of the standard scope of buy-side financial due diligence. Only when 'red flags' emerge during or after the negotiations does this sometimes trigger further analysis by the buyer.[173] If this reaches a point where the buyer engages forensic experts to assess the risk of fraud, then the transaction no longer follows a normal process.

The following is a list of common 'red flags' to look out for:

(1) Analysis of the financial statements:
   (i) sales or profits that do not turn into cash – red flags include deteriorating collection ratios, receivables ageing, and sustained cash outflow from operations despite profit growth;
   (ii) pressures on profitability – red flags include declining profit margins and a low level of provisions and impairments (indicated, for example, by increasing inventory turnover);
   (iii) straight line or 'hockey stick' earnings/profit growth;
   (iv) central adjustments/consolidation entries in group accounts that increase earnings and do not eliminate intercompany transactions – for example, the capitalisation of expenditures at group level. This setup can enable a small group of executives / central management to inflate

171. *Evlson Precision Holdings Ltd v. Hampson Industries plc*, CMS eAlerts, Share sale unwound for fraudulent misrepresentation, 11.10.2011, available at http://www.cms-lawnow.com/ealerts/2011/10/share-sale-unwound-for-fraudulent-misrepresentation.
172. *The Hut Group Ltd v. Nobahar-Cookson and another* [2014] EWHC 3842 (QB), para. 253.
173. An analysis of fraud cases shows, however, that many buyers ignore even multiple 'red flags'.

earnings without the involvement of local management and local accountants;
   (v) high financing costs compared to reported debt levels;
   (vi) opaque, expensive borrowings (which are necessary as profits do not turn into cash) that conceal the true indebtedness, for example, using off balance sheet structures.

(2) Analysis of organisational structure:
   (i) impending/recent flotation or buy-out;
   (ii) high level of related party transactions;
   (iii) unnecessarily complicated corporate structure or financing arrangements;
   (iv) dominant, overbearing senior leadership that operates outside of normal corporate governance structures and internal controls;
   (v) a weak finance function;
   (vi) a culture of consistently aggressive accounting; and
   (vii) involvement of non-financial management in accounting functions and with accounting and financial decisions.

(3) The sales process:
   (i) an overly aggressive reaction to legitimate questions; seller/target management constantly threatening to walk away from the deal;
   (ii) unusually/unnecessarily restrictive access;
   (iii) an 'artificial' and exaggerated sense of urgency;
   (iv) missing documentation.

Acts of fraud should be distinguished from the triggers that lead to their discovery. One important trigger is often the unexpected need for liquidity soon after closing. If this catches a buyer by surprise, then it raises further questions and post-closing due diligence. At that stage, the buyer has full access to the target's financials, and loyalties have likely shifted to the new owner. However, in the absence of a triggering event, there is often no post-closing review or effort to understand whether fraud was committed. It is, therefore, safe to assume that many frauds remain undetected, and indeed the statistics bear this out.[174]

Example: *The Hut Group Ltd v. Nobahar-Cookson and another* (High Court of England and Wales)[175]

In May 2011, The Hut Group Ltd (THG), acquired an online sports nutrition business known as 'MyProtein', the trading name of a company that was owned by the defendants (Cend). The purchase price amounted to GBP 58 million, of which GBP 30 million was paid in cash and GBP 28 million in shares in THG. The sellers were the founders of the MyProtein business and the family trust.

174. *See supra* n. 11.
175. *The Hut Group Ltd v. Nobahar-Cookson and another* [2014] EWHC 3842 (QB).

The SPA included sellers' warranties in relation to Cend's management accounts as well as warranties by THG, the buyer, that its draft statutory accounts gave a 'true and fair view' of its state of affairs, assets and liabilities and profit and loss as at 31 December 2010 (the THG Accounts Warranty), and that THG's management accounts 'fairly presented' its assets and liabilities and profits and losses for the period from 31 December 2010 to 31 March 2011 (the THG Management Accounts Warranty). The SPA limited the parties' liabilities for claims for breaches of warranty 'save insofar as it results from the fraud of [THG]' or '... the fraud of any of [the sellers]'. The relevant limitation was GBP 7.24 million for claims by the sellers against THG. The sellers' warranties will be discussed in Chapter 12.

Shortly after closing, THG started to prepare an initial public offering (IPO). As part of the IPO preparations, THG's group audit firm carried out a half-year audit of THG's accounts. In September 2011, it came to the auditors' attention that certain documents provided to it in its capacity as the group auditors had been false: the Financial Controller had been manipulating monthly profitability by overstating offline stock and debtors, and underreporting liabilities. An initial review revealed a number of occasions where it was apparent that the external auditor had been misled.

The external auditor then reviewed the audit of the preceding year-end, 31 December 2010, and identified a number of further issues. Before corrections, EBITDA had been GBP 4.1 million; after corrections, the restated figure was an EBITDA loss of GBP 1.5 million. There was also an adjustment to the 2011 management accounts, though no definitive revised accounts for the quarter were in evidence. The IPO process was halted.

In summary: a series of documents had been falsified during the audits of the year ended 31 December 2010 and the six months ended 30 June 2011, and the external auditors had also been misled as to the recoverability of certain assets and the extent of unrecorded liabilities. The three key areas of manipulation were:

(1) offline stock: On 31 December 2010, an entry had been booked to recognise GBP 1.6 million of 'offline' stock which was either double counted within the system stock balance, or which had been sold prior to 31 December;
(2) unrecorded liabilities: There were a number of unrecorded liabilities on 31 December 2010. Members of the finance function (including the wider purchase ledger team) had falsified a number of supplier statements and withheld certain invoices and supplier statements from the external auditors. The Financial Controller had also released a significant number of smaller accruals which would be below the audit materiality threshold; and
(3) recoverability of debtors: On 31 December 2010, a number of debtors were either recognised early or were not recoverable, despite formal representations from senior members of the finance team to the contrary.

It was not in dispute that THG was in breach of buyer's warranties, but whether fraud was attributable to the company (which would have effectively removed the contractual limitations of liability). While THG accepted that the breach of warranty was a result of the fraud of the Financial Controller, it submitted that his fraud was not to be attributed to THG. In its view, therefore; a contractual cap on damages of GBP 7.24 million applied, whereas, in the sellers' view, the fraud was to be attributed to THG, and the cap did not apply.[176]

The judge, commenting that there was an atmosphere within the finance department which allowed fraud to flourish, found that the fraud was to be attributed to THG. As a consequence, the contractual limitation of the claim did not apply.

176. *Ibid.*, para 285.

CHAPTER 11

Damages Valuation in M&A Disputes

§11.01 INTRODUCTION

The discussion so far was primarily concerned with the 'mechanics' of transactions and purchase price adjustments, earn-outs and fraud. This and the following chapter address the measurement of damages if a breach of contract (often the SPA) has occurred or other obligations have been breached.[177]

The basic compensatory principle is that a monetary award should restore the claimant to an economic position equivalent to the position but for the breach.[178] This has been expressed as follows:

> [A]s regards pecuniary loss, the claimant should be awarded the total of revenue (less costs) that would have been earned, less the total of revenue (less costs) actually earned.[179]

'Revenue' and 'costs' are accounting terms, and a claim for 'lost profits' references an accounting metric (profit).[180]

The measurement of damages in M&A disputes often starts from accounting figures. How these figures relate to 'value' – the valuation-relevance of accrual accounting – often plays a key role in the measurement of damages. It is the link between an alleged misrepresentation of the financial statements, or misstatements of

177. The discussion of 'value' is equally relevant to non-contractual claims. The difference to contractual claims, as it relates to damages, often arises from different counterfactuals. *See* §11.05 [A].
178. *See, e.g., Stephenson Blake (Holdings) v. Streets Heaver Ltd [2001]* Lloyd's Rep PN 44 at para 159.
179. Adam Kramer, *The Law of Contract Damages*, 496 (2nd ed., Hart Publishing, 2017).
180. The same is true for 'diminution in income'. *See, e.g., MMP GmbH v. Antal International Network Ltd* [2011] EWHC 1120 (Comm) at para. 82. In *Macquarie Internationale Investments Limited v. Glencore UK Ltd*, the judge explained that the accounts warranty, as its title indicates, '... is concerned with accounts, not with retrospectively perceived commercial value'. The dispute is discussed below in §12.01 [A].

individual elements of the financial statements (or their omission), and damages. The commercial basis of value that usually underlies the measurement of damages has not yet been discussed. This is the subject of this chapter.

The discussion in §2.01 [A] above already observed that the accounting measurement of assets and liabilities is different from their commercial value, but that the two are connected. It had linked the accounting equation to the relationship between firm value and the value of the claims on the firm, and observed that the two equations were taken from different contexts, but that they were of the same form. The difference was in the measurement basis.

Where does this difference arise? The starting point is that accounting is not a natural phenomenon,[181] but based on rules created by standard-setters or lawmakers. For example, the accounting principle of conservatism means that earnings recognition is deferred until uncertainty has been substantially resolved, whereas future losses may need to be recognised in the financial statements at an earlier and more uncertain stage. Conservatism in accounting is an objective that standard-setters or lawmakers who created the relevant accounting standards considered desirable. Conservative accounting tends to lead to outcomes that understate the book values of net assets relative to their commercial values.[182] Hence a difference.

While accounting rests on the authority of a standard setter or lawmaker, valuation does not. Value is not 'by fiat', not legislated or decreed by authority (other than secondary effects such as taxes that impact value). The correction of an accounting error and the question of damages are different matters: the wronged party is not restored to the position but-for an accounting warranty breach simply by receiving a corrected balance sheet. It is also usually not restored to the but-for position by an award of dollar-for-dollar compensation for the book value of an accounting error (unless that monetary amount coincides with the economic measure of damages).

It is not the intention here to summarise the literature on the relationship between accounting figures and value, or fundamental analysis, only to focus on matters relevant to damages valuation.[183] A key idea at the intersection of accounting information and value is that accounting information facilitates the valuation of firms or other assets. Market participants observe financial information, but it has been said that they 'see through' the accounting.[184] What markets look to is (presumably)

181. *See* the discussion in Stephen H. Penman, *On Comparing Cash Flow and Accrual Accounting Models for Use in Equity Valuation*, Contemporary Accounting Research Vol. 18, No. 4, Winter 2001, 681–692.

182. Stephen H. Penman, *Valuation Models: An Issue of Accounting Theory* (Columbia Business School, Columbia University, 2, in *Routledge Companion to Financial Accounting Theory* (Routledge 2015)).

183. A starting point in the literature to understand the relevance of accounting to valuation is Benjamin Graham, *The Intelligent Investor*, first published in 1949, rev. ed. 2005, HarperCollins New York, which outlines many of the ideas of fundamental analysis. *See also*: James A. Ohlson, *Earnings, Book Value, and Dividends in Equity Valuation*, Contemporary Accounting Research 11, No. 2 (Spring 1995), 661–687.

184. *See* the discussion in Stephen H. Penman, *Accounting for Value*, Columbia Business School Publishing, 2010, p. ix.

information about future cash flows.[185] In the process, they convert accrual accounting information into information that is relevant to the valuation. Accounting information enables markets to do that: it produces a representation of the underlying reality that is to be valued.[186] Indeed, it is an important purpose of the financial statements to help analysts and investors understand the commercial value of a business by providing information that aids in forecasting future payoffs.[187] Accrual accounting provides a basis for this. This is why the accounts have been called the 'building blocks of quantum'.[188]

So far, the commercial basis of value has not yet been defined. The chapter starts with a of discussion of what valuation models measure (§11.02). On the basis established there, it goes on to provide an overview of valuation standards (§11.03) and different approaches to damages valuation (§11.04). Lastly, the chapter addresses certain aspects of damages valuation that are common to M&A-related disputes, including the question of value versus price (§11.05 [A]), aspects of the cost of capital (§11.05 [B]), and taxes in damages valuation (§11.05 [C]).

§11.02 WHAT DO VALUATION MODELS MEASURE?

All rationalist valuation models start from the premise that individuals are concerned with consumption and that cash buys consumption.[189] An investor gives up consumption today in the expectation of more consumption in the future (in times of positive returns). Investment decisions represent a tradeoff between the two, and they are therefore forward-looking: today's value is the present value of the returns the investment is expected to generate.

Cash returns expected in the future must be discounted for the time value of money and the risk of not receiving them. More recent developments in behavioural finance notwithstanding,[190] it is fair to say that this rationalist view is a non-controversial basis of damages valuation in disputes.[191]

---

185. *Ibid.* Note that the market is not directly observing future cash in- and outflows, but rather information that allows their forecasting.
186. Similar to an eyewitness account of an event that is a source of information about the event. Whether the eyewitness is truthful in his or her description of the event does not affect the event itself.
187. Stephen H. Penman, [same as *supra* n. 181: *On Comparing Cash Flow and Accrual Accounting Models for Use in Equity Valuation*].
188. Gervase MacGregor, Andrew Maclay, and David Mitchell, *Overview of Damages and Accounting Basics* in John A. Trenor (ed.), *The Guide to Damages in International Arbitration*, 160 (2nd ed., Global Arbitration Review 2017). For example, the IASB's Conceptual Framework, which sets out the fundamental concepts for financial reporting, includes the following statement: 'The objective of general purpose financial reporting is to provide financial information about the reporting entity that is useful to existing and potential investors, lenders and other creditors in making decisions relating to providing resources to the entity' (Conceptual Framework, 1.2).
189. Stephen H. Penman, *Valuation Models: An Issue of Accounting Theory* (Columbia Business School, Columbia University, 2, in *Routledge Companion to Financial Accounting Theory* (Routledge 2015).
190. Robert J. Schiller, *Narrative Economics*, 277 (Princeton University Press, 2019).
191. Even where one or more parties in a transaction did not act rationally and, *e.g.*, the buyer overpaid (*see* §12.03 [C]), such nonrational, or boundedly rational outcomes only mean that

The discussion below is limited to the topics that are most likely to be of relevance to quantum experts in M&A disputes. It is not the intention of this book to summarise the literature on valuation and capital asset pricing models.[192]

§11.03 STANDARDS OF VALUE

[A] Introduction

Contentious valuations often require specific assumptions as to what to include in value. For example, these can relate to the nature of the counterfactual or whether to include synergies in the valuation. A practical approach to these questions can be found in the application of valuation standards.[193] In the context of disputes, standards of value can be viewed as conventions that capture a set of assumptions used for the measurement of value.[194] This chapter discusses the standards of value commonly encountered in M&A disputes.

[B] Fair Market Value

Fair market value is among the most commonly used valuation standards in disputes.[195] It has been defined as:

> [T]he price, expressed in terms of cash equivalents, at which property would change hands between a hypothetical willing and able buyer and a hypothetical willing and able seller, acting at arm's length in an open and unrestricted market, when neither is under compulsion to buy or sell and when both have reasonable knowledge of the relevant facts.[196]

---

the purchase price may not be the same as value, not necessarily that the damages valuation should replicate that outcome or lead to similar nonrational outcome.

192. For further reading on valuation approaches more generally, *see, e.g.*, Elizabeth A. Evans, Joseph J. Galanti, and Daniel G. Lentz, *Developing Damages Theories and Models*, in Roman L. Weil, Daniel G. Lentz and David P. Hoffman (eds), *Litigation Services Handbook* (5th ed., Wiley, 2012).
193. Also called the 'basis of value'. International Valuation Standards 2017 IVS 104 Bases of Value.
194. Note that the application of a standard of value is different from value being prescribed by a standard setter or legislated by a lawmaker. Valuation standards essentially tell the valuer what counterfactual to use, or whether to include or omit certain components in the valuation, such as synergies. In the context of damages valuation, these conventions can be useful to reflect legal considerations.
195. *See* Weil, Lentz and Hoffman *supra* n. 192, at 10.6., where it is called '*the most commonly used and accepted business valuation standard*'. In M&A-related disputes, *see e.g.*, *iSOFT Group Plc v. Misys Holdings Ltd. & Anor* [2002] EWHC 2094 (Ch) in which the SPA required the seller to offer to sell to the buyer, iSOFT, '*after-acquired competing businesses for a consideration equal to the then fair market value of such business*' (para. 4); *LBI EHF v. Raiffeisen Bank International AG* [2018] EWCA Civ 719.
196. *International Glossary of Business Valuation Terms*, American Society of Appraisers, ASA Business Valuation Standards, 2009.

Similarly, a definition provided by the US Supreme Court is as follows:

> [T]he price at which the property would change hands between a willing buyer and a willing seller, neither being under any compulsion to buy or to sell and both having reasonable knowledge of relevant facts.[197]

Both definitions of fair market value refer to a price agreed between a hypothetical willing buyer and seller in a transaction (as opposed to specific, identified parties). This price can be different from the price agreed in an actual transaction between specific parties, for a number of reasons: a specific seller may be forced to divest in a 'distressed' sale at a very low price. Or an acquirer may realise synergies from combining the acquired operation with its own, whereas similar benefits would not be available to a hypothetical, generic acquirer. Synergies that are unique to one particular buyer are generally included under the fair value standard (*see* below [C]) but not the fair market value standard.

Both definitions of 'fair market value' are also similar to the International Valuation Standards (IVS) definition of 'market value' (discussed below in section [D]), and some, therefore, consider fair market value to correspond to the IVS definition of 'market value'.[198]

[C] Fair Value

It is necessary to distinguish the term 'fair value' as it is used in valuation standards in a corporate finance sense (where it is nowadays usually referred to as 'equitable value')[199] from its use in accounting standards.

[1] Equitable Value

The equitable value measure is relevant to many types of disputes that relate to the acquisition or disposal of shares. An authoritative source is the International Valuation Standards Council (IVSC). The IVSC defines the term Equitable Value as:

> [T]he estimated price for the transfer of an asset or liability between identified knowledgeable and willing parties that reflects the respective interests of those parties.[200]

In contrast to both 'fair market value' and 'market value', the definition of 'equitable value' references specific, identified parties and their particular interests and circumstances.

---

197. *United States v. Cartwright*, 411 U.S. 546 (1973). This definition is also used by the US Internal Revenue Service, Regulation §20.2031-1.
198. For example, *see* Haberman and Perks, *Overview of Methodologies for Assessing Fair Market Value*, Global Arbitration Review, *The Guide to Damages in International Arbitration*, 3rd ed., 2018, 177. *See* below in §11.03 [D] for further discussion.
199. The International Valuation Standards issued in 2017 use the term 'equitable value'; previous versions used 'fair value'.
200. International Valuation Standards (IVS) 2017, 104 para. 50.

[2] 'Fair Value' in Accounting

The accounting meaning of 'fair value' can be relevant wherever there is disagreement over the fair value accounting basis of an asset or liability. This can be the case in completion accounts disputes. An example is *Mihail Tartsinis v. Navona Management Company* (the dispute discussed in §3.04 [A] above).[201]

The authoritative source of definition in an accounting context is the relevant accounting standards-setter. In IFRS, the term 'fair value' is defined by the IASB as:

> The price that would be received to sell an asset or paid to transfer a liability in an orderly transaction between market participants at the measurement date.[202]

This definition can raise complex questions in relation to the premise of a valuation (whether stand-alone or in combination with other assets or liabilities), the condition and location of the asset, the principal market, and estimating fair value when there has been a significant decrease in the volume or level of market activity.[203] IFRS 13 introduces a fair value hierarchy that ranks the inputs that might be used in the valuation:

- Level 1: Unadjusted quoted prices for identical assets and liabilities in active markets.
- Level 2: Other observable inputs for the asset or liability, such as quoted prices in active markets for similar assets or liabilities, or quoted prices for identical assets or liabilities in markets which are not active.
- Level 3: Unobservable inputs developed by an entity using the best information available where there is little or no market activity for the asset or liability at the measurement date.

The standard-setter prefers observable market prices wherever available over the preparer's estimates. Where available, Level 1 is therefore the preferable method, followed by other observable inputs (Level 2). Where such inputs are not available, fair value can be based on unobservable inputs (Level 3). Examples of assets for which there may not be observable inputs because there is no active market include certain long-dated derivatives (such as currency and interest rate swaps), and cash-generating units.[204]

The use of Level 3 inputs is sometimes labelled 'mark-to-model' accounting. It has been criticised in academic research[205] on the basis that, among other things, reliance on managerial assumptions in the valuation process can mean significant

201. *Mihail Tartsinis v. Navona Management Company* [2015] EWHC 57 (Comm). The court stated in para. 45: '*For present purposes, the concept of "fair value" can be treated as synonymous with "market value".*'
202. IFRS 13.
203. Applying IFRS 13 Fair Value Measurement, EY, November 2012, 21, 23, 24, 26, 46, 62.
204. *Ibid.*, 146.
205. Kalin Kolev, 'Do Investors Perceive Marking-to-Model as Marking-to-Myth? Early Evidence from FAS 157 Disclosure', Working Paper (NYU Stern School of Business 2009), with further references.

discretion and opening the door to intentional bias, rendering these mark-to-model estimates potentially misleading.[206] A similar concern was expressed by the investor Warren Buffett:

> Errors will usually be honest, reflecting only the human tendency to take an optimistic view of one's commitments ... [O]ften there is no real market ... and 'mark-to-model' is utilized ... In extreme cases, mark-to-model degenerates into what I would call mark-to-myth.[207]

Given the discretion that goes into Level 3 inputs, this is an area of potential dispute when accounting figures are used as the basis of a purchase price adjustment.

[D] Market Value

The IVS define the term market value as:

> The estimated amount for which an asset or liability should exchange on the valuation date between a willing buyer and a willing seller in an arm's length transaction, after proper marketing and where the parties had each acted knowledgeably, prudently and without compulsion.[208]

This definition is similar, though not identical, to that of the US Internal Revenue Service's definition of 'fair market value', and fair market value is considered by some experts to correspond to the IVS-defined 'market value'.[209] However, it has been suggested by those who argue that there is a difference between 'fair market value' and 'market value' that market prices are not necessarily always 'fair'.[210]

§11.04 VALUATION APPROACHES

[A] Introduction

There are generally three approaches used to value a company, an ownership interest, or any other asset. These approaches are generally also available for the measurement of damages. However, as the discussion below will show, there can be differences in how they are used in contentious and non-contentious valuations. Each approach is discussed below.

---

206. *Ibid.*, with further references.
207. Berkshire Hathaway Annual Letter to Shareholders 2002.
208. IVS 104, para. 30.
209. *See* Haberman and Perks, *supra* n. 198, at 177.
210. Herfried Wöss et al., *Damages in International Arbitration under Complex Long-Term Contracts*, Oxford International Arbitration Series (Oxford University Press 2014) 261 who state, *e.g.*, that '*while during* [the financial crisis of 2007 to 2009] *stock market prices properly reflected the economic conditions of the period, they did not satisfy the conditions to be called fair market values*'. It is not clear however what price level would have led the authors to conclude that market values were 'fair' at the time, or why.

[B] The Income Approach

[1] Overview

The most common form of the income approach is the DCF method.[211] The income that it discounts in order to get to enterprise value is usually free cash flow. An alternative is the Residual Income Method (RIM) which discounts accrual earnings, though it is far less commonly used in damages valuation.

Both the DCF method and the RIM are based on the idea (discussed above in §11.02) that the value of an asset is equal to the present value of the future cash flows it is expected to return.[212]

According to a 2015 PwC survey of published international arbitration awards, DCF and other income approaches were the most common valuation methodologies accepted by tribunals.[213] A recent update to the study concluded that 'Tribunals have become increasingly comfortable with DCF methodologies over the years but remain unwilling to accept valuations which they consider are based on overly speculative data.'[214]

Cases in which tribunals did not accept the income method primarily related to new ventures that were considered 'too uncertain' or 'speculative'.[215] While the majority of cases in PwC's sample related to investment treaty arbitration, the findings are relevant to commercial arbitrations as well, especially cases that involve companies with no established historical track record, such as young high-growth companies.

Discounting is an opportunity cost concept. It uses the weighted average cost of capital ('WACC') (if free cash flows are discounted), with the cost of equity in WACC commonly derived using the Capital Asset Pricing Model ('CAPM'), first published by Bill Sharpe in 1964.[216] The equation commonly used in damages valuation today is the

211. *See* David Saunders, Amit Arora, and Joe Skilton, *The Applicable Valuation Approach*, in John A. Trenor (ed.) *The Guide to Damages in International Arbitration*, 187 (2nd ed., Global Arbitration Review 2017), for references of empirical research.
212. This applies to the Residual Income Method too as accrual and cash income approaches are equivalent when the respective income measures are discounted to infinity and consistent assumptions are used.
213. PwC 2015 – International Arbitration Damages Research, Closing the Gap Between Claimants and Respondents, 8, and 2017 update, 6.
214. PwC International Arbitration Damages Research 2017 update, 6.
215. PwC 2015 – International Arbitration Damages Research, Closing the Gap Between Claimants and Respondents, 3. The rejection by tribunals of the DCF method on the idea that value cannot be determined because returns are 'too uncertain' or 'speculative' is not easy to reconcile with asset pricing theory and the extent to which risk can be reflected in the discount rate. *See* for risk and uncertainty Frank Hyneman Knight, 'Risk, Uncertainty and Profit' (Boston: Houghton Mifflin, 1921); *see also*: John Maynard Keynes, *The General Theory of Employment, Interest and Money* (New York: Macmillan) both cited in: Rubinstein, Rubinstein, *A History of the Theory of Investments*, Wiley, 2006, at 50 and 72 respectively under 'Risk vs. Uncertainty'.
216. William Forsyth Sharpe, *Capital Asset Prices: A Theory of Market Equilibrium under Conditions of Risk*, Journal of Finance Vol. 19, No. 3 (September 1964), 425–442.

single factor version derived by Eugene Fama in 1968.[217] Courts and tribunals frequently award damages on its basis.[218]

[2] Separating Operating and Financing Activities in a DCF Valuation

[a] Introduction

The distinction between operating and financing activities of a firm has been well-established in the finance literature since Miller-Modigliani.[219] It was introduced above in §2.01. To recap, enterprise value (or firm value) represents the present value of the free cash flows that a firm is expected to generate. Free cash flow is operating cash flow less cash investments.[220] If positive, free cash flow can be paid out to the providers of capital - the shareholders and debtholders. If negative, the operating deficits require funding, and the firm issues equity or debt securities in the capital markets. These are financing activities. The cash flows that relate to them are financing cash flows, and they are below free cash flow (for valuation purposes).

The equity bridge in §2.01 [B] demonstrated that (under certain assumptions), enterprise value is equal to the value of the debt plus the value of the equity.

[b] Dividend Irrelevancy

As indicated in §2.01 [B], the value of the equity can be calculated directly by projecting and discounting distributions to equity holders such as dividends.[221] As discussed there, this approach - the dividend discount or cash flow-to-equity-method - is not commonly used in practice, at least for non-financial businesses. It is, however, instructive as a way of thinking about value.

Secondary effects aside, dividends reduce the value of the enterprise dollar-for-dollar (as there would otherwise be arbitrage opportunities), and paying dividends is, therefore, a zero-net-present-value activity.[222] This observation is captured in Modigliani Miller's dividend irrelevance proposition which states that in perfect

217. Eugene F. Fama, *Risk, Return and Equilibrium: Some Clarifying Comments*. Journal of Finance. Vol. 23 No. 1 (March 1968) 29–40.
218. It has been observed that more empirical effort may have been put into testing the CAPM than any other result in finance, and that the results are mixed., *see* Rubinstein, *A History of the Theory of Investments*, Wiley, 2006, 172. Also *see* Eugene F. Fama and Kenneth R. French, *The Capital Asset Pricing Model: Theory and Evidence*, Journal of Economic Perspectives Vol. 18, No. 3, Summer 2004, 25–46. Note to future cross-examiners: the book does not take a position on the question of the validity of the CAPM.
219. Franco Modigliani and Merton Miller (Modigliani-Miller's Proposition I), *The Cost of Capital, Corporation Finance and the Theory of Investment*, American Economic Review June 1958, Vol. 48, No. 3, 261–297; Franco Modigliani and Merton Miller, *Dividend Policy, Growth and the Valuation of Shares*, Journal of Business 1961, 411–433.
220. Investing cash flow is considered to be part of operating cash flow in DCF valuations, i.e., above free cash flow.
221. This idea goes back to John Burr Williams, *The Theory of Investment Value* (Cambridge, MA: Harvard University Press, 1938), cited in: Rubinstein (Theory of Investments), 75.
222. Penman, *Accounting for Value*, *supra* n. 184, at 18.

markets, a firm's dividend policy will not have any effect on its current share price.[223] Dividends are the distribution of value, something that Modigliani-Miller separated from the generation of value which is the objective of the operating activities.

Forecasting involves a finite number of forecasting periods, followed by the forecast of a terminal value. Over such periods, the use of a dividend discount method seems difficult to reconcile with the dividend irrelevance proposition: value is the present value of future dividends, but forecasting the timing of dividend payments is irrelevant to the valuation.[224] Ohlson made the same observation when discussing the use of accounting information in valuation:

> [T]he paper highlights the key role of accounting data when one tries to come to grips with an apparent paradox in neoclassical security valuation: the present value of expected dividends determines a firm's value, yet the prediction of the dividend sequence is basically irrelevant if the underlying dividend policy is irrelevant. (Who wants to predict next year's expected dividends when all dividend policies yield the same market value?).[225]

Returning to the core idea of Modigliani-Miller, the apparent paradox is addressed in the observation that dividends are not the source of value, but the distribution of value.[226] Dividends themselves are not fundamental to the valuation. This is why the cash flow-to-equity-method, if limited to forecasting and discounting dividends, omits important information from the valuation.

A valuation based on free cash flow, on the other hand, determines enterprise value instead of projecting dividends to determine equity value. Free cash flow is the residual cash flow before distributions to shareholders and bondholders. Projecting free cash flow requires looking 'inside the firm', at its operating activities and the generation of value, not merely the distribution of value.

[c] *The Residual Income Method*

An alternative to discounting cash flows is to discount accrual earnings. This can take the form of the RIM; discounting residual operating income and adding it to the book value of net operating assets (before deducting net debt to arrive at equity value). The residual income method is an accounting-based valuation method, that is, it uses accounting information, usually taken from the financial statements. 'Residual' means

223. Merton H. Miller and Franco Modigliani, *Dividend Policy, Growth, and the Valuation of Shares*, The Journal of Business Vol. 34 No. 4 (October 1961), 411–433. This property can also be observed in the accounting equation (above at §2.01 [A]): Dividend payout increases net debt (by reducing cash) but simultaneously reduces the book value of equity. The two effects offset each other. The payment of a dividend has no effect on enterprise value.
224. These statements again requires certain assumptions, including perfect capital markets. Merton H. Miller and Franco Modigliani, *Dividend Policy, Growth, and the Valuation of Shares*, Journal of Business 1961, Vol. 34, 411–433.
225. James A. Ohlson, *Earnings, Book Values, and Dividends in Equity Valuation*, Contemporary Accounting Research Vol. 11, No. 2 (Spring 1995), 661–687, cited in: Rubinstein, *Theory of Investments*, 334.
226. Penman, *Accounting for Value*, *supra* n. 184, 40.

operating income in excess of a required return on net operating assets.[227] The difference between earnings and cash flows is the accrual accounting, that is, cash flows equal operating earnings minus the change in net operating assets.[228]

If the forecast horizon is infinite and consistent assumptions are used, then cash flow and earnings approaches are equivalent: projected earnings reconcile to cash flows by adjusting for the accruals. Accruals only bring future cash flows forward in time. This can facilitate finite-horizon valuation.[229]

This is also what a net debt deduction for a defined benefit pension obligation achieves (*see* above §4.02 [B]). It brings future cash outflows (to employees) forward in time (often by many years); more generally, this is really what a net debt deduction for *any* operating item achieves.

The fact that the financial statements on which the residual income method is often based can be the same financial statements as those warranted in a transaction would suggest that the RIM is a natural approach to damages valuation in financial statement warranty breach cases. At present, however, it does not play a significant role in damages valuation, and the book therefore focuses on the DCF method.

[d] The Distinction Between Operating and Financing Activities

As operating cash flows (including capital expenditures) are part of free cash flow, it is important to distinguish between the operating and financing activities in the valuation, that is, to allocate related cash flows correctly above or below free cash flow.

The cash flow statement, as prepared under generally accepted accounting rules, is a starting point. But accounting rules do not necessarily reflect the distinction between the operating and financing cash flows in the same way corporate finance theory does. One example where this distinction can be important in practice is factoring. Recall the discussion in Chapter §4.04 [A] [5] which concluded that the accounting for non-recourse factoring generally means that more operating cash flow is reported in a period than has in fact been generated by the business's operations.

Another consideration in this regard is that it is important for the valuation model to be consistent with SPA definitions of net debt and net working capital: projected cash flows that relate to items treated as net debt in the SPA should also be included in financing cash flows in the valuation model. Otherwise, there can be a risk of deducting the same item twice, a 'double dip'. Similarly, if the definitions do not interact seamlessly, an item might not be captured at all.

---

227. Residual income is alternatively referred to as 'economic profit' or 'economic value added', *see* Stephen H. Penman, *Financial Statement Analysis and Security Valuation*, 433 (4th ed., Mc Graw-Hill Education 2009).
228. Feltham and Ohlson.
229. Stephen Penman and Theodore Sougiannis, *A Comparison of Dividend, Cash Flow, and Earnings Approaches to Equity Valuation*, Contemporary Accounting Research Vol. 15, No. 3 (Fall 1998) 346.

Consider the criteria that suggest that an asset or liability is part of working capital (discussed above in §5.03). One of them was that working capital arises from operating activities, i.e., activities connected with the production of goods or services that are the object of the enterprise. It is consistent with this definition that working capital and related cash flows belong to the firm's operations: the collection of a trade receivable, the payment of a trade creditor, or the sale of an item from inventory all lead to operating cash in- or outflows that, in turn, are part of free cash flow. Only if part of working capital relates to a financing activity, such as factoring, then, to be consistent, the related cash flow should also be classified as a financing cash flow (provided the financing activity gives rise to a debt-like item in the SPA, which it generally should). Otherwise, there would be double counting.

Projecting cash flows usually amounts to preparing a set of pro-forma financial statements for the future. The starting point is very often the historical financials. There are a number of areas where cash flow statements – and the subtotals they show for net operating cash flow, investing cash flow, and financing cash flow – are not consistent with operating, investing, and financing cash flow in a corporate finance sense. Examples of potential inconsistencies under IAS include the following (similar inconsistencies exist under US GAAP[230]):

- Under IAS 7.31, interest and dividends received or paid may be classified in financial statements as either operating, investing, or financing cash flows, provided that they are classified consistently from period to period. In corporate finance, these cash flows would be considered to arise from financing activities (for a firm that is not a financial institution, in which case dividend or interest income can represent part of the operating business) as they concern the distribution of surpluses generated by operations or the funding of operating cash shortfalls rather than the creation of value. Further, in SPA definitions, these cash flows would also be typically classified as financing cash flows.
- Under IAS 7.35, cash flows arising from taxes on income are normally classified in the financial statements as operating, unless they can be specifically identified with financing or investing activities. From a corporate finance perspective, taxes that relate to operating activities (such as taxes due on operating income) should be considered to be operating items, while those related to financing activities (such as taxes due on interest income) are financing cash flows. This may collide with SPA definitions that include certain tax liabilities in the definition of net debt.

It is therefore important to restate, where appropriate, and to reformulate historical financial statements when performing a DCF valuation.

230. *Ibid.*, 124 for further discussion.

[C] The Market Approach

The market approach uses market data from comparable companies to value a company or an ownership interest in a company. It can be based on two types of transactions in the shares of comparable companies:

(1) transactions in shares of comparable companies that trade on a stock exchange ('trading comparables'); and
(2) M&A transactions involving substantial interests in comparable companies ('transaction comparables').

Both mean that the value of the business that is to be valued is derived from the market valuation of comparable companies or the 'peer group'. Differences in scale between the firm to be valued and the peer group are adjusted by expressing value in relative terms: the use of ratios to market price, or valuation multiples allows for comparison between different-sized firms (as long as the size difference itself does not render the firms insufficiently comparable).

The metrics used in the market approach are often taken from the financial statements (reported profitability measures are usually adjusted before a multiple is applied): sales, EBITDA, EBIT, operating cash flow, net income or the book value of equity. From these, the valuer calculates, respectively, EV/sales, EV/EBITDA-, EV/EBIT- and EV/cash flow to operations (CFO)-multiples; price/net income (P/E) and price/book (P/B) ratios. Sales-, EBITDA-, EBIT- and operating cash flow-multiples are enterprise value multiples. Net income and price-to-book multiples are equity value multiples.

Earnings-based multiples can be based on historical earnings (e.g., of the last financial year), current earnings (the 'current' financial year at the given valuation date), or projected earnings (usually the financial year following the acquisition or valuation date). When earnings-based multiples are used, the analysis of the quality of earnings and the identification and elimination of one-off or non-recurring elements to determine normalised, or underlying, earnings often take centre stage during the financial due diligence. To get a sense of the capacity of large corporates to influence, or manage, earnings, consider the following example.

Example of Earnings Management: Acquisition of Kidder Peabody by GE

In 1986, GE acquired Kidder Peabody, one of Wall Street's oldest investment banks. In 1994, it was discovered that a trader had created false entries over a number of years that artificially boosted Kidder Peabody's income. The SEC later concluded that the trader had committed securities fraud and banned him from the industry. Just after the discovery of this fraud, two days before a quarterly earnings release, GE determined that it was necessary to write off USD 350 million. This is how the CEO, Jack Welch, described the reaction of the senior business leaders upon hearing the news in his autobiography (it is not suggested that this should have given rise to a legal dispute):

> The response of our business leaders to the crisis was typical of the GE culture. Even though the books had closed on the quarter, many immediately offered to pitch in to cover the Kidder gap. Some said they could find an extra USD10 million, USD20 million, and even USD30 million from their businesses to offset the surprise. Though it was too late, their willingness to help was a dramatic contrast to the excuses I had been hearing from the Kidder people.[231]

Multiples can also relate market prices to non-financial metrics, for example, in the context of industry-specific valuations where specific metrics are important drivers of performance and cash flows. For example, energy companies can be valued on the basis of hydrocarbon reserves and hotel operators on their number of rooms.[232]

A limitation of the market approach is that it only provides information relative to other comparable firms. It adopts the view that similar firms should have similar valuations and, therefore, similar multiples and that markets are efficient at setting the prices of peer group firms. The market approach itself is not based on a fundamental analysis of intrinsic value. It derives a valuation implied by the given market valuation of other firms. Among other limitations, it cannot be used to challenge market prices.[233]

A further limitation of the market approach is that no two companies are exactly the same. Even comparable companies, usually in the same industry, trade at different multiples. This can be due to geographical differences, differences in expected growth rates, different accounting rules, different risk profiles (and therefore cost of capital), different investment requirements (outside the metrics captured in, say, an EBITDA multiple), and so on. In efficient markets, share prices reflect these differences. However, when valuing a firm using other firms' multiples, it is adjusting for such differences can be exceptionally complex, other than by narrowing the peer group.[234]

Nevertheless, the market approach is widely used in M&A-related valuation.

In damages valuation, on the other hand, its limitations can make the market approach unsuitable as the sole valuation method. It has even been called 'generally inappropriate for post-M&A damages disputes'.[235] However, the market approach is very common to serve as a cross-check on other valuation approaches, especially DCF valuations.[236] Further, there are some cases in which it was, in fact, the sole approach used in the valuation of damages. One example is the following case.

Example of Market Method Used in M&A-Related Damages Valuation (High Court of England and Wales)[237]

This is the same case as above in §10.01 in which a misrepresentation resulted in a breach of buyers' warranty. The case also considers a claim by the buyer, THG, for

231. Jack Welch, *Headline Book Publishing*, 225 (London, 2001).
232. Saunders, Arora and Skilton, *supra* n. 211, at 191 for further discussion.
233. Penman, *Accounting for Value*, *supra* n. 184, at 77.
234. *Ibid.*, n. 28, 264.
235. Gerhard H. Wächter and Christoph Wollny, *A Proposal for the Calculation of Damages in Post-M&A Disputes*, 2, SchiedsVZ, Heft 2, 80, 89 (2018).
236. Saunders, Arora and Skilton, *supra* n. 211, at 191.
237. *The Hut Group Ltd. v. Cookson & Barclays Private Bank Ltd* [2014] EWHC 3842 (QB). (There was an unsuccessful appeal from this decision in relation to issues unrelated to the quantum calculation: [2016] EWCA Civ 238).

breach of the sellers' 'true and fair view' warranty of the target's accounts. This claim is interesting not only because it was common ground between the parties that the market approach was the sole method on which the damages valuation should be based but also because of the question whether the valuation should reflect a reduction in the multiple used due to concerns over the reliability of the accounts or for other reasons.

The following was agreed between the parties in relation to quantifying loss:

- The target's value as warranted ('warranty true' enterprise value) was GBP 58 million, the purchase price, which consisted of GBP 30 million in cash and GBP 28 million in shares of the buyer.
- The appropriate valuation methodology on the 'warranty false' (i.e., actual position) basis was based on a multiple of EBITDA.
- A starting EBITDA (prior to any adjustments for the actual position given the breach of warranty) amounted to GBP 5.442 million.
- As a starting point for quantifying loss, it was appropriate to apply the transaction multiple, 10.7xEBITDA. However, this was subject to a 'reduced multiple' contention advanced by THG (*see* below).

Further, the treatment of certain adjustments for one-off items was undisputed.

The judge observed that using the EBITDA multiple method, arriving at the 'warranty false' valuation of the target business was in essence an 'arithmetical exercise'.[238]

The buyer's quantum expert argued for a reduction of approximately 18% in the transaction multiple on the basis of the 'existence of errors [...] [which] would call into question the accounts as a whole and the concern that further issues would arise would lower the value of the business to the acquirer'.[239] This reduction in the multiple would make a significant difference – to the loss of GBP 5.6 million based on the then 'base' multiple, the expert added a further loss of GBP 5.3 million based on the 'reduced' multiple.

The sellers argued that this was not a legally coherent position. They contended that the true value of the target business with fairly stated management accounts would not have been discounted by a purchaser to reflect that those fairly stated accounts might be unreliable. If anything, because the accounts would have been entirely accurate, they would have withstood all due diligence probing and would have enhanced, not reduced, a purchaser's confidence.[240]

In a subsequent submission, the buyer's expert changed the discount to arrive at a multiple of approximately 9.9x. Of the revised damages claim of GBP 8.6 million, about GBP 4 million was attributable to this reduction of the multiple. The rationale for the reduction had also changed. It was 'justified by an assumption of a stable gross margin with a sustained high growth in revenues, the combination of which is

238. *Ibid.*, para. 161.
239. *Ibid.*, para. 164.
240. *Ibid.*, para. 166.

necessary to give to a high growth in projected EBITDA', and by reference to comparisons with long-term growth forecasts that had been provided by the seller in 2011. The buyer's submission was that the 'elastic had snapped' such that a reasonable hypothetical purchaser and a reasonable hypothetical seller would have had to revisit the multiple as well as the EBITDA. Only by the reduced multiple could the further deterioration in the target business's growth rate and shortfall against its forecast growth be fairly reflected.[241]

The judge found that a reasonable hypothetical purchaser and a reasonable hypothetical seller would not have had to revisit the multiple as well as the EBITDA reduction, and that the application of a discount to the multiple would produce an unrealistic valuation of THG's loss. He therefore applied the agreed multiple of 10.7x.

[D] The Cost- or Asset-Based Approach

The cost or asset-based approach assesses a firm's value by identifying and adding up the market values of its assets. As assets are reported in the balance sheet at book value, an asset-based approach requires the valuer to convert these book values into market values. The value of the equity is then determined by deducting the firm's debt.

The asset-based approach must deal with the fact that many assets are not recognised on the balance sheet. For example, brand, knowledge or other intangible assets may account for much of a firm's overall value, but the firm may omit them from its accounts.

Further, relevant assets and liabilities may not trade in liquid markets. Those assets and liabilities that are on the balance sheet may be accounted for using historical cost accounting. Even if all operating assets and liabilities are accounted for at fair value, however, the aggregate of their individual fair values may not correspond to the value of the firm, as the fair value of the assets when put to use jointly usually exceeds the sum of their individual fair values (this is why assets and liabilities are organised in firms).

Asset-based approaches are often considered to provide a 'floor' to the valuation of a firm. This is because of the implicit break-up option inherent in any going concern: at any time, the owner has the option of discontinuing operations and liquidating the company. It may exercise this option if the liquidation value exceeds the present value of the going concern's expected returns.[242] Other than in this context, asset-based valuations are also used for specific types of companies. These include, for example, companies that hold individual income-generating assets (instead of trading entities) that are to be valued. The approach is also used in specific situations such as orderly liquidations.

241. *Ibid.*, para. 171. Note that the 'actual value' is discussed in hypotheticals.
242. Haberman and Perks, *supra* n. 198, at 182.

§11.05 DAMAGES MATTERS SPECIFIC TO M&A DISPUTES

This section discusses aspects of damages valuation that, while not necessarily unique to them, are frequently encountered in M&A-related disputes. The section starts with a discussion of the relationship between the value of an acquisition target and its price. Value and price are two terms that are sometimes used interchangeably in M&A disputes but that should be considered separately, especially for identifying the correct counterfactual. The section goes on to discuss the cost of capital, the treatment of taxes in damages valuation, and damages valuation clauses. It concludes with a note on event studies. Event studies use market measurements of value. They play a role in cases that involve public companies and can also serve as a 'cross-check' on other (more common) approaches to damages valuation.

[A] Value Versus Price

Introduction

In the case of a warranty breach, the price paid is often rebuttably presumed to be the same as the value warranted.[243] However, there can be situations in which price and value are not the same, perhaps especially in times of exceptionally high valuations.[244] For example, 2021 was a record-breaking year in M&A with global deal value of USD 5.9 trillion,[245] fuelled by access to cheap financing and driven by high valuations.

To be clear, a period of high valuations does not necessarily mean that markets, or individual acquisition targets, are overvalued. However, it does mean an increased scope for disappointment by parties in M&A transactions. Buyers can be left disappointed when the acquisition target falls short of the expected returns that were priced into the bid. Similarly, sellers can be disappointed in cases where a significant shortfall against expectations means lower earn-out payments. Disappointment breeds disputes.

The Counterfactual

Different types of breaches are associated with different counterfactuals that, in turn, can lead to differences in the measurement of damages. The differences start to matter more when price is different from value, as the following examples illustrate.

The first example is a claim for warranty breach, where the price paid is often rebuttably presumed to be the same as the value as warranted.[246] These types of claims often compare what was promised to what was delivered, or the value 'as warranted' to the value 'as is' (or the 'true value'). However, value and price need not necessarily

243. Kramer, *supra* n. 179, at 227.
244. Or alternatively in times of depressed valuations.
245. *See* Deal Insights, *Dealmakers ring out 2021 as the year of M&A*, Refinitiv Perspectives, 12 January 2022, available at https://www.refinitiv.com/perspectives/market-insights/dealmakers-ring-out-2021-as-the-year-of-ma.
246. Kramer, *supra* n. 179, at 227.

be the same and, as discussed further below, there can be situations in which bidders pay more or less than an asset is worth.[247]

Where price and value are different, measures of damages can differ, and the differences can be significant. To illustrate, consider the following example given in *Karim & Anor v. Wemyss*:

> Suppose that A owns a painting that he tells B was painted by a famous artist. If it had been, it would be worth GBP10,000. B pays GBP8,000 for it. It was not in fact painted by the famous artist and was only worth GBP100. If B can establish that what A said was a contractual warranty, then he is entitled to GBP10,000 – GBP100 = GBP9,900. But if he can only establish that the statement was an actionable misrepresentation, then he is entitled to GBP8,000 – GBP100 = GBP7,900, although if the misrepresentation was (or is treated as) fraudulent he may be entitled to consequential losses as well. Changing the facts, perhaps unrealistically, if the painting as warranted would have been worth GBP10,000 but is in fact worth GBP8,000, then on the contractual measure the buyer who paid GBP8,000 will recover GBP2,000; but on the tortious measure will recover nothing.[248]

In this example, the price of the asset is different from its value. The judge observed that, in a breach of warranty claim related to the quality of an asset, the measure of damages is the difference between the asset's true value and its value as warranted.[249]

Similarly, in *Merrill Lynch v. Allegheny*, a case that arose out of Allegheny's acquisition of Global Energy Markets (GEM) from Merrill Lynch, the US Court of Appeals for the Second Circuit, held that:

> A party injured by breach of contract is entitled to be placed in the position it would have occupied had the contract been fulfilled according to its terms .... It follows that appellant is entitled to the benefit of its bargain, measured as the difference between the value of GEM as warranted by Merrill Lynch and its true value at the time of the transaction.[250]

The second category is a claim in tort, such as fraudulent misrepresentation, where the measure of damages can be the difference between the true value of the asset and the price paid.[251] Again, in Merrill Lynch, the Second Circuit held that:

> we look to New York law that follows the well-established common law rule that fraud damages represent the difference between the purchase price of the asset and its true value, plus interest, generally measured as of the date of sale.[252]

247. The existence of a difference between price and value sometimes appears to be an implicit assumption when considering alternative approaches to the measurement of damages. For example, BGH (German *Federal Court of Justice), decision dated 15 March 2006, VIII ZR 120/04, NJW-RR 2006, 1185-1188, discussed in: Markus Altenkirch*: Calculation of Damages For a Breach of a Financial Statements Warranty, Baker McKenzie White Paper, 23 February 2017.
248. *Karim & Anor v. Wemyss* [2016] EWCA Civ 27 at [25]-[26].
249. *Ibid.; see also Merrill Lynch Co. Inc ML IBK v. Allegheny Energy Inc LLC* United States Court of Appeals, Second Circuit, Docket No. 05-5129-cv. Decided: August 31, 2007.
250. *Merrill Lynch Co. Inc ML IBK v. Allegheny Energy Inc LLC* United States Court of Appeals, Second Circuit, Docket No. 05-5129-cv. Decided: 31 August 2007.
251. *Karim & Anor v. Wemyss* [2016] EWCA Civ 27 at [23].
252. *Merrill Lynch Co. Inc ML IBK v. Allegheny Energy Inc LLC* United States Court of Appeals, Second Circuit, Docket No. 05-5129-cv. Decided: 31 August 2007.

A third category relates to *culpa in contrahendo* claims which are often associated with yet another measure of damages.[253] *Culpa in contrahendo* claims play a role in many M&A disputes in civil law jurisdictions.[254] These claims often relate to non-disclosure of information, or misrepresentation during the negotiations, and the damages claim can be for the 'negative interest',[255] which asks what a claimant (more often the buyer) would have done in a scenario in which all information had been disclosed truthfully:[256] the buyer may have walked away from the transaction, or alternatively paid a lower price. Damages are, therefore, often calculated as the difference between the price actually paid and the price a purchaser would have paid if all information had been disclosed truthfully.[257] Seller-friendly markets in which multiple bidders compete for a limited number of quality targets (as seen recently in 2021) can mean tightly managed auction processes and 'light' approaches to the buy-side due diligence. Both factors can make it easier for sellers to withhold information. It is easy to see how this could lead to an increase in these types of claims for misrepresentation during the negotiations.

The categories introduced above are summarised in Table 11.1, along with potential counterfactuals. (Note that these are simplified categorisations that do not represent a legal view on the appropriate choice of counterfactual.)

Table 11.1 Alternative Counterfactuals

	Comparison Between	
	Actual Position	*Counterfactual Position*
Breach of warranty of quality	True value	Value as warranted
Fraudulent misrepresentation	True value	Purchase price*
Culpa in contrahendo	Purchase price	(Lower) price that would have been agreed if the misrepresentation had not been made (or buyer may walk away from transaction)

*Note: Strictly speaking, the actual purchase price is compared to the actual value, neither of them a counterfactual.

253. Friedrich Kessler and Edith Fine, *Culpa in Contrahendo, Bargaining in good Faith, and Freedom of Contract: A Comparative Study*, Harvard Law Review, Vol. 77, No. 3, January 1964, 401. For further discussion of the culpa in contrahendo doctrine in M&A disputes *see* Wächter, *M&A Litigation*, 3rd ed. 2017, RWS Verlag Kommunikationsforum GmbH, at 261.
254. Friedrich Kessler and Edith Fine, *Culpa in Contrahendo, Bargaining in good Faith, and Freedom of Contract: A Comparative Study*, Harvard Law Review, Vol. 77, No. 3, January 1964, 401.
255. Wächter, *M&A Litigation*, 3rd ed. 2017, RWS Verlag Kommunikationsforum GmbH, at 551.
256. *See also* the discussion in *Altenkirch*: Calculation of Damages for a Breach of a Financial Statements Warranty, Baker McKenzie White Paper, 23 February 2017.
257. *Ibid.*

If the price paid for a target is assumed to be equal to its value, then the comparison of the actual and counterfactual positions as set out in the table above results in the same absolute difference in each of the three cases, although in culpa in contrahendo claims the actual and counterfactual scenarios are reversed.

Even if the difference is the same however, this does not necessarily mean that damages are the same, for a number of reasons: warranty claims are often subject to contractual limitations that may not apply to fraud[258] or culpa in contrahendo claims;[259] differences in valuation dates may lead to substantially different damages amounts; and a culpa in contrahendo claim may include elements of lost profits that would not necessarily be part of a warranty breach claim.[260]

Two recent cases that dealt with differences between value and price and their implications for the measurement of damages are *Glossop Cartons and Print Ltd & Ors v. Contact (Print & Packaging) Ltd & Others* and *Cardamon Limited v. MacAlister.*

[1] Glossop Cartons and Print Ltd v. Contact (Print & Packaging) Ltd[261]

In *Glossop Cartons and Print Ltd v. Contact (Print & Packaging) Ltd*, the Court of Appeal held that the buyer seeking damages from a seller for fraudulent misrepresentation was entitled to compensation despite agreeing a 'bad bargain'.

The purchaser was a packaging manufacturer called Glossop. It claimed damages for fraudulent misrepresentation against the sellers of certain business assets of a print company. The parties entered into three different simultaneous transactions, one of which related to assets that were worth less than the price paid.

The High Court found in Glossop's favour but held that a claimant in a deceit claim could not recover losses which directly flowed from the relevant transaction if those losses were the product of claimant's own commercial misjudgment. In order to ascertain the market value of the business assets sold, the High Court tried to establish what the claimants had subjectively factored into their calculation of the purchase price by deducting from the purchase price the cost of each flaw (or defect) that Glossop had not itself factored into its calculation of the price.

Glossop appealed the High Court's decision, arguing against what in the case was called the 'deduction method'. It argued that the High Court had failed to award damages for the direct loss caused by the fraudulent misrepresentations: the difference between the actual market value of the business assets sold and the price paid.

---

258. For example, *Abry Partners V, L.P., v. F&W Acquisition LLC*, 891 A.2d 1032 (Del. Ch. 2006) and *Online Healthnow Inc. and Bertelsmann Inc. v. CIP OCL Investments LLC et al.*, C.A. No. 2020-0654-JRS (Del. Ch. 12 August 2021) in which fraud claims survived despite contractual limitations.
259. *See, e.g.*, OLG Munich of 3 December 2020 NZG 2021. Vontractual exclusion of liability did not apply since such exclusion did not encompass breaches of pre-contractual disclosure obligations.
260. Wächter, *M&A Litigation*, 3rd ed. 2017, RWS Verlag Kommunikationsforum GmbH, at 551.
261. *Glossop Cartons and Print Ltd & Ors v. Contact (Print & Packaging) Ltd & Ors* [2021] EWCA Civ 639 (7 May 2021).

The Court of Appeal held that, as a general rule, damages for fraudulent misrepresentation should be assessed by deducting the actual value of the assets bought at the relevant date from the price paid. Glossop was therefore entitled to recover, by way of direct loss, the difference between the price it paid and the market value of the assets purchased at the relevant date. That difference was best represented by the amount of goodwill (mostly related to business contracts) which was considered to have had no real value.[262]

Glossop Cartons and Print Ltd v. Contact (Print & Packaging) Ltd shows the relevance of the correct counterfactual as the basis for quantifying damages.

[2] Cardamon Limited v. MacAlister[263]

In *Cardamon v. MacAlister*, a breach of warranty claim, the court found that the value 'as warranted' was greater than the purchase price.

The transaction related to the sale of a family-run insurance business for GBP 2.4 million, a significant discount against the initial asking price of GBP 5 million. The discount reflected that the seller needed to complete the transaction quickly for tax reasons and conducted limited due diligence.

Shortly after closing, material accounting errors in the 2014 financial statements came to light, and the accounts were restated.[264]

The seller's position was that the purchase price was the best evidence of the 'as warranted value'. The judge, however, dismissed this argument, holding that it would be wrong to take the purchase price as indicative of the target's value. She found that the value 'as warranted' was greater than the purchase price since the parties had entered into the SPA knowing that the purchase price was less than market value in return for a swift purchase without the usual due diligence process.

The SPA contained a *de minimis* provision which meant that the first GBP 500,000 of any warranty claim was irrecoverable. In addition, it contained a cap limiting the seller's liability to the purchase price of GBP 2.4 million. The court awarded the entire purchase price of GBP 2.4 million as damages: it found that the value as warranted was approximately GBP 3.0 million and deducted the GBP 500,000 *de minimis* amount, leaving GBP 2.5 million. It then applied the cap at GBP 2.4 million. The buyer recovered the full amount of the purchase price.

Escalation of commitment

When do value and price differ? In other words, why is someone willing to pay more or accept less than an asset is worth? In *Glossop Cartons and Print Ltd & Ors v. Contact*

262. The judge remarked that it was difficult to see how there could be any goodwill in a loss-making business. It is however not difficult to find examples of loss-making businesses (even those that sustain losses over longer periods) that nevertheless report goodwill. For example, Nokia Corporation which reported substantial losses in most years between 2016 and 2021 but goodwill in excess of EUR 5 billion at every year end throughout the same period (Source: CapitalIQ).
263. *Cardamon Limited v. MacAlister & Anor* [2019] EWHC 1200 (15 May 2019).
264. *Ibid.*

(Print & Packaging) Ltd & Ors, the court noted that the buyer may have simply misjudged the value of the business it acquired. In *Cardamon Limited v. MacAlister,* the parties had agreed a 'bargain purchase' in return for a swift transaction that the seller wanted for tax reasons, foregoing the usual due diligence process.

These are exceptional cases. Other, perhaps more common examples of situations where price is different from value can be the result of cognitive biases in the decision-making leading up to a transaction. For example, an irrational escalation of commitments, also called a 'bidding war', can result in prices that are not justifiable by reasonable assumptions.[265]

The case of Guidant, a manufacturer of medical products, illustrates the extent that price and value can differ in an escalation of commitments. The transaction escalated into the biggest and most contentious takeover battle in the medical devices industry at the time.[266] In December 2004, Johnson & Johnson (J&J) made a bid of USD 25.4 billion for Guidant. About six months later, before the transaction closed, the New York Times uncovered a flaw in one of Guidant's products, an implantable defibrillator, that caused it to malfunction in some instances. Guidant had not disclosed this deficiency, and this news, therefore, surprised J&J. The US Food and Drug Administration (FDA) opened an investigation into Guidant. The company announced a product recall.

A short time later, in November 2005, J&J reduced its offer to USD 21.5 billion over concerns about the FDA investigation and Guidant's new outlook. J&J later raised its offer again, to USD 23.2 billion.

On 5 December 2005, Boston Scientific, a competitor of J&J, fearing to be at a competitive disadvantage in the event J&J acquired Guidant, offered USD 24.7 billion for Guidant. The FDA investigation progressed, and Guidant's situation worsened. On 11 January 2006, Guidant tentatively accepted a revised bid by J&J of USD 23.2 billion. Boston Scientific raised its bid to USD 25 billion within a day, and J&J increased its bid yet again to USD 24.2 billion which Guidant provisionally accepted. On 25 January, Boston Scientific raised its bid yet again to USD 27 billion. Guidant accepted this revised offer, pending the approval of shareholders and regulators. J&J decided not to follow suit. Its share price had fallen every time it had raised its bid for Guidant.[267]

The day after Guidant accepted Boston Scientific's bid, Boston Scientific's share price dropped to USD 23.15, a decrease of approximately 15% since the company first announced the bid. By June 2006, after Boston Scientific had been forced to recall 23,000 Guidant pacemakers, it had fallen below USD 17.00.

265. Max H. Bazerman and Don A. Moore, *Judgment in Managerial Decision Making,* 123 (8th ed., Wiley 2013). However, even in instances where it can be shown that prices cannot be justified by reasonable assumptions, *e.g.*, when observing two prices that are each based on a set of assumptions where movements in the prices and assumptions produce a contradiction, it can be difficult to identify which of the prices is irrational.

266. B. Feder, *Quiet End to Battle of the Bids,* New York Times, C1 (26 January 2006). The bidding war was discussed in Bazerman and Moore *supra* n. 265, at 125–126.

267. Feder, *supra* n. 266, at C1.

Boston Scientific's winning bid of USD 27 billion was higher than the original bid by J&J of USD 25.4 billion, which was determined before any of Guidant's technological problems, which later developed into significant legal and reputational problems, had emerged. All else being equal, these problems would suggest a significant reduction in the value of Guidant, not an increase.

Why Else Might Value and Price Differ?

Why else might there be transactions where value and price differ? Agency theory and behavioural economics offer additional explanations.

Agency theory suggests that the separation of ownership (the shareholders) and control (management) of a firm can result in a strategic misalignment, or conflict, of interests. For example, it has been observed that managers have incentives to cause their firms to grow beyond the optimal size.[268] This can lead them to pursue M&A transactions that do not deliver the value that the acquiring firm paid for. Thus an acquirer can overpay, even when the management of the target firm (the agent) acts rationally, but self-interestedly (and against the interests of the target firm).

On the other hand, behavioural economics suggests the same outcome (overpaying) can occur as a result of nonrational, or boundedly rational, behaviour when a party agrees a price that is not justifiable by reasonable assumptions. Behavioural economists have examined the conditions that give rise to such outcomes.[269] The escalation of commitments discussed in the previous section is one such outcome. More generally, behavioural biases include overconfidence, or the competitive motive to 'win' rather than to seek one's own gain.[270] An example is an auction process in which a bidder who – in the event it loses – would experience a loss in market share or competitive position, and who becomes determined to beat the other side. This can lead to an escalation of commitments and spiral into an outcome where price is not justifiable by rational assumptions, and, indeed, both sides can lose.[271] A seller-friendly market is more likely to breed such conditions than a buyer-friendly market.

[B] Which Cost of Capital?

Non-contentious Valuations

A bidder who uses the income approach in the (non-contentious) valuation of an acquisition target must decide whether to discount projected cash flows at the cost of capital of the stand-alone target or alternatively at the cost of capital of the target when integrated into the acquirer's business after the acquisition. As with other capital investment decisions, the cost of capital will depend on the investment's perceived level of systematic risk. The discount rate the buyer uses must reflect this risk

268. Michael C. Jensen, *Agency Costs of Free Cash Flow, Corporate Finance, and Takeovers*, American Economic Review, May 1986, Vol. 76, No. 2, 323.
269. Bazerman and Moore, *supra* n. 265, 119–131.
270. *Ibid.*, at 131.
271. *Ibid.*

appropriately. As different companies have different exposures to systematic risk, acquirers will use different cost of capital assumptions for different target companies.

A similar question arises when acquirers use a multiple-based valuation (a form of the market approach): should an acquirer limit the peer group to companies comparable only to the target (in terms of the type of the business or geography) or should the peer group include companies similar to the acquiring group as it is expected after integrating the acquisition target?

These decisions can have a considerable effect on the target's valuation. The effect can be especially significant for cross-border transactions into emerging markets or for acquisitions of young, high-growth businesses by larger acquirers. In these cases, the difference between the cost of capital of the acquirer and that of the target entity can be significant.

In non-contentious M&A valuations, many acquirers, as a matter of policy, use the target firm's cost of capital, not their own or the expected cost of capital of the combined operations.[272] The reason usually given, consistent with corporate finance theory of capital investment decisions, is that the objective is to discount at a rate that reflects the systematic risk of the investment, not the investor.

An acquirer who uses the market approach and who selects a peer group on a set of criteria that relate solely to the target, not the acquirer or the combined group, essentially takes the same approach to considering systematic risk in the valuation.

The systematic risk of an acquisition target will be influenced by the acquirer's plans for the time after the deal has closed, including the extent of the integration of the target into the acquiring group. In many PE transactions, the target effectively continues to operate as a stand-alone business after acquisition, and neither its operations nor the financial structure will be merged into those of the acquirer (even though the stand-alone financial structure often changes after an acquisition with debt effectively pushed down into the acquired entity). Strategic buyers and PE buyers in bolt-on acquisitions, on the other hand, often plan to integrate the target at least partially into their own operations and their financing structure. That can mean that the acquired entity will share corporate functions with the acquirer, or participate in a cash pooling or other financing arrangement. If a target is embedded in the acquirer's financing structure, lenders may be effectively secured by the acquiring group's assets, or cash flows (even if the arrangement is implicit rather than explicit).

A decrease in the target's cost of capital after an acquisition is a benefit to the acquirer. It is a type of synergy.[273] As with other synergies, the extent the buyer is willing to share them with the seller impacts the price it will offer. The availability of synergies that can be shared can be central to the bidding strategy of corporates, and something PE bidders can find difficult to compete with in situations where synergies are not available to them.

272. For example, *see* James R. Hitchner, *Financial Valuation: Applications and Models*, 858 (Wiley 2003).

273. Aswath Damodaran, *The Value of Synergy*, Working Paper, 29 (Stern School of Business, October 2005).

Contentious Valuation

The measure of damages in a post M&A dispute is often different from the original valuation of the acquisition target, a non-contentious situation. One of the differences can arise from the question whether to use the same cost of capital in the actual and hypothetical scenarios, or alternatively whether to reflect in the damages valuation the differences in the capital structures that result from the two scenarios. If each scenario reflects optimal leverage, then the debt and equity weights in weighted average cost of capital (WACC) can be different.

For example, the target may generate more cash in the hypothetical scenario, and this additional liquidity can affect the capital structure and lead to different weights of debt and equity in the WACC. Further, if the target company carries out multiple activities, each with its own systematic risk, and the breach affects one of these disproportionately, then the overall systematic risk may be different in the two scenarios. For example, if a target company consists of a portfolio of commercial real estate and solar projects, and the breach affects only the solar projects, then the risk profile of the overall target business may change as a result of the breach.

The standard of value may also affect the extent to which the damages valuation reflects synergies specific to a buyer (and claimant). As discussed above in §11.03, a commonly used standard of value is fair market value. This is the value at which property would change hands between a hypothetical willing and able buyer and a hypothetical willing and able seller, acting at arm's length in an open and unrestricted market, when neither is under compulsion to buy or sell and when both have reasonable knowledge of the relevant facts.[274] The generic, hypothetical buyer this standard refers to will usually not benefit from synergies related to any specific buyer, and, as a result, synergies are often not included when the fair market value standard is used.

In contrast, the fair value standard references specific, identified parties and their circumstances.[275] If this standard of value is used, then the valuation, including the discount rate used, may reflect synergies that relate to a specific buyer.

[C] Taxes

The general principle is that compensatory damages should put the claimant in the position it would have been in but for the wrongful act. This is a position after taxes, in relation to both lost profits and the award. With marginal tax rates in many countries being above 20% (many significantly higher),[276] notwithstanding the multitude of deductions from the tax base when calculating taxable income, taxes can have a significant impact when calculating loss in the context of an award for damages.

---

274. *International Glossary of Business Valuation Terms*, American Society of Appraisers, ASA Business Valuation Standards, 2009.
275. *See* above §11.03 [C] [1].
276. *See Corporate Income Tax Rates around the World, 2021*, https://taxfoundation.org/publications/corporate-tax-rates-around-the-world/ (accessed in April 2022).

There are two distinct aspects when considering taxes in damages valuation: the corporate income tax on lost profits (often those of the acquisition target), and taxes on the damages award payable by the claimant (if any). These two may be subject to entirely different tax rules, deductions, and so on.

Taxes on Lost Profits

The corporate income tax on lost profits is the difference between taxes on taxable income in the hypothetical and in the actual scenario. As the wrongful act may affect the tax base, the tax rates are not necessarily the same in each scenario. They will also usually be applied to different projected taxable incomes, meaning the effective tax rates can be different.

Estimating future corporate income tax payments can be a complex area of the damages claim that often requires specialist knowledge of local tax rules. Estimating future taxes further requires assumptions in respect of (future) tax rates, depreciation and amortisation, the appropriateness of transfer prices, the treatment of tax-losses carried forward, and other future changes to the tax basis such as the availability of deductions and allowances, to name only a few.[277] This is often an area of significant complexity.

Taxes on operating income are operating costs, and tax payments on operating income are operating cash flows. Taxes are no different in this respect from the cost of purchasing supplies, or the cost of rent, salaries, or wages. Conversely, income taxes on financial income are financial expenses, and their payment belongs in the financing section of the cash flow statement. For example, the tax shield benefit of financial leverage and the associated cash flows are part of the firm's financing. Taxes on operating income reduce free cash flow, whereas tax effects related to financial income or expenses are below free cash flow.

Tax on the Damages Award

It is usually necessary to consider in a damages award any taxes that will be payable on the award. A claimant who is taxed on the award would otherwise be undercompensated. On the other hand, if an award is 'grossed up' to reflect taxes that the claimant is ultimately not liable for, the claimant would be overcompensated. Taxes on the award should therefore be considered separately from taxes on the target's lost profits. In fact, the two can be considered to be entirely different matters.

Approaches in Damages Valuation

One approach that some quantum experts use is to omit all corporate income taxes from the damages calculation.[278] This means determining damages on the basis of pre-tax lost profits while also not considering any taxes that may be payable on the

277. James Nicholson, *The Impact of Corporate Taxation on Economic Losses*, FTI Consulting White Paper, 2, (January 2018).

278. *See* the discussion in James Nicholson, *Taxation and Currency Issues in Damages Awards*, in: *The Guide to Damages in International Arbitration*, 265 (2nd ed., Global Arbitration Review 2017).

award. Unless there is a subsequent 'true-up', this approach implicitly assumes perfect symmetry between the tax rates at which each of the two would have been taxed so that the benefit to the claimant from omitting taxes in the calculation of lost profits (which are therefore higher) is exactly offset by the taxes payable on the award. However, there is usually no reason to assume such symmetry, and the tax situations of the claimant and that of the target entity are often different.

It is also not at all straightforward to move a DCF valuation from a post-tax to a pre-tax basis. Stock market returns used in the CAPM are on a post-tax basis, and investors' return expectations are generally after taxes. An approach sometimes used to calculate pre-tax cash flows is to 'gross up' post-tax cash flows at a rate equal to one minus the marginal corporate tax rate. However, this will usually not give the same result as discounting post-tax cash flows at post-tax discount rates since it ignores the difference between accrual accounting taxable income (on which the tax payable is based) and cash flows (which are grossed up).

It can be shown that except in no-growth perpetual cash flow scenarios, post-tax cash flows are not equal to pre-tax cash flow multiplied by a factor equal to one less the marginal corporate tax rate.[279] It is therefore important to use post-tax cash flows and post-tax discount rates in DCF valuations.[280]

[D] Damages Clauses

It is common for SPAs to contain clauses that govern the assessment of damages. Beyond limiting damages, such clauses frequently exclude indirect or consequential damages or the use of specific valuation methods when calculating damages (such as multiple-based methods). Damages clauses also frequently exclude 'loss of profits', 'diminution in value', or a 'loss in value' of the sold shares, frequently without defining these terms. Some damages clauses also specify that internal costs should not be included in the damages calculation, or limit the calculation of damages to a 'dollar for dollar' basis, again frequently without clearly defining what these exclusions mean.

A purpose of these clauses is to protect sellers from what they feel can be overly aggressive approaches to quantum, such as the mechanical application of a multiple to a correction of EBITDA, or the inclusion in damages of internal costs that would have been incurred in any event, even without the breach. The discussion here is limited to certain financial aspects of these clauses; their legal aspects are outside the scope of this book.

It is rare for damages clauses to set out a specific damages valuation method that is to be used in the case of a breach. In fact, the more specific a valuation clause, the less it may fit the (hitherto unknown) circumstances in the event it becomes relevant. More generally, limiting the degrees of freedom in a damages valuation risks removing valid, and required, valuation approaches. Assessing a monetary amount that restores

279. *See* Wayne Lonergan, *Pre and Post Tax Discount Rates and Cash Flows: A Technical Note,* The Journal of Applied Research in Accounting and Finance, Vol. 4 No. 1 2009, 41–45.
280. *Ibid.*, p. 45.

a claimant to the position but for a breach is a commercial matter, that, as observed above in §11.01, usually cannot be predetermined and contractually prescribed. Clauses that aim to do so by specifying valuation methods or specific assumptions to use in the process, thereby limiting valid options, risk outcomes that do not restore the claimant to the position but for a breach. It is usually simply not possible for the SPA to consider all possible circumstances and their implications for damages before these circumstances are known.

Damages clauses also often leave important terms undefined. For example, a 'dollar-for-dollar' basis for the calculation of damages (which to many accountants has echoes of a 'dollar-for-dollar' balance sheet adjustment) may sound straightforward but can mean different things to different experts.

The following is an example of a valuation clause in an SPA that led to a dispute. The example illustrates the difficulty of prescripting valuation approaches in a contract.

Example: Valuation Method of Shares Subject to a Put Option (International Arbitration)[281]

The example relates to the valuation of shares on the exercise of a put option by the seller. Two companies had entered into an SPA under which the respondent sold 51 % of the share capital of a Swiss target to the claimant. The claimant (buyer) also received a put option which allowed it to require the respondent (seller) to purchase shares in the target company held by the claimant during the seven years following the third anniversary of the SPA. The shares were to be sold at their 'fair market value'. Fair market value was to be determined by an independent expert having regard to the following criteria:

- The target's existing and historical financial performance over the preceding three-year period.
- An analysis of relevant market factors during the same period, including multiples of financial indicators (i.e., turnover, net profits, cash flow, net assets) paid for comparable companies in recent M&A transactions in comparable countries and industries.
- An analysis of trading multiples of any existing comparable companies trading on the local stock exchange or other relevant stock exchanges.
- An analysis of the status of the subsector in the country where the target was located and its expected future development, with consideration given to any relevant market information and recent or expected legislative and regulatory developments which would impact the market value of the company.
- A DCF analysis.

The claimant exercised the put option during the agreed period, but the parties could not agree on the valuation of the shares. They appointed an audit firm to

281. ICC Case 11786, in: The Arbitration of Disputes Relating to Mergers and Acquisitions: A Study of ICC Cases, Andrea Carlevaris ICC International Court of Arbitration Bulletin Vol. 24 Number 1/2013, p. 29.

determine the shares' fair market value. However, the audit firm's valuation was not considered binding on the parties, and the case went to arbitration. The tribunal performed a detailed analysis of twenty-seven valuation issues over which the parties disagreed and applied the criteria set out in the SPA.

From a valuation perspective, the provisions in the SPA referenced different (seemingly arbitrary) methods and criteria, without defining their relationship to each other. This may have given the parties a sense that something had been agreed, but the provisions were not in fact helpful to an independent expert who was engaged to assess fair market value. A better outcome may have been achieved by setting out a clear expert determination process in the contract, binding on the parties, without being overly prescriptive as to how precisely the expert should go about the valuation.

[E] Event Studies

The final aspect of damages valuation in this chapter relates to disputes that involve public companies. In these cases, a market valuation (in the form of a share price traded at a public exchange) is normally readily available.

Event studies have been used in financial economics, accounting research, class actions, investigations of market manipulation and other contexts for many years.[282] They were first introduced in academic research in 1933[283] and significantly refined in the late 1960s.[284] They are also occasionally used in the valuation of damages in M&A disputes (though significantly less than in some other types of disputes such as class actions).

The market constantly values the shares of public companies, and, by extension, constantly establishes their market capitalisations (i.e., their equity values). The idea behind the use of an event study in damages valuation is that the behaviour of a share price immediately after the disclosure of an event (such as the discovery of accounting fraud, or other – usually adverse – event) can be used to determine the effect of the event on the share price. This idea is not only used for public companies that are the subject of a dispute but also for private companies for which public companies can be identified that have been affected by comparable events.

The price of a share that is traded on a public exchange continuously reacts to a multitude of news – some firm-specific, others relating to the general market.[285] For example, share prices react to the announcement of a central bank's monetary policy

282. *See* S. P Khotari and Jerold B. Warner, Econometrics of Event Studies Center for Corporate Governance, Tuck School of Business at Dartmouth, p. 4. *See also* Meloria Meschi and Ravi Kanabar, *Event Studies in International Arbitration: A Primer, the* American Review of International Arbitration (ARIA), Vol. 31, No. 1 (December 2020).
283. James Clay Dolley, *Characteristics and Procedures of Common Stock Split-Ups*, Harvard Business Review Vol. 11, No. 3 (April 1933, 316–326).
284. Ray Ball and Phillip Brown, *An Empirical Evaluation of Accounting Income Numbers*, Journal of Accounting Research Vol. 6, No. 2 (Autumn 1968), 159–178 and Eugene F. Fama, Lawrence Fischer, Michael C. Jensen and Richard Roll, *The Adjustment of Stock Prices to New Information*, International Economic Review Vol. 10, No. 1(February 1969) 1–21.
285. *See* Wöss et al., *supra* n. 210, at 313. In some cases, news can be sector-specific (rather than general market-specific) which can require the use of an industry-specific index.

decisions, the release of a firm's last quarter's earnings, or the discovery of accounting irregularities in a local subsidiary. An event study isolates the part of a price movement that is due to a firm-specific event (such as the earnings announcement or disclosure of accounting irregularities) from general market events (such as monetary policy announcements). It uses regression analysis to predict the normal return on a firm's daily stock price over a period of time. Put simply, the difference between the predicted return and the actual return is the abnormal, or excess, return – the part of the stock's total return that cannot be explained by general market events.[286] The abnormal return is a measure of the change in price of the share associated with the event that is being analysed.

The use of an event study requires that the event has been disclosed to the market and that the relevant company's shares trade in informationally efficient markets.[287] The event study can then be used to analyse the following question: what value does the market assign to the difference between the value that could have been expected but-for the release of information about the adverse event and the actual value that reflects the event? This is very similar to a damages valuation that compares a hypothetical 'warranty true' scenario (what was expected) and the actual scenario (what was the actual value).

Event studies are less common in M&A disputes, many of which either do not relate to public companies or for other reasons do not lend themselves to the use of statistical analyses as those used in event studies. For example, this may be the case where a public company discloses information over time, or where it is difficult to identify the exact timing of market reactions when the release of information is in a foreign language or across time zones. The disclosure date may also differ from the damages valuation date, for example, in cases where accounting errors are announced months or even years after the date of the accounts which they relate to (although statistical techniques are available to remove the effects on price in the interim period); or it may be difficult to separate the effect on price of the disclosure of an alleged breach from other significant firm-specific news around the disclosure date.

For these reasons, the use of event studies in M&A damages valuation is the exception. Nevertheless, there are examples of M&A-related disputes where event studies have been used, at least as a cross-check on other approaches to the assessment of damages.

Example: Transaction involving a Public Company Purchaser's Shares as the Acquisition Currency

An example of a situation where an event study was used to assess damages is a dispute where the buyer was a public telecom firm that acquired a mobile operator and paid part of the consideration of several billion dollars in the acquirer's shares. The value of the acquirer's shares were an important part of the overall consideration.

286. Litigation Services Handbook, Federal Securities Acts and Areas of Expert Analysis, Nicholas I. Crew, Kevin L. Gold and Marnie A. Moore, 24.19 for further discussion.
287. *Ibid.*, at 24.16.

Several weeks after closing, the buyer announced that it had uncovered accounting irregularities in one of its significant subsidiaries. On the day of the announcement, the buyer's market capitalisation decreased by more than a fifth, an effect of several billion dollars, and the acquisition currency, which had made the seller a minority shareholder, was worth significantly less as a result. The accounting irregularities dated back several years, to the period before signing, and the seller argued on this basis that the shares had already been worth less at the time of the transaction, only that the market had been unaware of their true value.

The seller's expert used an event study to isolate the effect on the share price after the disclosure of the accounting irregularities. The result of this analysis was used as a measure of damages. (The parties settled).

CHAPTER 12

Damages for Breaches of Representations and Warranties and Other Obligations, and Quantum of Indemnities

§12.01 OVERVIEW

[A] Breach of Warranty

The SPA in every transaction contains representations and warranties from each party to the other. The principal purposes of representations and warranties include:

- the allocation of risk between the buyer and the seller. Representations and warranties identify which party assumes the risk for which item, including the risk of unknown conditions and liabilities;
- to force disclosure;[288] and
- to serve as a closing condition (e.g., 'bring-down' of representations and warranties or MAC clauses).[289]

A warranty is a promise made in a contract by one party to another that a state of affairs exists.[290] A breach arises when the state does not exist.[291] Alleged breaches of warranties in SPAs are a common cause of post-deal disputes. Alleged breaches of warranties that relate to the financial statements are also a reason why many purchase

288. Representations and warranties are typically qualified by reference to any matters disclosed to the other party, including in a formal 'Disclosure Letter' typically sent by the seller to the buyer. Any matter fairly disclosed in the Disclosure Letter or other circumscribed disclosure cannot found a claim for misrepresentation or breach of warranty.
289. Latham & Watkins, *Key Provisions of Acquisition Agreements*, February 2016, p. 10, available at https://www.lw.com/admin/Upload/Documents/OilAndGasMandA/General%20Concepts/Consolidated_General_Concepts_Part_II_Key_Provisions.pdf.
290. Kramer, *supra* n. 179, at 225.
291. *Ibid.*

price adjustment disputes that would otherwise have been resolved in an expert determination end up in litigation or arbitration.

Sellers' SPA warranties typically relate to the title to shares, insolvency, commercial contracts, intellectual property, litigation, employees, pensions, environmental damages, taxes, compliance with law, and financial statements. The focus of this chapter is on sellers' warranties that relate to the financial statements – usually (although not necessarily) those of the target company.

Below is an example of a financial statements warranty:

> The Audited Financial Statements for the financial year []:
>
> (i) have received an unqualified audit opinion;
> (ii) have been prepared in accordance with [relevant GAAP]; and
> (iii) give [to Sellers' Knowledge] in all material respects a true and fair view of the financial position and affairs of the Company as at the Accounts Date and of the financial performance of the Company for the financial year ended on the Accounts Date.

A frequent element of a financial statements warranty is the promise that the target's historical accounts give a 'true and fair view' of the state of affairs at the end of the period, and the profit or loss for the period (or similar wording, as in the example above). This is a 'true and fair view' warranty.

Financial statements warranties can also relate to specific elements of historical profit and loss accounts or alternatively metrics that can be derived from them, such as minimum EBIT or EBITDA figures of a specific period. Alternatively, warranties can relate to specific line items in the balance sheet, such as working capital, (minimum) equity, total assets, or total debt figures. In legal terms, these types of warranties are considered to be similar to a warranty of quality, i.e., a warranty as to the characteristics of the business and its past.[292]

Warranties can alternatively be promises that reasonable care was taken when financial information (e.g., a business plan) was prepared. 'Warranties of reasonable care' are legally different from 'warranties of quality' and damages may be measured on a different basis. These are discussed separately below in §12.02.

The following is an example of an alleged 'true and fair view' warranty breach where the judge remarked on the distinction between and accounting breach and commercial value.

Example: *Macquarie Internationale Investments Limited v. Glencore UK Ltd*[293]

Approximately three months after Macquarie acquired Corona Energy Holdings Limited ('Corona'), one of Corona's main suppliers presented an invoice for GBP 2.4 million relating to meter charges that had been missed previously by the supplier due to an error that occurred during an IT system change. The charges were unknown to

292. *Ibid.*
293. Court of Appeal of England and Wales: *Macquarie Internationale Investments Limited v. Glencore UK Ltd* [2010] EWCA Civ 697.

both the seller and the target, and the target's liability could not reasonably have been discovered before signing. The seller was, therefore, not at fault by reason of their failure to disclose the existence of the liability.

The SPA included the following warranty:

> The Accounts:
>
> (a) have been prepared in accordance with Relevant Accounting Standards and in a manner consistent with that adopted in the preparation of the annual accounts of the Group and/or the Company or Subsidiary to which they relate (as the case may be) for the Financial Years ended 31 December 2003 and 31 December 2004;
>
> (b) give a true and fair view of the assets and liabilities of the Group and/or the Company or the Subsidiary to which they relate as at the Accounts Date and the profits and losses of the Group and/or the Company or the Subsidiary to which they relate (as the case may be) for the Financial Year ended on the Accounts Date (including all related party transactions) ....[294]

The buyer argued that the seller had breached the 'true and fair view' warranty. Even if the liability was unknown and the process in accordance with the relevant accounting standards, not including the liability meant that the accounts did not present a 'true and fair view'.

The Court of Appeal held that (unless there are exceptional circumstances, which in its view were not present in the case) accounts show a 'true and fair view' if they have been prepared in accordance with the relevant accounting standards. The relevant accounting standards did not require to record a provision for a liability that was unknown at the time, and the accounts had therefore been 'true and fair'. The Court held that the target group of companies did not know about and could not reasonably have discovered the missed meter charges at the relevant time. Furthermore, it held that it could not be said that the target group or its accountants made an 'error' within the meaning of paragraph 63 of FRS 3, which required or permitted the accounts for the year ended 31 December 2005 to be reopened or restated.

The judge stated that the accounts warranty, as its title indicates, '... is concerned with accounts, not with retrospectively perceived commercial value'.[295] The buyer's claim for breach of warranty failed.

[B] Indemnities

An indemnity is a promise to reimburse the claimant in respect of a specified loss it has suffered or might suffer. Indemnities are often appropriate for specific matters which are known to the parties, but where there is significant uncertainty over the amount of the obligation. They often include potential liabilities arising from environmental risks, litigation, product liability, or taxes relating to the seller's period of ownership.

294. *Ibid.*, para. 23.
295. *Ibid.*, para. 84.

The quantum of an indemnity depends on its terms.[296] These need to be set out clearly in the SPA. A seller undertakes to indemnify a buyer for loss suffered as a result of a particular event, then if the event occurs (subject to thresholds and other conditions) the seller has to reimburse the buyer dollar-for-dollar for the loss suffered as a result. There is no obligation to prove that any such loss has occurred as a result of inaccuracy in the information that the seller provided.[297]

§12.02 COMPENSATORY DAMAGES AND THE BUT-FOR FRAMEWORK

[A] Overview

The award of damages is the principal remedy granted by courts and tribunals for breach of contract.[298] A modern formulation in European law for the basic measure of contract damages is:

> [S]uch sum as will put the aggrieved party as nearly as possible into the position in which it would have been if the contract had been duly performed. Such damages cover the loss which the aggrieved party has suffered and the gain of which it has been deprived.[299]

This approach is referred to as the 'expectation' measure (in contrast to 'reliance' damages), as the claimant is entitled to be put in the same position as he or she 'expected' to be in had the contract been performed as promised.[300]

[B] The Principles of Compensation and the But-For Framework

The general principle is that the expectation measure must put the claimant in the same position he or she would have been in 'but-for' the breach. The basic compensatory calculation is a factual comparison between what actually happened (the breach position) and what would have happened but for the breach (the non-breach position).[301] The but-for framework is a way to capture this comparison: it compares the (hypothetical) position the aggrieved party would have been in had a contract been

296. Kramer, *supra* n. 179, at 237.
297. Although there may be additional terms ensuring that the seller has some oversight over or involvement in the handling of disputes that emerge between the target company and a third party, in order to protect the seller from a buyer whose motivation to fight the liability is reduced by knowledge of the indemnity.
298. Kramer, *supra* n. 179, at 4. For example, it was set out by *Baron Park Robinson v. Harman* in 1848 and cited many times. Kramer, *supra* n. 179, at 13 with further citations.
299. Article 9:502 of the Principles of European Contract Law. There is a similar principle in bilateral investment treaty (BIT) arbitrations, based on Chorzow Factory (1928), which states that compensation should '*wipe out all the consequences of the illegal act and re-establish the situation which would, in all probability, have existed if that act had not been committed*'. *See* Wöss et al., *supra* n. 210, at 6.26.
300. Kramer, *supra* n. 179, at 13 with further citations.
301. *Ibid.*, at 249.

performed with the (actual) position it found itself in as a result of the breach. This was expressed by a High Court judge as follows:

> I take the governing principle to be that damages should be such as will restore the plaintiff, so far as a monetary award can do so, to the position it would have occupied had the breaches found to have been committed by the defendants not occurred. On that basis an inquiry into damages should therefore normally take the form of a comparison, in financial terms, between the events which have actually happened and those which would have happen[ed] had the relevant breach not occurred, the former being susceptible of direct evidence, the latter being necessarily hypothetical.[302]

A graphical depiction of the factual comparison between what would have occurred and what actually occurred but for the breach is shown in Figure 12.1.

Figure 12.1 The But-For Framework

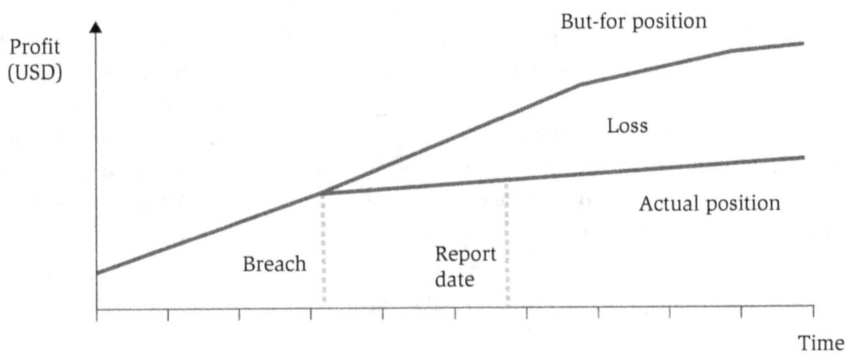

The two paths represent actual returns (lower line) and hypothetical returns (upper line) that the target generated or would have generated had a breach not occurred. The two lines diverge from the date of the breach onwards.[303] The damages period can be finite, i.e., the two paths may converge after some time, or they can alternatively remain separate. Closely related, especially over longer time horizons, are often the questions of causation and mitigation. As these are legal matters, they are not discussed here further.

[1] The Actual Position (The Breach Position)

The actual position, or breach position, is what in fact happened. As monetary damages should put the claimant in the position he or she would have been in had the

302. *Stephenson Blake (Holdings) Ltd v. Streets Heaver Ltd* [2001] Lloyd's Rep PN 44 para. 159 (Hicks QC).

303. They could alternatively diverge only at some point *after* the breach if, for example, it takes time before the breach affects the returns.

breach not occurred, the actual position aims to measure the value 'as is'. In warranty breach cases, this is often considered to be the value on the basis of restated accounts (corrected to represent reality), that is the accounts 'with the right figures' in them.[304]

When considering a claim for breach of contract, the actual position is generally more straightforward to develop; what is more difficult is to calculate what would have happened had the contract not been breached.[305]

In a warranty breach case in an M&A dispute, on the other hand, the actual position (reflected in the financial statements after any error corrections) can be more difficult to establish. The parties themselves have already valued the non-breach position, thinking that was reality.

Consider a true and fair view warranty where the buyer's valuation was based on the reported EBITDA of a historical period. It turns out that this EBITDA figure was overstated. The actual value represents what the company was really worth, not what the overstated EBITDA suggested it was worth, or what the buyer may have assumed it was worth.

Establishing the actual position - this is the lower line in Figure 12.1 above between the date of breach and the report date - is often based on the last available historical financials at the time of the damages valuation, frequently interim financials. The financial information relevant to assessing damages in this scenario often extends beyond the time at which the valuation takes place. This is the part of the lower line in Figure 12.1 to the right of the report date, and it is this forward-looking aspect that can make the actual scenario so complex as it requires projected information, often based on management's expectations.

[2] The Hypothetical Position (The Non-breach Position)

The hypothetical position is what would have happened had the breach not occurred. In warranty breach cases, the purchase price is often considered to be the value as warranted.[306] The purchase price is, therefore, often considered to be the value associated with the non-breach position.

In any event, the assumptions used to establish the hypothetical position should be realistic (at least at the relevant valuation date).[307] The following sources are often used as a basis for the hypothetical position:

- The assumptions the parties made when they valued the target firm before signing.
- Other company projections (ideally prepared just before the time of the breach - that is, unaffected by the breach).[308]

304. *Sycamore Bidco Limited v. Sean Breslin/Andrew Dawson* [2012] EWHC 3443 (Ch).
305. For example, MacGregor, Maclay and Mitchell, *supra* n. 188, at 160.
306. As discussed above in §11.05 [A], price and value are not necessarily always the same.
307. *Ibid.*
308. Depending on the use of hindsight (a legal matter) these projections may possibly be adjusted to reflect new information.

- Trend extrapolation from historical financial statements, particularly relevant for companies with a stable track record of trading.
- Profitability metrics and balance sheet ratios of comparable companies (a peer group).
- Analysts' expectations in respect of market growth rates, market share, and other drivers of financial performance.

The non-breach position is represented by hypothetical returns. If the income approach is used, the relevant metric is usually projected free cash flow.[309] In order to project these returns, they can be broken down into their constituent parts: projected trading, working capital (and other balance sheet movements) and capital expenditure; trading can be broken down further into variable and fixed cost components in order to model how each responds to changes in sales. The damages expert usually prepares an integrated set of financial statements from which he or she derives the free cash flows the business could have been expected to return had the warranties been true.

[3] Discontinuing operations

In cases where a target company discontinues trading, actual free cash flows will go to zero (or below in case there are costs of liquidation). This situation is depicted in Figure 12.2.

Figure 12.2 The But-For Framework: The Actual Position Goes to Zero

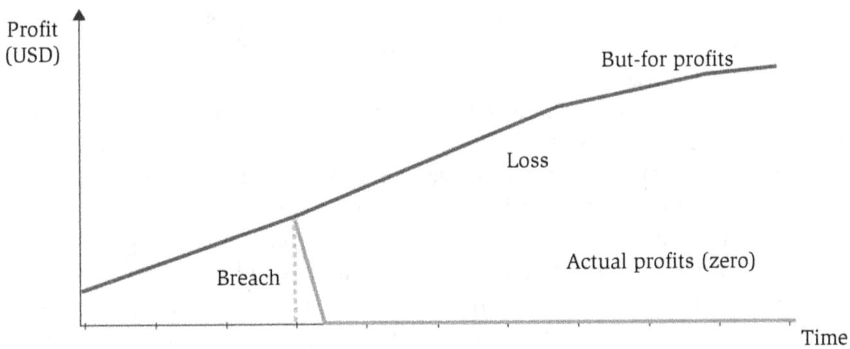

Example: Joint Venture Dispute over Lost Profits (International Arbitration)

Two joint venture partners entered into a joint venture agreement for the production and distribution of technology used in shipbuilding. Party 1, a start-up, contributed technology it had developed and patented. Party 2, a manufacturer and distributor of technology solutions for the shipbuilding industry, contributed access to its existing

309. §11.04 [B].

distribution network and financing of the start-up phase (during which the entity was expected to be loss-making). The joint venture agreement entitled each party to a 50% share of the joint venture's profits over an initial term of several years.

At the inception of the joint venture, Party 1 licensed its proprietary technology to the joint venture. Party 2 provided start-up funding. A short while later, while the entity was still ramping up operations, Party 2 was acquired by a large corporate. The acquirer had its own technology which competed with that Party 1 had licensed to the joint venture. Shortly after the acquisition, Party 2 withheld additional financing from the joint venture entity, which was soon forced into liquidation.

Party 1 argued that the joint venture agreement was breached as Party 2 had withheld the funding. It claimed damages as the difference between the actual value of its ownership interest in the joint venture entity (zero) and the counterfactual, in which the joint venture entity would have received funding and continued to trade. The hypothetical position was largely based on a business plan that the two parties had agreed a short time before the acquisition of Party 2.

[4] Loss of Business Value Versus Lost Profits

The discussion above used the term 'loss' in a broad sense that encompassed both lost profits and a reduction in the value of an ownership interest. However, claims may be for lost profits, lost, or diminished, business value, or a combination of these, and the distinction can be important.

When damages experts refer to 'lost profits', they usually mean lost cash flows,[310] the metric many experts most closely associate with 'value'. Even if the term lost profits refers to a measure of accrual earnings, these accrual earnings will reconcile to cash flow according to the accounting equation (for an infinite forecast horizon).

The idea underlying the income approach discussed above in §11.04 [B] is that the value of an asset is the capitalised value of the future income stream it generates. The 'flow' of a (lost) income stream reconciles to the (loss in) present value of 'stock'. This same idea is captured in the stocks-and-flows accounting relationship: in the closing accounting entry, a period's earnings are added to the book value of equity (from which dividends are paid).[311] It is 'flows' that lead to a change in 'stocks'. In concept, 'lost profits', when capitalised at a point in time therefore mean a reduction in the value of a business at that point in time. All else equal, 'lost profits' and 'lost business value' are two sides of the same coin; the terms can be interchangeable.[312]

However, all else is often not equal, and there can be legal reasons that make it necessary to distinguish between lost profits and the loss of business value. First, many SPAs exclude certain types of losses, such as lost profits or the diminution of value. This can make the distinction relevant and raise complex legal questions.

310. *See, e.g.*, Evans, Galanti and Lentz, *supra* n. 192, at 4.16.
311. Penman, *Accounting for Value, supra* n. 184, p. 168.
312. Evans, Galanti and Lentz, *supra* n. 192, at 4.17.

Further, differences can arise in relation to the valuation date and the use of hindsight: the valuation of a business (or an ownership interest) at the time of a breach can sometimes mean that a valuation should reflect only what was known at the time. In contrast, a claim for profits that would have been generated after the date of the breach (but were not) may, in some instances, incorporate additional information.[313]

Lastly, a difference may arise if a company itself is the claimant – it may be able to claim a loss of profits, but not a diminution of its own value. In contrast, shareholders in a company may only be able to claim a diminution in the value of their shares. These are, however, legal considerations outside the scope of this book.[314]

[5] The Valuation Date and the Use of Hindsight

It is common to assess loss at the date of the breach and based on the information available to the parties at the time (though this is a legal matter). In M&A disputes, the date of breach is frequently the date of the financial statement warranty, which is often signing and (in case of a 'bring-down') closing. With the valuation date typically comes the question of hindsight: to what extent should subsequent events be considered in the assessment of damages?

Both the valuation date and the question of hindsight can have significant effects on damages. For example, this was a central issue in *Ageas v. Kwik-Fit & another* which concerned the breach of a financial statements warranty.[315] After closing, it emerged that the warranted accounts on which the buyer had based its valuation of the target contained errors in the treatment of bad debt as an incorrectly calculated bad debt reserve had resulted in the overstatement of both profits and assets of the target. The judge explained:

> Damages for breach of contract will normally be assessed by reference to the position at the date of breach. But a later date may be used for the assessment if in all the circumstances of the case to do so would more accurately reflect the overriding compensatory principle.[316]

The judge held that, under the terms of the SPA, the buyer had assumed the risk connected with the reserve post-acquisition. The judge made specific reference to the fact that the purchase price was a fixed price. The bargain embodied in the SPA was the allocation of risk to the buyer of any benefit or loss arising either from the way the buyer chose to run the business or as a result of external influences on the success of the business.[317] The court did not, therefore, cut across this allocation of risk by allowing hindsight to influence the calculation of damages.

---

313. For example, this was the issue in the Canadian case *RBC Dominion Securities Inc. v. Merrill Lynch Canada Inc.* [2004] B.C.J. No. 2337.
314. For further discussion *see* Kramer, *supra* n. 179, at 497.
315. *Ageas (UK) Ltd v. Kwik-Fit (GB) Ltd & anr* [2014] EWHC 2178 (QB).
316. *Ibid.*, para. 30.
317. *Ibid.*, para. 50.

The discussion above in §3.05 of post-balance sheet events addressed accounting guidance when to reflect new information after the balance sheet date in the accounts. This is often relevant in completion accounts disputes and expert determination, but can be different in warranty breach cases as the question of hindsight is a legal matter in these disputes.

[6] Measure of Damages Related to Warranties of Reasonable Care

A different measure of damages applies for warranties of reasonable care. This type of warranty is a promise that the seller has taken reasonable care in preparing financial information.[318]

An example is the case *Esso Petroleum v. Mardon*.[319] A warranty of a forecast was found not to be a warranty of the forecast being true, but a warranty of the seller having taken reasonable care in preparing the forecast. The measure of damages was not the 'loss of bargain', but compensation for having been induced to enter into a contract which turned out to be disastrous for the claimant. The Court of Appeal found that the damages were to be measured by the loss the claimant suffered, as:

> [The claimant] can say:
>
>> I would not have entered into this contract at all but for your representation. Owing to it, I have lost all the capital I put into it. I also incurred a large overdraft. I have spent four years of my life in wasted endeavour without reward: and it will take me some time to re-establish myself.
>>
>> For all such loss, he is entitled to recover damages. It is to be measured in a similar way as the loss due to a personal injury. You should look into the future so as to forecast what would have been likely to happen if he had never entered into this contract: and contrast it with his position as it is now as a result of entering into it. The future is necessarily problematical and can only be a rough-and-ready estimate. But it must be done in assessing the loss.[320]

---

318. Kramer, *supra* n. 179, at 233.
319. *Esso Petroleum v. Mardon* [1976] QB 801, discussed in Kramer, *supra* n. 179, at 233.
320. *Ibid.*

CHAPTER 13

Material Adverse Change Clauses and Pre-signing Disputes

§13.01 INTRODUCTION

Material adverse Change and Material Adverse Effect clauses aim to protect a buyer by providing a mechanism to terminate a transaction before closing in the event of a MAC.[321] MAC clauses are usually either closing conditions or sellers' representations (and sometimes both).

The wording of MAC clauses can vary significantly. MAC clauses are sometimes categorised into 'Company' MACs and 'Market' MACs, (but they can combine elements of both): a 'Company MAC' is tested relative to the target company and usually references changes of company-specific metrics such as a reduction in sales or EBITDA by a certain percentage. A 'Market MAC' references changes in the overall market situation or the target's industry.

A MAC clause in an SPA should be aligned with MAC clauses in debt financing agreements (especially in private equity deals), the idea being that in the event a senior lender invokes a MAC and debt financing may become unavailable, or delayed, the buyer can also invoke a MAC under the SPA and avoid closing.[322]

Courts have generally been reluctant to allow buyers to invoke MAC clauses in order to walk away from signed deals.[323] Most alleged MACs do not lead to the transaction not closing, but instead to renegotiations of the price. For example,

321. The terms 'Material Adverse Change' and 'Material Adverse Effect' clause are used interchangeably in this publication.
322. Even if perfectly aligned, however, there can be a disconnect between the two MAC clauses. For example, cases may be heard in different jurisdictions or courts.
323. For examples of events that did not constitute a MAC, *see S.C. Johnson Son, Inc. v. Dowbrands, Inc.*, 167 F. Supp. 2d 657 (D. Del. 2001) and *Frontier Oil Corporation v. Holly Corporation*, C.A. No. 20502 (Del. Ch. 29 April 2005). For further discussion *see Mergers and Acquisitions Disputes*, AICPA Forensic and Valuation Services Section Practice Aid, American Institute of Certified Public Accountants, New York, NY 2012, 49.

Delaware courts had never allowed a MAC clause to invalidate a deal until *Akorn, Inc. v. Fresenius Kabi*, in which a combination of multiple serious misrepresentations and a sustained and substantial decline in financial performance of Akorn's business led to the court's conclusion that a material adverse event had occurred (the Delaware Supreme Court affirmed the decision).[324] To put the magnitude of the adverse developments in the case in context, after closing, Akorn announced year-on-year declines in quarterly revenues and earnings per share of 29% and 96%, respectively (followed by significant declines in subsequent quarters).

In most other cases, rather than leading to a transaction not closing, alleged material adverse events lead to a renegotiation of the price. An example of this is the acquisition of Yahoo by Verizon (*see* the discussion in §13.02).

§13.02 DEFINITION OF A MATERIAL ADVERSE CHANGE

A key element of a MAC clause is the definition of what changes or events are 'material'. A MAC clause can make reference to specific changes or events or alternatively include only general wording (sometimes in combination with carve-outs that exclude certain events, for example, a 'pandemic'). Broad MAC clauses, generally in the interest of the buyer, increase the scope for disagreement.

The meaning of 'material' in a MAC context was recently addressed by the High Court in *Decision Inc Holdings Proprietary Ltd v. Garbett*:[325]

> One way of testing whether a change is material is to ask whether it is so significant that the other party, had they known of the change, would not have entered into the transaction at all, or would have entered into it on significantly different terms... However, the test is an objective test – evidence of the actual states of mind of the parties is not – and should not be – admissible in this regard. The question is as to whether a reasonable person who had entered into the transaction with the aims and objectives of the buyer would have sought to withdraw from or renegotiate the transaction had he known of the change. That is the true test of materiality.

The court found that the sellers had breached a warranty that there had been no material adverse change in the target company's prospects since the date of its last accounts. The judge also rejected the idea that 'materiality' in this context should be informed by the accounting concept of materiality:

> I do not think that there is any necessary read-across between the accounting concept of materiality and the use of the term in a contract. In fact the two perform entirely different functions.

324. *Akorn, Inc. v. Fresenius Kabi* (C.A. No. 2018-0300-JTL Del. Ch. 1 October 2018). *See also* https://www.skadden.com/insights/publications/2018/12/delaware-supreme-court-affirms-akorn.
325. *Decision Inc Holdings Proprietary Ltd v. Garbett* [2023] EWHC 588.

§13.03 OTHER CASES

The acquisition of Yahoo by Verizon for USD 4.8 billion in July 2016 is an example of a MAC clause that led to a renegotiation of the price. The SPA included a MAC clause that defined a MAC event as one that 'has had, or would reasonably be expected to have, a material adverse effect on the business, assets, properties, results of operation or financial condition of the business, taken as a whole'.[326]

After signing, Yahoo disclosed that it had become aware of two cyber-attacks dating between 2013 and 2014 that compromised more than one billion of its customer accounts. Verizon renegotiated a reduction in the purchase price by USD 350 million. Reuters cited federal filings that Verizon's CEO initially proposed a discount as high as USD 925 million.[327] The financial question underlying the measurement of any discount relates to putting a value on the compromised customer accounts.

The covid pandemic brought a fresh wave of MAC-related disputes. Among the first buyers to claim that the target experienced a MAC because of the pandemic in 2020 was PE firm Sycamore Partners which sued Victoria's Secret parent, L Brands, in April 2020, seeking to end its deal to acquire a 55% stake in the lingerie brand.[328] The case settled, allowing Sycamore to pull out of the proposed deal.

Another early-pandemic case was *Travelport v. WEX*.[329] In May 2020, WEX notified the sellers that it was pulling out of a USD 1.7 billion acquisition of two companies that provided business-to-business payment services in the travel industry, as, in its view, conditions resulting from the pandemic constituted a material adverse effect. Travelport turned to the courts to force WEX to close the transaction. Although Travelport did not succeed (on a preliminary issue), the deal did eventually go through, however, at a much lower valuation of USD 577.5 million.[330]

Buyers invoked MAC clauses in numerous other pandemic-related disputes, many of which were resolved by renegotiating the price.[331]

The pandemic also brought into sharper focus other contractual clauses that could prevent a transaction from closing or alternatively lead a buyer to claim damages.

326. *See* 'How Yahoo's Data Breach Could Affect Its Deal with Verizon', *The New York Times*, 23 September 2016.
327. Verizon sought USD 925 million discount for Yahoo merger, got USD 350 million, Reuters Business News, 13 March 2017, available at: https://www.reuters.com/article/us-yahoo-m-a-verizon-idUSKBN16K2ID.
328. *Sycamore Partners III, LP, et al. v. L Brands, Inc. [Victoria's Secret]*, C.A. No. 2020-0306-, compl. (Del. Ch. 24 April 2020).
329. *Travelport Ltd v. Wex Inc* [2020] EWHC 2670 (Comm) (12 October 2020).
330. *See* Financier Worldwide Magazine, *Deal certainty in M&A agreements – current concerns*, September 222 Issue.
331. For example: *Bed Bath & Beyond, Inc. v. 1-800-Flowers.com, Inc.*, et al., C.A. No. 2020-0245-, compl. (Del. Ch. 1 April 2020); *Snow Phipps Group, LLC v. KCAKE Acquisition, Inc., et al.*, C.A. No. 2020-0282-, compl. (Del. Ch. 14 April 2020; red. 17 April 2020); *Carlyle Roundtrip v. Juweel Investors, Ltd., et al.*, C.A. No. 2020-0351-, complaint (Del. Ch. 8 May 2020; red. 13 May 2020); *Forescout Technologies, Inc. v. Ferrari Group Holdings, LP, et al.*, C.A. No. 2020-0385-, compl. (Del. Ch. 19 May 2020).

An example is *AB Stable VIII, LLC v. MAPS Hotel and Resorts One, LLC, et al.*[332] The buyer, Mirae Asset Financial Group, a Korean financial services company, walked away from the acquisition of Strategic Hotels & Resorts LLC when the pandemic hit. The court affirmed that the seller's actions permitted the buyer to terminate the SPA because the seller, the owner of fifteen luxury hotels, had breached a covenant requiring that the target business operate 'only in the ordinary course consistent with past practices in all material respects' by shutting two hotels entirely and limiting operations at the other thirteen severely in light of the covid pandemic. Mirae terminated the transaction not because of a material adverse event, but because of a breach of the ordinary course covenant.[333]

§13.04 EXAMPLE OF A PRE-SIGNING DISPUTE

Disputes can arise in the period before signing, for example, over binding parts of (otherwise non-binding) documents such as letters of intent, exclusivity agreements, break-up fees, or non-disclosure agreements.

Gemini v. AmeriPark was a dispute over an exclusivity agreement. Gemini, a private equity firm, entered into an exclusivity agreement to finance the proposed acquisition by AmeriPark of MileHi, a competitor of Ameritrade. AmeriPark and Gemini executed an 'Outline of Key Transaction Terms', which specified the terms of the proposed financing. While the rest of this term sheet was expressly non-binding, the paragraphs entitled 'Exclusivity' and 'Confidentiality' were binding. The exclusivity provision in the term sheet mirrored that in a separate arrangement between MileHi and AmeriPark. The exclusivity provision stated, in relevant part, that:

> AmeriPark 'agrees not to discuss this opportunity or reach any agreement with any person or entity regarding financing for this Transaction or the pursuit of any sale or major other financing' for a certain period.

The term sheet contemplated a recapitalisation of AmeriPark and a redemption of the shares of Greenfield Partners LLC, a large shareholder in AmeriPark. AmeriPark, therefore, required Greenfield's approval for the proposed financing.

As work on the MileHi acquisition progressed, AmeriPark management began to distrust Gemini and, before the exclusivity period expired, asked its shareholder Greenfield whether Greenfield would be interested in financing the MileHi acquisition instead of the Gemini-led financing. Also, during this period, AmeriPark management approached the CEO and sole shareholder of MileHi, the acquisition target, about the possibility of seller financing. After some negotiation, the CEO and shareholder of AmeriPark agreed to finance the acquisition, and AmeriPark completed the acquisition of MileHi using seller financing. Gemini had been dropped from the deal.

332. *AB Stable VIII, LLC v. MAPS Hotel and Resorts One, LLC, et al.*, C.A. No. 2020-0310-, compl. (Del. Ch. 27 April 2020; pub. 30 August 2020).

333. *See also Delaware Court of Chancery Provides First Guidance on COVID-19 Broken Deal Issues*, Jones Day Commentary, December 2020, available at https://www.jonesday.com/en/insights/2020/12/delaware-court-of-chancery-provides-first-guidance-on-covid19-broken-deal-issues.

Gemini sued AmeriPark for breach of the exclusivity provision by pursuing financing for the MileHi acquisition from both Greenfield and the MileHi shareholder. The parties had differing views about the meaning of the exclusivity provision in the term sheet: AmeriPark argued that the phrase 'any person or entity' referred to the persons or entities expressly set forth elsewhere in the term sheet – investment banks, PE funds, etc. As the funding did not come from any of those sources, AmeriPark argued that it was not in breach. Gemini argued that the exclusivity provision was unambiguous and prohibited discussions with 'any person or entity' and that this included Greenfield and the shareholder. Gemini lost in a jury trial in Federal court. The court found that the exclusivity provision was ambiguous. On appeal, it was affirmed that the exclusivity provision was ambiguous. Further, the court stated that it assumed the discussions with Greenfield about the Gemini financing would be necessary in the context of a redemption of the Greenfield stake.

It was pointed out by attorneys Kirkland & Ellis that, if the court's logic is extended, a PE sponsor 'obtaining a broadly-worded exclusivity at the end of an auction nevertheless would be exposed to being displaced, during the exclusivity period, by a management buyout or a transaction led by a significant target shareholder. Equally, a lender who bargains for exclusivity to finance an acquisition would be at risk of being dislodged by the target's or buyer's existing lender whose consent may be required'.[334]

334. 'Exclusivity' – Not as Preclusive as It Sounds?, Kirkland & Ellis LLP, Kirkland M&A update, 19 July 2011.

CHAPTER 14
Lessons Learned

§14.01 INTRODUCTION

The focus of this publication is technical, with an emphasis on financial and accounting matters insofar as they affect deal mechanics. The discussion in earlier chapters offers a number of lessons as to how disputes might be avoided. These lessons are summarised below. Even so, any such discussion would be incomplete without mention (albeit brief) of other factors that influence a transaction and which - whether or not by design - can contribute to creating the conditions for a dispute. These include behavioural biases.

Anyone who has been involved in multiple M&A transactions will know that dealmakers are humans: individuals subject to various biases in negotiation or, in the words of John Maynard Keynes, 'animal spirits'.[335] While this is the domain of behavioural economics and outside the scope of this publication,[336] it would not be appropriate to ignore behavioural aspects entirely. They are, therefore, incorporated in the following practical considerations that may help avoid disputes.

§14.02 RECOMMENDATIONS

Ensure the SPA Is Specific and Unambiguous

Many of the examples in this book demonstrate that ambiguous wording or vague measurement concepts in the SPA are common causes of disputes. The parties and

335. John Maynard Keynes, *The General Theory of Employment, Interest and Money*, 1973 (1936), 149–150, 161–162, (New York: Macmillan), quoted in: George A. Akerlof/ Robert J. Shiller, *Animal Spirits*, 3 (Princeton University Press 2009).

336. For further reading, *see* Managerial Judgment and Decision Making by Max Bazerman and Don Moore and Raymond S. Nickerson, *Confirmation Bias: A Ubiquitous Phenomenon in Many Guises*, Review of General Psychology 1998, Vol. 2, No. 2, 175–220 with further references.

their advisors should ensure definitions (such as those of accounting policies) are clear and unambiguous. If even specific wording can leave room for potential disagreement, the parties should consider using fixed values or a formula-driven approach.

Raising a sensitive topic that relates to a potential dispute during negotiations, like the definition of a MAC, can be difficult even for experienced dealmakers. It may seem that there is never a good time to discuss what could (theoretically) go wrong in future. Avoiding such topics, and thereby accepting ambiguity, can facilitate the negotiations and increase the probability of signing the deal. Ambiguity of this kind has been called 'constructive ambiguity'.[337] The parties may feel that the benefit of getting to the finish line outweighs the increased risk of disagreement later, and it can often be a rational decision to accept some ambiguity. A dealmaker who is only concerned with avoiding a post-deal dispute may not sign many deals. However, it is useful to be aware that there is a trade-off between unambiguous wording and the risk of disagreement later.

Another aspect relates to situations in which only one party benefits from ambiguity. For example, an ambiguous rather than a narrowly defined MAC clause may allow a buyer more scope to claim that a MAC occurred. Similarly, the party that prepares the completion accounts may prefer ambiguous accounting rules over narrowly defined ones. In these cases, clarity protects the other party.

In any event, if the objective is to avoid disputes, then accepting ambiguity can be counterproductive, and thus precise drafting is generally preferable. Experienced buyers and sellers will set aside a time and place during the negotiations in which these matters are discussed, and invest sufficient time to ensure SPA definitions are clear.

Be Aware of the Risk of a Dispute

Recent research suggests that warranty breaches and fraud are more common than many participants in M&A transactions assume. The authors of one recent study, for example, estimate that on average 10% of large publicly traded firms are committing securities fraud every year – even without the pressures of a transaction – and that only about one-third of frauds in public companies are detected.[338] Research published by W&I insurers suggests that the average reported claim frequency per policy recently exceeded 20% for all categories of deal size except the smallest deals worth less than USD 100 million (17%).[339] Other surveys report somewhat lower figures.[340] While the

337. Khaled Elgindy, When Ambiguity is Destructive, 22 January 2014, Brookings Institution, https://www.brookings.edu/opinions/when-ambiguity-is-destructive/.

338. Detection likelihoods are between 29% and 52%, depending on the type of fraud. Dyck, A., Morse, A. and Zingales, L. *How Pervasive Is Corporate Fraud?* Review of Accounting Studies, 2023.

339. M&A: *Elevated claim levels put focus on due diligence*, AIG Claims Intelligence Services, 2021. The survey suggests that claims related to financial statements warranties are the most common type of contractual breach, followed by tax and compliance with laws. It covers the period to the end of 2019, i.e., before the covid pandemic. The data do not include non-contractual claims (such as fraud), or disputes resolved by expert determination. The data

statistics of W&I insurers relate only to insured transactions (a subset that is not necessarily representative of all transactions), they are nonetheless informative.

It is likely that many dealmakers underestimate the 'base rate' (in Bayesian terminology) of the occurrence of fraud or warranty breaches. A lesson that emerges is that buyers should actively review red flags for fraud (*see* above §10.03) and, where appropriate, incorporate forensic aspects in their financial due diligence procedures. Further, both parties should acknowledge that a dispute is possible, actively consider strategies to avoid disagreement, and agree on the appropriate dispute resolution mechanism.

Employ a Diverse Range of Skills on the Deal Team

Deal teams, led by the CFO or head of M&A, often include lawyers, accountants, bankers and others with industry, technology, IP, valuation, and complementary areas of expertise.

A range of voices with varied qualifications and not only professional but also cultural experiences can help bring important issues to the surface. Diverse teams approach a problem from different angles. They are more likely to find solutions, and members of a diverse team who speak out can help avoid 'groupthink'[341] and other cognitive biases.

Communicate Constantly

It is a recurring theme in this book that many issues that lead to M&A disputes originate at the interface of disciplines. For example, if the valuation team is not sufficiently aware of how the completion mechanism works, the same item may be captured twice in the purchase price (*see* §9.03).

Members of the deal team should, therefore, as a matter of routine throughout the transaction process, share findings with each other. The leadership should ensure there is a forum for such exchanges.

Recognise Behavioural Biases

The M&A process consists of a series of decisions, large and small, faced by principals and their advisors. Even highly intelligent and experienced dealmakers do not always reason rationally.

---

naturally also do not include uninsured transactions; the deals at greatest risk of a warranty breach that are not capable of getting W&I insurance are therefore excluded.

340. Insights into W&I Insurance Claims in Asia, *What half a decade of data tells us*, Marsh Insights, April 2020. This survey reports that the average rate of notification of all policies in the last five years in Asia was approximately 15%.

341. *See* Shireen Meer, 28 July 2017 Diversity needs to be more than skin deep, Management Today.

Behavioural scientists who have studied decision-making make a distinction between 'System 1' and 'System 2' thinking.[342] While System 1 thinking refers to intuitive thinking, which is fast, effortless, and emotional, System 2 thinking refers to slower, conscious, more considered and logical reasoning.[343] Studies suggest that people are more likely to rely on System 1 thinking when they are rushed and have more on their minds.[344] The pace of many M&A negotiations means dealmakers and their advisors are prone to rely on System 1 thinking. No matter how intelligent or qualified a person is, errors or biases are more likely to occur when System 1 thinking is engaged.[345]

It is fair to say that biases in decision-making at the very least facilitate M&A-related disputes. Behavioural scientists have analysed the anatomy of decision-making and developed recommendations on how to keep biases in check.[346] It can be useful for decision-makers in transactions to be aware of these recommendations. Being open to feedback and appropriately humble about one's judgment can play an important role in becoming less reliant on System 1 thinking and being less vulnerable to biases. Decision-makers should treat their beliefs not as 'sacred possessions' but as testable hypotheses.

Provide Opportunities to Raise Concerns

Confirmation biases, overconfidence, or 'deal fever' can all present a hazard. If there is apparent consensus in a deal team, it can require courage for an individual to raise concerns and challenge the consensus: after all, the concern raised could (and often does) turn out to be unimportant.

While challenging assumptions can lead to uncomfortable situations, it is often an important element of a successful acquisition process. Effective teams give their members a sense that it is okay to speak up. Senior leadership should, therefore, create an environment where members of the deal team are encouraged to challenge assumptions and ensure that all concerns are addressed. Surround yourself with colleagues who challenge your thinking.

Consider How Unexpected Events Could Impact the Transaction

The parties should consider how unexpected events might impact the deal. Where could volatility find its way into the purchase price adjustment, represent a MAC, or cause a breach of warranty? The potential effects of volatility should be carefully

342. Bazerman and Moore, *supra* n. 265, at p. 3.
343. Stanovich, K.E. and West, R.F., 2000, *Individual Differences in Reasoning: Implications for the Rationality Debate.* Behavioural & Brain Sciences, Vol. 23, pp. 645–665; D. Kahnemann, *A Perspective on Judgment and Choice: Mapping Bounded Rationality*. American Psychologist, Vol. 58 No. 9, 697–720.
344. Bazerman and Moore, *supra* n. 265, at pp. 3 and 4 with further citations.
345. *Ibid.*, p. 4.
346. *Ibid.*, pp. 15, 216, 217.

considered, in particular when they meet 'soft' accounting standards or vague measurement concepts.

One way to address this risk is to use fixed values in the completion mechanism instead of measuring at closing. This is common practice, for example, for pension obligations (*see* above §4.04 [C]), but fixed values or a formula-driven approach can also be considered for some aspects of inventory valuation, the measurement of restructuring provisions, expected profit margins inherent in long-term contracts, etc.

Ensure Proper Documentation/Note Taking

It can often prove difficult to retroactively understand the basis on which a certain decision was reached or a particular action taken. Documenting financial information provided or important assertions made by the other party, as well as your own thought processes, serves as a valuable reference and can also support your case should a dispute result in litigation. For example, it may be helpful to preserve trial balances at a historical reference date. This will ensure a seller has access to this information in a dispute even when it can no longer access the internal reporting systems.

A court or tribunal will, in considering a case, take into account the decision processes of the parties not only as given in oral evidence, but (arguably even more so) in contemporaneous documents.

Recognise the Constraints

There is never enough time or perfect data available to identify and address every risk. We have yet to meet a purchaser who was entirely happy with the information provided by the seller. The objective, therefore, is to form sufficiently robust judgments as to risks involved, to protect against them contractually to the extent possible or to reflect them in price.

Successful dealmakers understand what can realistically be obtained, recognise the constraints, make the most of the available data, and thus make avoidable errors less likely.

Index

R

S

T

www.ingramcontent.com/pod-product-compliance
Lightning Source LLC
LaVergne TN
LVHW020000031026
849161LV00021B/766